TITAN OF TEHRAN

*From Jewish Ghetto
to Corporate Colossus
to Firing Squad —
My Grandfather's Life*

Shahrzad Elghanayan

The Associated Press
200 Liberty Street
New York, NY 10281
www.ap.org

Hardcover: 978-1-7338462-7-1
E-book: 978-1-7358459-2-0
(Published by The Associated Press, New York)

Cover design by Alicia Tatone
Interior design by Kevin Callahan/BNGO Books
Project Oversight: Peter Costanzo

Visit AP Books: www.ap.org/books

Contents

Contents

To Doug

Foreword

On February 1, 1979, Ayatollah Ruhollah Khomeini returned to Iran from exile, landing in Tehran in a dramatic climax to an Islamic revolution that toppled the Pahlavi dynasty and shifted the course of Middle Eastern history.

To those of us journalists helping inform the world of these momentous events, it was a time of urgent, headline-making news.

But "what we call 'news' is always personal to someone," Shahrzad Elghanayan observes in *Titan of Tehran*, "and can turn a family's world upside down."

In these pages, Ms. Elghanayan weaves a rich and engrossing tapestry that draws the reader into the world of 20th century Iran, into the story of a family whose enterprise and ambition won it wealth and respect in its ancient homeland, and into the upheaval that in a matter of weeks plunged them into an almost medieval abyss.

The story of Habib Elghanian, the author's grandfather, is the inspiring story of a poor Jewish boy rising from a Tehran ghetto, a slum called the "edge of the pit," to create an industrial empire through decades of hard work, daring and foresight. From trading in secondhand clothing and watches, he moved into pioneering the making of plastic products in Iran, and then on to mining, real estate, construction, aluminum. He helped modernize his country, rising to the pinnacle of its commercial world, all the while seeking the best for his family and community.

That uplifting story ended, however, in a sudden storm of religious fanaticism, anti-Semitism and death.

The author's determination to bring Habib Elghanian back to life and to vindicate his name is evident in the wide-ranging, yearslong research that underpins this compelling narrative, a work full of insight, too, into Iran's history and even into today's U.S.-Iranian enmity.

Just as evident is the author's own deep love for and embrace of family, and a steadfast devotion to truth and justice, to at long last righting a historic wrong.

Charles J. Hanley
Pulitzer Prize-winning former AP correspondent

PART I

FROM PIT
TO PLASTICS

CHAPTER 1

⁓

We Hear the News

"Sorry, sir, we're unable to get through to Tehran."
Fed up with the telephone operator's recurring inability to get a line to Iran, my father hung up and dialed the garage attendant in our Midtown Manhattan apartment building.

"This is Karmel Elghanayan from apartment 31-H," he said. "Would you please bring my car out?" Soon he was heading down the FDR Drive in his brown-and-beige Cadillac toward a shop in Greenwich Village where he'd buy a shortwave radio.

He needed news.

Just a few days earlier, on March 15, 1979, Ayatollah Ruhollah Khomeini had locked away my grandfather, a powerful businessman and Jewish community leader, in Tehran's Qasr prison. Since talking with our few relatives and friends still in Iran had become increasingly difficult, Radio Iran's shortwave broadcasts became the next best option for the most up-to-date details on the Iranian Revolution's progress.

My father unpacked the big black box and tested the radio's reception around our 31st floor apartment in The Sovereign. He settled on a corner of the bathroom sink near a narrow window facing east, where the sounds were clearest from 6,000 miles away.

That spring, when I was turning 7, Farsi-language news blared from the radio every day. My father never missed the morning broadcast, New York time, for Tehran's evening news, and again at night, for early morning developments.

Some weekend mornings, I'd sit on the floor outside the bathroom and watch him shave while he listened to Radio Iran before heading out for breakfast with my mother Helen and my younger brother Shahram at the Greek diner across the street on 58th Street and First Avenue.

We had moved to New York almost two years earlier, in the summer of 1977, after my father decided he didn't want to raise us in Iran. Two years before that, in 1975, it was the shah's secret service — not Khomeini's revolutionaries — that had taken my grandfather from his house in the middle of the night and held him for months before releasing him. Now a theocratic ruler had taken over from the monarch, and imprisoned my grandfather again. By the first week of May, revolutionary firing squads had executed some 200 people, almost all of them members of the deposed shah's government, military and secret service.

At 10:30 p.m. on May 8, my father tuned in as he did every night for the 6 a.m. news from Tehran. He planned on getting up early the next morning for synagogue services to mark my grandmother Nikkou Jan's *yartzeit*, the traditional religious ceremony marking the one-year anniversary of her death in Tehran. In his striped cotton pajamas and burgundy leather slippers, he stood facing the mirror in the white marble bathroom, to listen.

Eight men were executed today. Among them was millionaire businessman Habib Elghanian.

As the announcer went on with the report, my father stood motionless in stunned silence. My mother, hearing her father-in-law's name on the radio, ran into the bathroom. My brother and I were asleep in our rooms.

We Hear the News

On Long Island, my father's youngest brother Sina had nodded off with his shortwave radio murmuring on. His pregnant wife Sheryl heard the news and shook him awake.

As word of my grandfather's execution spread in the middle of the night, friends and family from Long Island and Queens hurried to our place. Others who lived in our building threw on robes and took the elevator to our apartment. The morning of May 9, 1979, I woke to a house full of dishelved and tired people — folks I was used to seeing in our apartment at lunch or dinner. I had no idea something cataclysmic had occurred. My mother fed me breakfast, then took me down to the lobby where a small yellow school bus waited outside to take me to the Lycée Français, where I was finishing first grade.

My father's sister, my aunt Mahnaz, who was in New York, was spared the late-night phone call. Shortly after her two boys had gone off to grade school, her cousins arrived at her Upper East Side place, their faces telegraphing the sorrow they were about to utter.

The family began mourning my grandfather even as it marked my grandmother's *yartzeit*.

By that evening, reports of my grandfather's execution had spread around the globe.

On ABC's "World News Tonight," anchor Peter Jennings, with a map of Iran chromakeyed over his left shoulder, showing the capital Tehran and a silhouette of a rifle across the yellow outline of the nation, announced the news. "Elsewhere overseas today, there were more executions in Iran," he intoned. "They've become almost commonplace. But today's give rise to increased concern for Iran's minority groups. Among the eight men who faced an Islamic firing squad today was a leading Jewish businessman, the first member of that troubled community to be convicted of associating, in the words of the court, 'with Israel and Zionism.' Jews in Iran fear that accusation from militant Muslims more than any other."[1]

---

1. Peter Jennings, *ABC World News Tonight*, Vanderbilt Television News Archive, May 9, 1979.

On the "CBS Evening News," Walter Cronkite reported: "An Iranian firing squad in Tehran today executed eight more persons, including a prominent Jewish businessman accused of having links with Israel. In Washington, the State Department renewed its strong disapproval of the summary trials and executions." As to the businessman's death, Cronkite said, "it was indicated that he was tried as an individual, not as a Jewish leader."[2]

What the initial reports did not immediately presage was that the execution would be a watershed for both Iran's economy and the future of the nation's Jewish community. That evening's news also couldn't foretell how the U.S. Congress' reaction to my grandfather's execution would become Khomeini's excuse for cutting diplomatic relations with the United States — with repercussions still felt today.

In Tehran early that May morning, my father's older brother Fereydoun, whom we call Fred, and his wife Eliane were also preparing for Nikkou Jan's *yartzeit*. They were gathering with relatives to drive out to her grave at the Giliard Jewish cemetery, east of the capital in Damavand. They hadn't turned on the radio all morning.

Amir Victory, my grandfather's cousin and president of one of the family enterprises, arrived at the meeting place, blurting: "Terrible news, terrible news, I have terrible news."

Then: "They executed Habib, they executed him before dawn."

Fred dropped the two bottles in his hands — one with wine to recite prayers and the other with *golab*, rose water, to sprinkle over his mother's grave. He stood crying in the puddle of rose water, wine and shattered glass.

Earlier that night, Revolutionary Guards pulled into my grandfather's driveway with large trucks to empty the home of its furnishings. The longtime nanny Layla Khanoum and the caretaker Vali were still there. They

---

2. Walter Cronkite, *CBS Evening News*, Vanderbilt Television News Archive, May 9, 1979.

watched the Guards stuff the trucks with beds, sofas, chairs, tables, even family albums.

"Please," Layla Khanoum pleaded with one of them, as he plundered the house. "I raised these children. Please let me keep some of their pictures."

"Stop," the guardsman admonished her. "These albums are not yours."

"Please let me keep just a few of the children," she begged, tears cascading down her wrinkled face.

Back in New York, when my father tried calling his brother Fred, the overseas operator offered the same maddening refrain:

"Sorry sir, we're unable to get through to Tehran."

While our black shortwave droned on in the cold marble bathroom, my grandfather's bullet-riddled body languished in the prison morgue, with a cardboard sign around his neck. It read: "Habib Elghanian, Zionist Spy."

⌇

CHAPTER 2

In the News Again

Twenty-five hundred feet under the Iranian desert, technicians and scientists stood bewildered, trying to figure out what caused the recurring explosions inside the heavily guarded uranium enrichment facility at Natanz. By summer 2010, about 2,000 aluminum canisters, centrifuges used to enrich uranium, had blown up inside the facility in north-central Iran. This happened month after month without any apparent military strikes, bombs, or even the slightest hint of infiltration.

Natanz, the target of a cyberattack, had been hacked. A virus called Stuxnet had spread through Natanz's computer system, crippling the Siemens computers' mechanism that regulates the speed at which turbines spin inside the nearly 6-foot-long centrifuges to enrich uranium — which, if spun long enough, can be used to make nuclear weapons.

The virus switched the electric current from high to low speeds in quick succession, disrupting the steady, 1,000 revolutions per second speed of the spinning turbines. As the current accelerated and then slowed, the uranium-filled turbines spun out of control, causing the centrifuges to burst apart.

Stuxnet had been designed to make the computer readings of the electric current look as though the turbines were spinning at their normal speed, making it impossible to detect what sabotaged a quarter of Natanz's 9,000 centrifuges. The cyberattack was silent and invisible. In the battle to slow down Iran's nuclear capability, a new weapon of war that caused no human casualties had been created. And no one claimed responsibility.

Hidden from view deep under the desert, the damage at Natanz — unlike the damage of conventional wars — had been un-photographable. Working as a photo editor at The Associated Press in New York, I had edited thousands of pictures from the wars in Iraq, Afghanistan, Lebanon and Gaza where death and destruction had been visible. But the attack in Iran had escaped my attention — until Nov. 19, 2010, when I opened an e-mail from my father.

"I heard there was a mention of my dad in the NYT today," he wrote. "Do you know anything about this? If so, let me know."

My heart racing, I searched *The New York Times'* website for my grandfather's name. Known as one of the titans of Iran's business world, as famous in pre-revolutionary Iran as John Jacob Astor IV, Cornelius Vanderbilt or Andrew Carnegie during the American Industrial Revolution, he had also been the secular leader of Iran's nearly 100,000-strong Jewish community from 1959 until shortly before the Iranian Revolution. A self-made success, he had built a business empire after World War II with his six brothers, helping modernize Iran with, among other things, the introduction of the plastics industry and the construction of the country's first private-sector high-rise, the iconic Plasco Building.

I found "Habib Elghanian," the spelling most commonly used by the news media, in a paragraph toward the end of a Page 1 article probing the origins of Stuxnet: "Worm in Iran Can Wreck Nuclear Centrifuges." It said: "Last month, researchers at Symantec also speculated that a string of numbers found in the program — 19790509 — while seemingly random might actually be significant. They speculated that it might refer to May 9, 1979, the day that Jewish-Iranian businessman Habib Elghanian was executed in Iran after being convicted of spying for Israel."[1]

Seeing his name in the story jolted me back to the darkest day of my family's history when the radio delivered the news of his execution to our home.

Sitting on the couch in my apartment in New York, I reread the story, trying to make sense of the speculation. Hackers mischievously drop clues about who they are inside their code, and researchers looking for such signatures inside Stuxnet pointed to "19790509" as a possible guide to who might have created the virus. At the time, neither the U.S. nor Israel had taken responsibility for the attack.[2] If the speculation was correct, and the digits "19790509" really did refer to the date of my grandfather's execution, was the inclusion cyber warfare's version of "Habib, this one's for you"?

Could it be, I wondered, that the numbers embedded in the virus amounted to a 21st century equivalent of messages painted on World War II bombs to memorialize the fallen? Could this have been a warning to Iran from Israel, the country most threatened by Iran's nuclear program, that the Jewish state remembered how in 1979 when the Islamic Republic was establishing itself, the new regime had hand-picked Iran's most eminent Jew as the first well-known civilian to face the firing squad? Had Israel kept my grandfather's execution on a secret list of wrongs against Jews that it would never forget?

Impossible to know. Stuxnet is classified — and no one will address if the code was a hidden message.

The virus had infiltrated more than tunnels in the Iranian desert. Reading about Stuxnet sparked a reaction deep inside me, where the past quietly sits. For four decades, my family has not been able to return to our homeland

---

1. William J. Broad and David E. Sanger, "Worm in Iran Can Wreck Nuclear Centrifuges," *The New York Times*, Nov. 18, 2010.
2. David E. Sanger, "Obama Order Sped Up Wave of Cyberattacks Against Iran," *The New York Times*, June 1, 2012.

after the Iranian government stripped us of our citizenship. In defiance, we've relied on our own web of indestructible tunnels to travel back in time, to relive memories of life in Iran, and safeguard the days that made my family who they are. Throughout much of my life, I regularly accompanied relatives, as their yearning hearts sought a temporary balm, down these tunnels to the past: a walk down one of Tehran's old sycamore-lined streets, a visit inside an old house, a trip to a favorite coffee shop or cabaret, gatherings at my grandparents' house, to bask, if only for a few soothing hours, under sunny, happy days.

We learned of our official status as exiles prior to my grandfather's execution when, weeks before our passports expired, my father took the documents to be renewed at the Iranian consulate in New York. "I've been given orders to confiscate these," the consulate worker informed him after reading our names. Without our passports, we became stateless refugees overnight — even though in 1979 Iran belonged to us as much as we belonged to Iran.

Jews have a long and storied history there dating back to biblical times when the first Jews were forcibly brought to what's now Iran by King Nebuchadnezzar II of Babylonia after he conquered Jerusalem in 597 B.C. Among his captives were King Jehoiachin of Judah. After Nebuchadnezzar appointed Jehoiachin's uncle Zedekiah as the new king of Judah, Zedekiah wanted independence, leading Nebuchadnezzar to lay siege to Jerusalem a second time, this time destroying the Temple and carrying away more Jews who eventually spread throughout the land. In 539 B.C., Persian King Cyrus II defeated the Babylonians and freed the Jewish slaves, allowing them to return to Jerusalem to rebuild the Temple. Those who didn't return to the Promised Land stayed in the Persian Empire.[3]

---

3. Mayer I. Gruber, "The Achaemenid Period," in *Esther's Children: A Portrait of Iranian Jews*, ed. Houman Sarshar (Beverly Hills: The Center for Iranian Jewish Oral History, 2002) p. 3-8.

Staring at my grandfather's name in that paragraph in *The New York Times*, I exhumed the few memories from our outdoor lunches on the patio of his house in Shemiran in the north of Tehran. When he'd take his afternoon swim, I'd watch him, shaking my head "no" when he'd urge me to jump into the freezing pool fed by the fresh stream flowing directly from the Alborz Mountains.

What quietly shaped my life was growing up knowing an injustice had been committed against my family. What I learned from my father's attention to the shortwave broadcasts of Radio Iran and the hundred or so news clippings neatly taped inside two gray-blue notebooks he had once shown me, was that what we call "news" is always personal to someone, and can turn a family's world upside down. Much of what I decided to study at school and many of the jobs I pursued were informed by this history. I studied political science at Columbia University, worked for a human rights group, then moved on to news organizations, where I could seek out and give voice to the voiceless.

Seeing the long shadow my grandfather cast decades after his execution, I was determined not to let his story remain the way his killers intended: shattered and forgotten. Just a month after *The New York Times* story, I quit my job at The Associated Press and set out to restore what Khomeini had destroyed on May 9, 1979.

I traveled to Los Angeles, home to many Iranian exiles, and to rural Ohio, to San Diego and to Jerusalem, digging for every shred and shard, gathering information about my grandfather's life by talking with his business associates, diplomats he knew, friends and family. I collected piles of books, newspaper and magazine articles, congressional records and national archive documents, transforming my home into a labyrinth to the past. My most prized discoveries were an unpublished memoir my grandfather's older brother Davoud left to his children, along with my grandfather's own private letters, photographs, and several videos of him during my father's bar mitzvah and my parents' engagement party.

In the News Again

I began to piece together all these fragments to try to replicate what had been — emulating Kintsugi, the Japanese art of restoring broken pottery by gluing pieces with gold-, silver- or platinum-colored lacquer. Inspired by the shiny-seamed relics created by Kintsugi masters, I set out to resurrect my grandfather's bullet-shattered life with glistening new veins.

By reconstructing the story of his life, I was hoping to figure out something that had bothered me for as long as I could remember: Why hadn't my grandfather left Iran? Why had he stayed in Tehran during the Iranian Revolution — when he could have easily been with us, his family, in New York, or in London with his brother, or in Israel, the country created so that Jews in a position like his had a place to go? Was he simply like the integrated German Jews who felt at home in 1930s Germany? Was there more to his story?

Surviving, after all, is what Iranian Jews had done for millennia: Generations of resilient men and women had outlasted centuries of oppression and poverty along with decades of famine and epidemics. Living as a minority group in isolated pockets in cities across Iran, they had forged ahead without breaking the bond with Judaism or the past.

When I walk down my own secret tunnels to find my grandfather on that spring evening in 1979, I see him standing blindfolded in the prison courtyard, ready to face the bullets. I'm a kid, just turned 7, and I'm holding on tight to his hand. I don't want him to be alone. He's whispering the traditional last words of Jews, *"Shema Israel, Adonai Eloheinu, Adonai Echad."* Before I can turn my head to say goodbye, the sound of gunfire rips through Tehran's silken night, and he falls to the ground. I'm kneeling next to him. Streams of blood have begun to dye the land.

I promise to never let go.

CHAPTER 3

Born on the Edge of the Pit

Bundled-up and rosy-cheeked, young Habib with his older brothers John and Davoud fought the hissing winter wind as they climbed the steps of the Jewish public bathhouse to street level, where they waited for their mother Khanoum Jan and sister Saltanat. Down in the steamy *hammam*, using pumice stones and wool rags, the boys had washed off a month's worth of grime. Now they stood at the top of the stairs, scrunching their freshly scoured faces in the wind.

Khanoum Jan arrived, her smiling eyes skipping like sparrows from son to son. She squeezed each boy's face before kissing their foreheads and checked that they hadn't left anything behind. John held the copper wash basin and Davoud, the bath bag filled with the family's pumice stones and rags.

"Watch out for your clothes," she urged as they began their trudge home through the mud along the narrow, winding street turned doughy by the thawing snow. And try they did, tiptoeing to avoid splashing the slush. Amid the symphony of her children's squishing feet and the whistling of the wind through her own tchador, Khanoum Jan cursed the never-ending struggle to keep her kids clean. Barely 10 minutes passed before their clothes were soiled, and she knew she would have to endure the cold in the courtyard where she did the laundry in a large tub with bare hands.

With the winter sun setting early, dusk surrendered to night when they reached their rented room in one of the Jewish ghetto's typical flat-roofed adobe and brick houses. The children left their well-worn galoshes — passed down from older to younger sibling — at the top of the stairway, to keep mud out of their one-room home on the second floor.

Inside, Khanoum Jan added a few pieces of coal to the brazier, the small box that served as a heater. The children played while she ran back down to the kitchen she shared with the family living below them, to warm up dinner from what little was left of lunch. Only on Sabbath eve did the family always have a full meal, often the traditional chicken soup over rice — even if they had to borrow money.

After supper, which they ate on the floor, she unfolded the thin mattress out of the corner of the room and pulled the heavy quilt over herself, John, Davoud, Habib and Saltanat.

Only in the winter months did Khanoum Jan take care of young Habib and his siblings alone. Her husband Ostad "Oussa" Babai, a tailor, spent two or sometimes three months in Ghasvin, 90 miles northwest of Tehran, where he traveled to sell the men's suits he sewed with a pair of apprentices. He would return by the first day of spring, to celebrate the Persian New Year, *Nowrooz*. When he was around, he'd take the boys to the *hammam* when it opened at dawn.

No one was wealthy in Tehran's Jewish quarter, Sarechal, or *Mallaleh*, meaning neighborhood, the residents' own name for their squalid section inside the eastern edge of the central district of OudLajan, one of Tehran's oldest enclaves. Of the 5,000 to 6,000 Jews who lived there in the early 20th century, Khanoum Jan and Oussa Babai were among the poorest. For decades, they could only afford to rent a small room. They could neither buy a house nor rent one in a safer place tucked away deep in one of Sarechal's cul de sacs at the end of the neighborhood's serpentine streets, sheltered from the occasional Muslim looters who'd swoop in to harass the Jews. Khanoum Jan's father, Haim-Saghi, owned a grocery store called Saghi Baghal in Sarechal, where he also made wine and liquor and cheese. Even though Islam forbids drinking alcohol, Jews, segregated in their own neighborhood, were permitted to make their own wine for the weekly Sabbath and the Jewish holidays. Other food vendors included fruit and vegetable sellers, a couple of bakers and butchers.

Haim-Saghi — who along with two of his three sons would play a key role in his grandson Habib's rise — was one of the neighborhood elders and lived in a bigger, four-room house with his family.

Sarechal means "the edge of a pit," where layers of chicken bones, animal carcasses, vegetable and fruit peelings decayed in a large hole where residents dumped their garbage, causing a stench to waft over the neighborhood until the garbage was burned.[1]

Probably no place smelled quite as pungent as the edge of the pit, but most of Tehran, like parts of other big cities around the world at the time, reeked of fetid decaying garbage, too, and lacked running water and a sewage network. Only the capital's wealthier residents could escape the stench and heat of the city's baked summer days by heading to Tehran's northern districts in Shemiran to enjoy the cool air of the nearby Alborz Mountains.

But the *Mahalleh* had amenities too. Aside from six synagogues, it had four pharmacies, four bankers who lent money out of their homes, several doctors, a small inn where travelers could spend the night, two small bazaars, even a perfumer. Among its delights were the mulberry vendors who carried from home to home freshly picked large, juicy, tangy berries on large trays balanced on their heads.[2] Gifted musicians would play the

---

1. Amir Afkhami, Skype conversation with author, March 3, 2015.
2. Nourollah Khorramian, "Oh Hear the Story of Mahalleh Palace," www.sarechal. com, Los Angeles, Feb. 1992.

ney, a Persian flute, or *tar*, a string instrument, creating soothing, at times melancholy melodies that would drift across a street.

Unlike European Jews who had forcibly been penned inside walled ghettos, Habib's ancestors had voluntarily congregated into segregated Jewish neighborhoods to resist converting to Islam. In the 16th century under the Safavid dynasty that established Shiism as Iran's official religion, the *ulama*, scholars trained in Islamic law who were determined to convert all religious minorities to Islam, passed oppressive decrees to prevent them from prospering. Those who didn't accept Muhammad as their prophet and the Quran as God's final revelation were deemed impure, filthy, *najes*.

To humiliate the *najes*, the *ulama* forbade them from using Muslim public baths, drinking from public fountains, leaving their houses when it rained or snowed, touching anything when entering Muslim shops, opening shops in the bazaar, building homes taller than a Muslim's, buying homes from Muslims or giving children Muslim names.

Considered *najes* and segregated in their own ghettos, the Jews washed in their own bathhouses, shopped in stores owned by other Jews, bought and sold homes amongst themselves, lived within walking distance of their synagogues, homes and businesses. They could come out when it rained without worrying that drops would bounce off them and onto Muslims who considered water contaminated if it rebounded from any minority.[3]

Part of a resilient community with deep roots in Iran, Jews had lived on the land centuries before Islam's arrival.

When Islam reached Iran in 642 A.D., Jews could convert or escape execution by paying a poll tax. In the 11th and 12th centuries, some Jews became important government figures though dozens of communities were destroyed during Genghis Khan's Mongol invasion of northern and eastern

---

3. Houshang Ebrami, "The Impure Jew," in *Esther's Children: A Portrait of Iranian Jews*, ed. Houman Sarshar (Beverly Hills: The Center for Iranian Jewish Oral History, 2002) p. 101.

Iran in 1221. Between 1501 when Shiism became the official state religion and the end of the 19th century, organized massacres around the country wiped out entire Jewish communities. Except for a few relatively tolerant interludes during the zealously religious Safavid kingdom beginning in the 16th century, Jews, like other religious minorities, suffered discrimination and hostility.

The Jewish families who survived into the 1900s were tough. By the start of the 20th century, Khanoum Jan and Babai were among 50,000 surviving Jews living in ghettos in Tehran, Isfahan, Shiraz, Yazd, Kerman and Hamadan.[4]

My grandfather was born on April 5, 1912,[5] an accident of timing that would prove both lucky and unlucky. He was born in a sweet spot of Iranian Jewish history, when Jews got a break from the conservative Shiite clergy's cruelty — turning out to be what a historian called a "Golden Era." But it would end abruptly.

By 1912, the status of Iran's Jews was slowly improving — on paper at least, and in fits and starts. First, in 1905, Muslim merchants began pushing for a Western-style constitution and a parliament to safeguard their property against the ruling Qajar dynasty king's arbitrary powers. The clergy split into two camps. Liberal clergymen sided with the merchants, while conservatives, seeing their traditional religious authority under attack, sided with the king, deriding parliaments and laws as Western ideas they were staunchly unwilling to embrace. In 1905-06, the merchants and liberal clergy prevailed, winning the Constitutional Revolution that gave Iranians the right to thrive and live side by side in relative harmony.

Minority groups' rights were enshrined in Article 2 of the Constitution of Dec. 30, 1906, and in Article 8 of the Supplementary Fundamental Laws

---

4. Ervand Abrahamian, *A History of Modern Iran*, (Cambridge, U.K.: Cambridge University Press, 2008) p. 18.
5. Mayo Clinic medical records.

of October 1907. The first said: "The National Consultative Assembly represents the whole of the people who thus participate in the economic and political affairs of the country." And the second: "The people of the Empire are to enjoy equal rights before the Law."

Iran's Jews now had outlets to speak out. A May 1907 letter that a young man named Yousef from the *Mahalleh* was emboldened to write to Parliament's newspaper reflects the cultural realities underlying the legal change.

"I'm a 16-year-old and a tailor," he began, explaining the efforts of himself and three others to improve their community, installing lights and hiring unemployed residents to clean and sweep up. "We did all this for (two) reasons: for the comfort of the pedestrians and for relieving the Jews from the stigma (of uncleanliness) attached to them." Noting the descent of both Judaism and Islam from "one father," Abraham, he concluded: "We beg of you wise men and compatriots to stop those who harass the Jewish community. God almighty advised in the Blessed Quran against cruelty."[6]

Neither the new Constitution nor the Parliament could legislate away centuries of the prejudice and stigma of being considered *najes*. It would take several more decades for most Jews to leave the *Mahalleh* and live more or less as equals among Muslims. In fact, immediately after the Constitutional Revolution, hardline clergy and the Qajar king Mohammad Ali Shah waged a six-year civil war against the liberal camp which had granted minority rights — until the conservatives were defeated on March 12, 1912, and the king left Iran.

A mere three weeks after that liberal victory, Khanoum Jan gave birth on April 5. Eager to embrace their new status as equals, she gave her son a name used by Muslims, Habibollah, meaning "God's Beloved."

---

6. Janet Afary, "From Outcasts to Citizens, Jews in Qajar Iran," in *Esther's Children: A Portrait of Iranian Jews*, ed. Houman Sarshar (Beverly Hills: The Center for Iranian Jewish Oral History, 2002) p. 165-166.

If the political gains for Iran's Jews through Habib's lifetime would indeed be blessings, his family still had to overcome the disruptions of World War I and the famine, cholera and typhus outbreaks that ravaged the nation. Most lethal of all was the 1918-19 worldwide influenza pandemic that in one week killed Habib's paternal grandfather and two paternal uncles.

During the *ghaati*, a famine from 1917 to 1921, people waited in line for hours sometimes just getting burnt bread. Still, they persevered. "Our father worked hard and did not let us feel the pinch," Habib's brother Davoud wrote in his memoir. "He perpetually worked hard, often until midnight." When Khanoum Jan cooked meals, she would hand out food in little tea dishes to passersby. Her brother Hajji Mirza Agha, working through an association called *Kaneyeh Kheyrkha Nikkha* that he and friends created, distributed food to the poor, with financial aid from Jewish organizations abroad.

The famine didn't stop Khanoum Jan and Babai from paying the tuition to send their children to school. By 1918, at age 6, my grandfather Habib was in the small minority of Iranians going to school. Along with his brothers John and Davoud, he went to the first school in Iran for Jews. The Alliance Israélite Universelle school was established in the *Mahalleh* in spring 1898 by French Jewish statesman Adolphe Crémieux. France's Jews had been granted equal rights during the French Revolution a century earlier. Crémieux created the first Jewish organization to defend and promote the political and civil rights of Jews in the Middle East as well as Eastern Europe, the Balkans and North Africa. Along with Iran's Jewish community leaders and organizations of British Jewry, most notably the Anglo-Jewish Association, Crémieux began interceding on behalf of Iran's Jews as early as the 1870s. Two decades later, the first Alliance school, Ettehad, was established in Tehran's Jewish quarter and additional schools were set up in other Iranian cities during the first decade of the 20th century. The Alliance Israélite schools, where French, Farsi and Hebrew were taught, provided a modern secular education, facilitating Jewish assimilation.

"Soon after their establishment, Alliance Israélite schools became the most important community centers for Iranian Jews," Faryar Nikbakht writes in *Esther's Children*. "Social gatherings, functions and community meetings were held there. Sometimes major official and religious leaders from the Muslim community were invited to gatherings, and gradually warmer relations between Jews and Muslims as well as increased respect for Iranian Jews started to develop." [7]

At home, the boys learned at a young age that the family couldn't rely on their father alone to make ends meet. Yearly tuition at the school was 1,200 francs, approximately 240 tomans at the time, and the family couldn't always keep up with the payments. Faced with the prospect of her two oldest boys having to drop out of school because the family was broke, Khanoum Jan sold her only valuable, a silver spouted hookah that was part of her dowry. It covered one month's tuition.

"This little act of sacrifice made a huge impact on me," wrote Davoud, a beneficiary of the heirloom's sale. "I will never forget it."

To supplement Babai's income for several years, Khanoum Jan also worked selling fabric door-to-door four or five days a week with another Jewish woman in the *Mahalleh*, instilling in young Habib that women were independent and resourceful.

By the time my grandfather started at the Alliance in 1918, the school was taking its students on outings, gym classes were offered, and the older students were staging Molière plays. Habib studied French from ages 6 to 9, until 1921, when the Alliance began putting more emphasis on Farsi and to a lesser extent Hebrew. The school had "very good teachers," recalled Davoud, who stayed through the 10th grade at age 16. Habib, who didn't like studying much and was good only at math, dropped out at 12 or 13, having

---

7. Faryar Nikbakht, "As With Moses in Egypt, Alliance Israélite Universelle Schools in Iran," in *Esther's Children: A Portrait of Iranian Jews*, ed. Houman Sarshar (Beverly Hills: The Center for Iranian Jewish Oral History, 2002) p. 203.

gone only to primary school. Still, when he stopped, he was in the minority of Iranians who had attended any school. By *Encyclopaedia Iranica*'s estimate, the Alliance schools throughout the country had 4,150 boys and girls in 1906. By 1941, the 15 Alliance schools had 6,500 students. In 1924, the entire country had 83 primary schools with 7,000 students and 85 secondary schools with 5,000 students.[8]

Thanks to Crémieux, three generations of my family eventually became francophile, enrolling in different French schools in Tehran and later New York. My maternal grandmother was among the Iranian Jewish women who attended the Alliance Israélite. She enrolled all four of her children in French schools, including my mother who went to Jeanne d'Arc, a well-known Catholic girls' school in Tehran. Then, my mother enrolled me at a co-ed secular school, the Lycée Razi of the Alliance Française, which I attended for a year until we moved to New York and I started the Lycée Français.

In the early 20th century, only 15 percent of Iran's 12 million residents lived in cities. In Tehran, the capital with 200,000 inhabitants, Jews numbered 5,000 to 6,000, or about 2.5 percent.[9] Living in an urban area, when Iran was still rural, semi-feudal and tribal, made Tehran's Jews a minority within a minority. Despite the shortages, famine and epidemics, Khanoum Jan and Babai's family, like many Jewish families, kept growing. After Saltanat, John, Davoud and Habib, Khanoum Jan had four more sons between 1915 and 1924: Nourollah, Nejatollah, Sion and Attollah, called "Eddy."

In 1921, Babai purchased a house a few blocks outside the *Mahalleh* on a street, with both Muslims and Jews, called *Seraheh Dongi*, not far from the Alliance school. The new home offered much more space with four rooms,

---

8. Djavad Hadidi, "FRANCE xv. FRENCH SCHOOLS IN PERSIA," *Encyclopaedia Iranica* online edition http://www.iranicaonline.org/articles.

9. Ervand Abrahamian, *A History of Modern Iran*, (Cambridge, U.K.: Cambridge University Press, 2008) p. 6.

a cellar, toilet and kitchen; it also came with a small water reservoir in the yard and a tiny decorative pool surrounded by four small orchards.

But the new place didn't lead to much better living conditions because the family rented out rooms. Habib, 9 at the time, and his siblings and parents continued to live in one room.

"Everyone sat and ate on the floor," Davoud recalled. "All of us slept on the floor. Two or three people would sleep on one mattress with one quilt."

Despite years of liberalization, a year after the family moved, Jewish persecution persisted. As Habib was entering fourth grade in September 1922, one of the school's Jewish workers and a mullah's servant got into an argument. When Muslims heard the Commissariat authorities had ruled in the Jewish worker's favor, a mob rushed into the *Mahalleh* and headed for the Alliance school, which consisted of a huge garden and two compounds with large rooms. The French Embassy was nearby, and gendarmes were dispatched to escort the teachers and students home. The school closed for several days.

Starting Sept. 19, rioting forced Jews to shutter their shops. Habib's maternal grandfather Haim-Saghi was sought out and attacked in his home by a dagger-wielding man from Pamenar, a mixed Muslim-Jewish street nearby. Iranian police made themselves scarce, and the mayhem finally stopped on Sept. 22 when the French gendarmes fired on the rioters.

Haim-Saghi got his arm stitched and bandaged. Wounded and feeling pushed to drastic action, he resolved to complain about the attack to the most powerful man he knew, a man who had visited his store to drink his homemade red wine — a man who would become Iran's king.

Once he recovered enough, Haim-Saghi marched several blocks north into the Baharestan neighborhood. He stood outside the gates of the two-story Parliament building, waiting for the man to come out.

Soon he would get his audience — with a bold, impromptu move.

CHAPTER 4

⁓

The Formative Years

Habib's grandfather Haim-Saghi kept a keen eye on the carved wood door behind the columns of the Parliament building, where he knew Reza Khan would eventually walk out. In 1922, Reza Khan was the Iranian army's commander-in-chief and the soon-to-be Reza Shah, founder of the Pahlavi dynasty. The building, white brick-and-stucco with blue tiles, once served as the summer residence of former Qajar King Naser al din Shah, who had granted oil and mineral concessions in 1872 to Reuters founder Baron Julius de Reuter for payments the king personally pocketed. Now, deputies met in sumptuous rooms and grand halls where the Constitution that enshrined Haim-Saghi's rights as a Jew had been signed during Parliament's first session in 1906. Though the building's new occupants, the people's representatives, were more enlightened and less corrupt than the Qajar dynasty kings who had taken over from the Safavid dynasty in 1785, room for progress remained, especially for minorities.

As he waited, Haim-Saghi may have ruminated on how the conservative clerics and rulers had fought a six-year civil war over the 1906 Constitutional Revolution that gave Jews the right to have their own representative. It was impossible for all Iranians to be equals, the ranking conservative cleric Sheykh Fazlollah Nuri had argued, because Muslim religious laws separate its believers from the non-believers. Jews were pressured into giving up their right to a representative who was replaced with liberal Muslim cleric Seyyed Abdollah Behbahani. Nuri's demands didn't stop there. The following year, he organized a coup against Parliament with Qajar King Muhammad Ali Shah's backing and the Russian government's help. While laying siege on Parliament in 1907, the anti-constitutionalists marched into the *Mahalleh*, demanding Jews join the insurgents. Fearing death if they didn't, some participated in the demonstrations, chanting against the Constitution. Nuri was tried and executed in 1909, the conservatives lost the civil war in 1912, and Loqman Nehurai became the Jewish representative in Parliament, pushing hard to eliminate discrimination.[1]

Still, Haim-Saghi was emboldened to appeal to a higher authority. If a Constitutional Revolution, civil war and a Jewish representative couldn't stop Jews from being attacked in the country they had inhabited for thousands of years, he'd complain directly to the army's commander.

Confident that Reza Khan would recognize him from having patronized his store for wine, Haim-Saghi waited. Finally, when Reza Khan emerged from the building, Haim-Saghi charged toward him. Guards rushed to intervene. As they seized him, Reza Khan indeed recognized the grocery store owner and instructed his men to stand down.

Haim-Saghi showed his bandaged arm, explaining how he was wounded during the attack in the *Mahalleh*. Family lore has it that Reza Khan assured him that he was aware of the problem and was working to help improve the

---

1. Janet Afary, "From Outcasts to Citizens, Jews in Qajar Iran," in *Esther's Children: A Portrait of Iranian Jews*, ed. Houman Sarshar (Beverly Hills: The Center for Iranian Jewish Oral History, 2002) p. 174.

Jews' condition. In the meantime, he advised Haim-Saghi to tell his sons to move out of the Jewish neighborhood. [2]

That fall however, it had not been Iranian but French forces that intervened to stop the riots. Further, that September, Reza Khan cut off the Jewish quarter's water supply, allegedly to create an international incident that might bring down Qajar King Ahmad Shah's government. (Rabbi Joseph Saul Kornfeld, the U.S. ambassador to Persia from 1922 to 1924, helped to restore the water.)[3] [4]

Reza Khan had forged an illustrious career in the military, ascending to the post of army commander the previous year. He first joined the Cossack Brigade around 1894 and rose steadily through the ranks. In an attempt to reverse the 1917 Russian Revolution, Britain attacked Russia from Iran, took over and purged the Cossack Brigade, substituting Russian officers with British and Iranians, including Reza Khan. Russia fought back, first annexing parts of northern Iran and gradually other parts, until the Iranian government lost all power outside Tehran in 1920. In winter 1921, Reza Khan, promoted by the British to brigade commander, led a coup d'état and seized control over Tehran, forcing the Qajar king to appoint him head of the Iranian army and minister of war. He subsequently secured the rest of the country before Parliament appointed him prime minister in 1923. Two years later, he crushed an Arab nationalist rebellion, persuaded Parliament to depose the Qajar king and appointed himself king in December 1925.

Reza Khan's advice to Haim-Saghi to get his sons to move out of the Jewish neighborhood fit his plans to build a united, integrated nation he could easily rule over as future king. By the time he gave this advice,

---

2. Pari Elghanian-Tabibnia, interview with author, 2011.

3. Hossein Abadian, *Foundation of Pahlavi Dynasty*, Iranian Institute of Political Studies and Research, p 460 - 467.

4. Mohammad Gholi Majd, *Great Britain and Reza Shah*, (University Press of Florida: 2001), p.169.

Haim-Saghi's sons, Habib's uncles, Hajji Mirza Agha and Hajji Aziz, were business partners and on their way to prosperity. They first owned a grocery store on Darvazeh Ghazvin Street, then bought a shop where they sold menswear on Lalezar Street, Tehran's most prominent retail thoroughfare inspired by Paris' Champs-Elysées. They also had an office in the high-traffic bazaar's Serah-e Timcheh Haji Mohammad Ismail section. For Jewish merchants, who decades earlier were not permitted to own stores outside of their own neighborhoods, having an office in the religiously conservative and status-conscious bazaar constituted a major breakthrough.

Maternal uncles grooming and nurturing their nephews became a family tradition.[5] Habib's uncles had succeeded under the tutelage of their maternal uncle, Agha Baba Elghana. In the early 20th century when restrictions were lifted on minority participation in the economy, Agha Baba Elghana traveled to France and returned to Tehran with fabrics that he sold in a store called *"Ensaf,"* or *"Equality,"* on Lalezar Street. He continued to live in the *Mahalleh* until he could afford to move with his wife and three children into a mansion in the city's prime area near the Russian and British embassies. He financially supported his sons without insisting that they learn his business, while mentoring his nephews.

Agha Baba Elghana was born around 1870, after his father, the family's earliest known forebear, moved to Tehran's Jewish quarter. Family members speculated that the father, known simply as Elghana, had come from Kashan because his descendants in Tehran continued to pronounce Farsi words for aunt and uncle with a Kashani accent. Kashan, in the province of Isfahan, is where most of Iran's Jews hail from.

After being groomed by their mother's brother, Hajji Mirza Agha and Hajji Aziz did the same for their sister Khanoum Jan's sons, my grandfather and his brothers. Mirza traveled to Russia and Beirut to import fabrics, and

---

5. Iraj Elghanian, phone interview with author, August 2015.

Aziz moved to Paris with his wife Heshmat where they opened an office for their business.

In 1926, Aziz took John, then 19, to Paris. Because John had studied at the Alliance school, he spoke passable French and could help his uncle export goods from Paris to Tehran. The following year, Davoud, 17, joined his brother John in Paris to work in the family import-export business, using his strong math skills.

At first, Davoud recollected, "I mostly stayed at home and paid the bank drafts. After three months I registered at a night school called Ecole Pigier where I learned accounting and French." Soon he was keeping accounts for the business.

From the apartment at 164, rue Montmartre, Davoud accompanied his uncle and brother to the nearby rue d'Aboukir in the Sentier, Paris' predominantly Jewish clothing wholesale district. There they bought leftover factory fabrics to send to Mirza to sell in Iran, which was then in the midst of a transformation engineered by Reza Shah, king since December 1925.

Aiming to unify and cement control over his splintered country — its 636,000 square miles populated by various ethnicities and tribes ruled by tribal leaders, Shiite clerics and provincial governors — Reza Shah was instituting new rules.

In 1925, when Habib was 13, the king required every Iranian to get birth certificates and pick a last name. This is how we got ours.

Habib's maternal grandmother understood the value of name recognition (what the 21st century zeitgeist calls branding). Exercising her matriarchal sway, Khorshid, who was Haim-Saghi's wife, said everyone in the family should take on the Elghana name. Her reasoning: Her brother Agha Baba Elghana and their two sons already were well-known businessmen. To Elghana, they added the patronymic plural suffix "yan" or "ian" to their earliest known male ancestor's name.

Around the same time, after my grandfather Habib dropped out of school, he tutored neighborhood kids in math for a while and worked briefly as an office boy at his great-uncle Agha Baba Elghana's store.

While his older brothers John and Davoud were in Paris in 1927 traveling by ship and then train via Baku and Moscow, Habib's formative years were spent in Iran. His uncle Mirza began to mentor and groom Habib, 15, at his recently finished hotel Gilan-No, a little north of the *Mahalleh*.

Habib first worked as a front-desk clerk, taking care of guests, did some accounting and changed money for international tourists. The hotel, elegant in its heyday until the late 1940s, had about two dozen rooms on two floors and a large room for receptions. Happy with his nephew's drive and outgoing personality, Mirza promoted him to hotel manager. At Gilan-No, Habib observed European and Western tourists and businessmen. He further polished his persona by devouring a book titled *Adaabe Moasherat*, similar in content to George Washington's *Rules of Civility and Decent Behavior in Company and Conversation*.[6]

Habib was also showing signs he was entrepreneurial. One day at the hotel, he picked up a magazine a Swiss guest had left, and, after reading about Swiss watches, he decided to order one. Pocket watches were still common, wristwatches a novelty in the 1920s. When the watch arrived from Switzerland, Habib sold it at a good profit. He soon ordered two more and began importing and selling them.[7]

No one was making watches in Iran, where hardly anything was manufactured. Most of the country's needs were met by imported goods, with the urban economy centered in the bazaars. The entire country had fewer than 20 modern industrial plants. The largest included an arsenal, a sugar refinery, a match factory and two textile mills. Fewer than a thousand people in all of Iran earned wages in large factories. Besides a few smaller plants that

---

6. Ruhollah Cohanim, interview with author in Los Angeles, April 2011.

7. Manouchehr Omidvar, interview with author in Great Neck, New York, March 2011.

produced electricity and brewed beer, the economy was largely an agricultural, feudal one that Reza Shah wanted to modernize.[8]

In 1929, while serving as a protégé in his uncle's hotel, Habib was drafted into the military under the newly instituted conscription. As part of the army, he was immersed in a national institution, designed to be an ethnic and religious equalizer and to teach order, discipline and allegiance to the ruler and the nation Reza Shah was building.

In a photo dated 1929, my grandfather is dressed in an army uniform with a military Pahlavi hat, similar to the French kepi. He's sitting sideways with his legs crossed and both hands resting over knee-high socks. At 17, his hard gaze suggests determination and self-confidence. Three friends, also in uniform, stand around him.

In another black-and-white photograph, dated Feb. 29, 1935, my grandfather's gaze is softer as he stands inside Gilan-No's yard. He's dressed in a light double-breasted suit with a pocket square and light-colored leather shoes, his dark wavy hair combed back. About a month shy of 23, his thin frame has filled out. He looks strapping, friendly and self-assured, his hallmark look.

Setting the two pictures side by side, I imagine him looking to the future with hope and optimism. Formidable events and institutions had shaped his life — from the Constitutional Revolution and the Alliance school to his military service and his uncle's mentoring — and had prepared him for what lay ahead in a country angling to enter the modern age.

Reza Shah's modernization plans, shifting the center of economic and political power from Iran's heavily rural and tribal areas to the country's urban centers, were about to enrich a new class of capitalists: merchants who would supply the goods to meet the rising demands of a population the

---

8. Ervand Abrahamian, *A History of Modern Iran*, (Cambridge, U.K.: Cambridge University Press, 2008).

king wanted to pull out of its feudal shell. Iran — open for change, progress, modernity — belonged to the entrepreneur.

But Reza Shah's aggressive goal to modernize Iran, beneficial for liberal Iranians, minorities and the urban class, was anathema to Iran's entrenched religious and economic elites who loathed change and feared losing their own sources of income. Like Kemal Ataturk in Turkey, Iran's king wanted to declare his nation a republic but there were clear risks. While some land-owners prospered by selling their agricultural products to the expanding urban centers, others lost their land; some were reportedly imprisoned until they agreed to sell. Tribes that once guarded their own territories were forced to give up their defense capabilities in favor of a unified army. Landowners, tribal leaders and the powerful Shiite clergy were sidelined. They were losing their status, tax exemptions and local authority. And they were fuming.

Reza Shah's authoritarian proclivities and his constant fear of being overthrown by the Soviets made him drift away from the notion of constitutional monarchy that intellectuals and bazaar merchants had fought for in 1906.[9]

Pondering all of this, I look again at the two black-and-white photographs of my grandfather, and they show me something more: After his parents raised their family in the ghetto, surviving segregation, famine and epidemics, after he served in the army and worked in Iran instead of going abroad like his brothers, his attachment to his homeland was taking root.

And yet, though I know he will soar, I feel dread as I stare at these pictures. I see what my grandfather, on his way to becoming one of Iran's most famous industrialists and the Iranian Jewish community's leader, cannot see: the traditionalist forces watching with disdain the rise of a new class of entrepreneurs, among them minorities, determined to modernize Iran. I see the clergy, lying in wait.

---

9. Robert Graham, *Iran: The Illusion of Power*, (New York: St. Martin's Press, 1979), p. 56.

CHAPTER 5

⌇

Unveiling the Future

Vast societal changes envisioned by the king were taking shape as Habib went through his 20s. Reza Shah was establishing universities and hospitals and building roads and railways to connect the entire country. Though massive, these projects were easy enough to engineer. Changing society's long-held beliefs and customs was not. Instead of embracing the country's rich ethnic, tribal and religious diversity, Reza Shah set out to redesign Iran's tapestry.

Imposing a nationwide dress code turned out to be a drastic step. Overturning widely accepted traditions, the code forbade women to wear veils and headscarves and forced men to dress like Westerners, all in the cause of modernity. But far from being truly modern — allowing freedom to choose — the code was intrusive and oppressive. Unifying by Westernizing aggravated a rift in Iranian society, further pitting the religious and traditional against those who yearned to be part of a larger world that they were discovering, a rift that persists today.

Iranians who had traveled to Europe in the 19th century, feeling insecure about their dress, opted to wear Western clothing, which came to represent modernity.[1] Religious Iranians who opposed wearing "infidel" clothing mocked them, calling them "fokoli" from faux col, French for false collar. The so-called "fokolis," mostly educated members of the elite, opposed the veil and Iran's patriarchal system. Since the Constitutional Revolution, women and intellectuals had also expressed their opposition to the veil. Soon, educated Iranians living in cities, along with some of Tehran's newspapers, also opposed the veil, which was fast becoming a sign of being unenlightened.

In 1928, Reza Shah started a campaign to forbid women from wearing the tchador, stripping them of their religious and traditional identity. His fiats extended to men, too: To be modern meant they too had to dress like Europeans, with the exception of several religious classes. Traditional menswear — such as *sardari* (frock pleated around the waist), *aba* (loose sleeveless cloak open in the front) and *ghaba* (long tunic open in the front) — was no longer acceptable, and even seen as embarrassing by some.

The unveiling program began at schools where female teachers were forbidden to work with their hair covered. Senior officials' wives also were ordered to attend public functions with uncovered heads.

Habib felt the tremors of this seismic change in his own home and in the streets. Despite the gradual phasing in of these rules and despite the fact that Reza Shah wanted to empower women, most Iranians were furious because covering heads in public was deeply ingrained as a sign of respectability. Even some Jewish women, including Habib's mother, were concerned about the decorum of going in public with their heads bare.

Going back at least to the early 16th century, Jewish women in Iran, like their Muslim counterparts, also had to cover their entire body. But for Jews, there was a detail meant to demean and set them apart: They were forced to sew bells on their veils' hems to signal their presence. In the mid-17th

---

1. Details about the unveiling come from this essay: Houchang E. Chehabi, "Staging the Emperor's New Clothes: Dress Codes and Nation-Building under Reza Shah" *Iranian Studies*, volume 26, numbers 3-4, Summer/Fall 1993.

century, Jewish women had to wear a two-color veil and leave their face uncovered because they were considered unworthy of respect. By the mid-19th century, all women covered their hair with a large scarf augmented by a veil and a piece of fabric worn in front of the face — white for Muslims, black for Jews.[2]

The custom of covering women predated even Islam's seventh-century arrival in Iran. The Greco-Roman historian Plutarch commented on the practice of hiding women during Iran's first royal dynasty of the Achaemenids (550-330 B.C.): "The Persians especially are extremely jealous, severe, and suspicious about their women, not only their wives, but also their bought slaves and concubines, whom they keep so strictly that no one ever sees them abroad; they spend their lives shut up within doors, and when they take a journey are carried in closed tents, curtained on all sides and set upon a wagon."[3]

The fear of a man being aroused by women's hair was so prevalent that most Iranians, men and women alike, didn't question the notion that hiding their hair protected women from men.

Even the shah's most intimate political adviser, the minister of court, Abdolhossein Taymourtash, who is credited with playing a crucial role in Iran's modernization and who was a proponent of unveiling, predicted resistance and a future demand for hats. In fact, while rural, tribal, poor and religious women refused to give up their veils, a small number in urban areas compromised and replaced their veils with hats, if they could afford them.

Absorbing the tensions of these years was Ruhollah Khomeini, who would shake the world as the founder of Iran's theocracy in 1979. In 1925,

---

2. Haideh Sahim, "Clothing and Makeup" in *Esther's Children: A Portrait of Iranian Jews,* ed. Houman Sarshar (Beverly Hills: The Center for Iranian Jewish Oral History, 2002) p. 177-178.

3. Plutarch, *Lives of the Noble Grecians and Romans (Parallel Lives),* Modern Library Series.

as a 23-year-old, he had moved to the holy city of Qom, about 100 miles south of Tehran. After memorizing the Quran at a theological center, he enrolled at Qom's Faizieh theological school, a center of Shiite scholarship founded in 1920. The Faizieh school became a gathering place for clergymen opposed to Reza Shah's modernization effort.

These clergymen were not alone. In summer 1935, *ulama* and preachers at the Gowharshad mosque, which was close to the shrine of Imam Reza in the northeastern town of Mashhad, delivered speeches against men's hats and women's unveiling. Over two days beginning July 13, 1935, security forces first tried to disrupt the gatherings by storming both the shrine and the mosque. The troops withdrew after killing some of the demonstrators but returned the next day with reinforcements and attacked the mosque, killing more people, arresting and exiling senior *ulama*.

Amid the upheaval, Habib saw the needs of a changing society — and he saw opportunity. "When Reza Shah banned the veil, I sat and thought about it," he said, as one of his friends recalls. "The women who were used to wearing a veil would still not come out of the house without covering their hair. So I decided to sell hats."[4]

At the time, European and American women were sporting short hair under bell-shaped hats, called cloches, followed by slouchy, short-brimmed fedoras. Hats were also manufactured in Iran, and women's magazines like *Alam e-Nesvam* carried numerous advertisements for hatmakers in the 1930s. At the bazaar, Habib picked up a few hats, which quickly sold, giving him a bigger idea. "I went to Lalezar Street," he continued explaining to his friend, "rented a store and ordered a case of hats from France." When those sold well, he said, "I went to Paris and purchased more hats to bring back home."

---

4. Manouchehr Omidvar, interview with author in Great Neck, New York, March 2011.

Despite restrictions on imports, women's hats were allowed into Iran. Over time, restrictions on what could and could not be imported would play a big role in Habib's future business ventures and ultimately lead to establishing factories in Iran.

Another entrepreneurial brainstorm came as Habib was walking one day in Tehran's Sheikh Hadi neighborhood, a mixed, progressive area with Muslims, Jews, Christians and Zoroastrians, where his family began renting a house from his uncle Hajji Mirza Agha in 1933. On his walk, Habib spotted a pretty young Armenian woman and hired her on the spot as a model for his store.

"The model looked good in all the hats, so women thought they would all look as good as she did," Habib said. Sales of hats soared. "There was a line every morning to buy them."

Even as the old guard stiffened its resistance to the veil ban, Habib's business flourished. He decided to look for an office in Tehran's grand bazaar, a centuries-old marketplace in the city's largest shopping area dominated by Muslim merchants called *bazaaris*. Like the clergy, the *bazaaris*, mostly middle class and religious, feared losing their status as the monarchy pushed to modernize and secularize Iran; this made the bazaaris and clergy natural allies. Decades later, their alliance would help topple the monarchy and reintroduce the obligatory head covering.

Undaunted, the sociable Habib found an old bearded man sitting in a bazaar office and asked him if he could put a table in a corner and work next to him. Once his hat business took off by 1936, Habib settled into his own second-floor bazaar office inside the Haji Mohammad Ismail arcade, the same section as his uncle Mirza. Like many of Iran's future industrialists, Habib first established roots in the bazaar.

All the while, he held his finger to the winds of a changing society. And he always knew how to sell what a modernizing nation wanted.

CHAPTER 6

⌣

A Pivotal Year

A pair of white gloves in his left hand, Habib stands tall in a black tuxedo. With the widow's peak of his wavy dark hair and the dimple in his chin accentuating his warm smile, the 24-year-old groom looks dashing. His right hand holds the arm of his petite bride, dressed in a long-sleeve white V-neck cinched-waist gown and satin shoes. The halo-shaped bouffant veil rises almost a foot above her face and cascades down around her feet. Cradling a large bouquet in her hand, she smiles. Nestled inside the flowers is a string of white lights that turn on and off with a small button at her fingertip. The bride is Habib's first cousin Nikkha, the 15-year-old daughter of his mentor and uncle Hajji Mirza Agha. The bride and groom are in a photographer's studio in 1936, posing for their wedding picture.

My grandmother had several names. Mahsoltan was her official name, though no one used it. Nikkha, meaning "the one who does good deeds," was her middle name. Those closest to her called her Nikkou Jan, literally "Nikkou Dear."

Soon after she was born in 1921, her father's business began to flourish. So Mirza considered Nikkha his good-luck charm. Family and friends took so seriously the idea that Nikkha filled her family's house with good luck that, during her wedding planning, relatives suggested that Mirza buy his daughter's luck from Habib — to keep for his own house. He refused, saying, "I want Nikkha to take it with her to enhance good fortunes in her new life."[1]

During a pre-wedding ceremony, it was customary for the father of the bride to wrap a scarf filled with bread, cheese and fresh herbs around the bride's waist to take her *barakat*, blessings, to her new home. When her father wrapped the symbolic *barakat* around her waist, he whispered in her ear, "Please leave some of it for me, too." And so it was that Mirza gave his good-luck charm to the nephew he had groomed for a decade. Her luck aside, Nikkou Jan brought a down-to-earth warmth and fierce loyalty to her husband and his work.

A few days before the wedding, came the *jahaz baran*, when the bride's dowry was delivered. A procession of hired men and women carried large trays of cakes, candy and fruit stacked in the shape of pyramids on their heads, while others bore her dowry on wooden planks. Musicians and dancers entertained hundreds of guests during the weeklong wedding festivities. Mirza gave Habib a gift of a small diamond ring and a matching diamond necklace to Nikkha. He also bought them a house near his on Zal Street, where Habib and Nikkou Jan lived until the end of World War II.

Nikkou Jan grew up without her husband's hardships. Though Habib had spent his childhood poor in the *Mahalleh*, by the time Nikkou Jan turned 5 in 1926, her family lived in a mansion. Mirza had lent money to a Qajar prince who couldn't pay back the debt; so, the prince relinquished his house in the Sheikh Hadi neighborhood on a street nicknamed Sadtomani Avenue (something similar to Millionaire's Row, even though "Sad Toman" literally meant 100 tomans). The property was large enough for six houses and needed three gardeners. Mirza, his wife Khanoum Jan (the same name

---

1. Mahnaz Elghanayan Fouladian, interviews with author.

as Habib's mother) and their children lived in the original mansion. At the back of the property, Mirza built a number of apartments that he rented out.

In the early 1930s, Mirza purchased a car with a manual crank that started the engine, one of just a few in Tehran at the time. During one of his trips to a neighboring Arab country, he brought back a chauffeur named Nasser who drove family members on errands, appointments and dates.

Mirza helped the community's poorer members. Between 8 and 10 every morning before going to work, he'd receive people at home seeking loans to get married, find a home or start a business. With the help of other Jewish merchants, he raised the needed money or found an available room for rent.[2]

As my grandmother moved out of her father's house in 1936, Mirza's luck did wane, while Habib's grew, advancing the superstition that Nikkou Jan was a good-luck charm. What had really happened was that years earlier, in 1931, Reza Shah had restricted imports to Iran, forcing Hajji Aziz to return from Paris with Habib's brothers John and Davoud. By 1933, the boys' uncles had sold off the inventory of fabrics imported from France and heavily invested in real estate. In the meantime, as hats were still allowed into the country, Habib's business was taking off.

Shortly before the inventory of imported goods was depleted, Mirza informed John and Davoud he had no work for them and gave them a total of 2,700 tomans. Aziz tried to help his nephews by suggesting they get their own license to import whatever goods they could. They followed his advice and after some successful ventures from 1933 to 1936, John and Davoud formed a partnership with Habib and their other brother Nourollah — it was called Elga LLC.

Noting that Habib needed help with banks as he ran his business, Davoud describes in his memoir a scene at the bazaar. "Habib went to his own office on the second floor of Haji Mohammad Ismail arcade, shut the door on himself and didn't come out at noon for lunch. He had a disagreement with

---

2. Pari Elghanian-Tabibnia, interview with author in Great Neck, New York, 2011.

Hajji Mirza Agha. He needed a bank signature for Bank Usmani but Hajji Mirza Agha had refused. Convinced that a big dispute would ensue from this, I discussed the matter with John. The same week, we talked to brother Habib and Nourollah and became partners."

Davoud and John loaned money, charging interest, to the new company. The four brothers, John, Davoud, Habib and Nourollah, with Lotfollah Victory, their maternal aunt's husband (who had not changed his name to Elghanayan), established a partnership, each owning 20 percent of Elga LLC.

Staying in the import business for now — even though Reza Shah's government was building manufacturing plants for everything from cigarettes to cement and offering low-interest loans — the Elga partners each took charge of one aspect of their new company. Habib, who had honed social grace at the hotel, had formed relationships at the bazaar and had displayed ingenuity in selling, took charge of sales. Nourollah, who had graduated from business high school in 1933, served as the idea man and sought out the foreign companies that could still export their goods to Iran. John, most fluent in French, corresponded with those companies. Davoud, with his excellent math skills, focused on finances. And Lotfollah Victory applied for quota allocations for imports at the Ministry of Economy.

Iranians' demand for luxury goods, coveted as status symbols, was growing. The brothers identified Switzerland as the best place from which to import watches and silk. "Business with Switzerland was open and many people did not know that at the beginning," Davoud remembers.

The Depression had shrunk Swiss export markets, but government and business interests worked together to negotiate bilateral trade deals to meet remaining demand. A Treaty of Friendship, Establishment and Commerce was signed with Iran, effective by summer 1935.[3] Nourollah got names of

---

3. "Convention d'établissement entre la Confédération suisse et l'Empire de Perse" April 25, 1935 and "Traité d'amitié entre la Confédération suisse et l'Empire de Perse," June 1, 1935.

watch and silk factories from the Swiss commercial attaché in Tehran, and in 1936, Elga LLC began importing luxury goods from Switzerland.

As business flourished, Habib and Nikkou Jan's first son, Fereydoun, "Fred," was born on March 21, 1939. Mirza kept an ambulance ready outside in case of an emergency that would require rushing his daughter to a hospital.

As World War II broke out in Europe, the brothers had made enough money to buy a big house for their parents and their unmarried brothers. Under the house's gabled roof on Massoud Saad street, the brothers established their new Elga LLC offices.

Business was about to boom.

CHAPTER 7

∿

War Years, Boom Years

With the coming of global war, so much would be changed forever. The world order would be reshaped, as would the Iranian monarchy, and with them, the fortunes of Habib, his brothers and our family.

Even before World War II broke out, Reza Shah had cultivated a complex relationship between his country and Germany, in service to advancing his modernization efforts and preventing Soviet and British influence from growing in Iran. In the late 1920s, after the British and Soviets opposed Reza Shah's plans for the Trans-Iranian Railway project, German companies stepped in, and in 1928, Julius Berger, a general contractor for mostly German and American firms, was awarded the construction contract for the first section of the rail system. It was ultimately to link Tehran with the Persian Gulf in the south and the Caspian Sea to the north. In 1930, German companies were also contracted for new textile and sugar plants.

Reza Shah relied on German citizens for financial expertise. A senior adviser in the Finance Ministry was Otto Schniewind. In 1927, when the National Bank of Persia (Bank Melli) was established with a mission to help bolster trade, industry and agriculture, the head was Kurt Lindenblatt. Later, following an inquiry into losses by the bank, he would be dismissed.

As Adolf Hitler rose to power in Germany, he had no plans for Iran. It was Alfred Rosenberg, the chief Nazi Party ideologist, who revived Iran's relations with Nazi Germany in spring 1934 with plans for a German sphere of influence stretching over the Balkans, Turkey and Persia up to the frontiers of India.

A 1935 agreement boosted Nazi Germany's role in the economy; the Germans became Iran's primary trading partners in the next five years. That same year, Reza Shah requested that the world community start referring to Persia as Iran, the name Iran called itself and which means "Land of The Aryans." The Nazis had rewritten the meaning of Aryan, which is an ancient nomenclature used to refer to the noble class and a geographic location called "Aryavarta."

Relations warmed: In 1936, the Reichsbank head and economic minister Hjalmar Schacht visited Iran. New commissions were given to German firms. In 1937, the Iranian parliament Speaker Hasan Mohtashem-al-Saltana-Esfandiari had an audience with Hitler. That winter, an emissary brought Hitler's invitation for Reza Shah to visit him in Germany, a trip he never made.

In August 1939, the Nazi-Soviet Pact that delineated each of the powers' spheres of interest was welcomed by Reza Shah, who thought it would benefit Iran's commercial relations with Germany and allow Iran to use Soviet routes to trade with Germany.

At the same time, however, he never formally aligned himself with any country. He punished allegedly Nazi circles in Tehran and gave refuge to persecuted intellectuals who fled Germany. When the war broke out in Europe in September 1939, Reza Shah declared Iran neutral.

In spring 1940, Iran began to fear it might be the target of a German-approved Soviet attack – and quietly approached the British for help. When

Germany attacked the Soviet Union on June 22, 1941, Iran welcomed the move because now it felt certain that the Soviets couldn't attack.

But maintaining Iran's claim of neutrality in the war would prove fateful when Reza Shah refused to allow the Allies the use of Iran's newly built rail system as a transport corridor to ship arms to Russia to fight Germany. On July 29, 1941, he rejected the Allies' request to expel Germans in Iran who were helping build factories, roads and bridges. Worried that those Germans could spy for Hitler's Axis, the Allies renewed their request on Aug. 16. A week later, Reza Shah ordered the Germans to leave, but he had waited too long.

The Anglo-Soviet invasion of Iran came two days later with a sea, air and land assault. More than a dozen Iranian divisions surrendered. In exchange for keeping his family in power, Reza Shah abdicated and went into exile on Sept. 16. His eldest son, 22-year-old Mohammad Reza Pahlavi, who had studied in Swiss schools since age 11, became king.[1]

Reza Shah had failed to understand how claiming to be neutral on the one hand and displaying pro-German leanings on the other would do him in. Worse, he had miscalculated the power and resolve of Britain and the Soviet Union to protect their vital interests.[2]

Living through this historic tumult were my grandfather and his family. They would adjust to the new Iranian reality. Shielded from the horrors of the Holocaust and remembering that they had once benefitted from foreign Jewish support, the family joined with other members of the Iranian Jewish community to help those escaping the Nazis.

With Britain and the Soviets occupying Iran and in charge of the nation's road transportation and military affairs, the Persian Corridor became an

---

1. "GERMANY I, German-Persian diplomatic relations," *Encyclopaedia Iranica* online edition.
2. Robert Graham, *Iran: The Illusion of Power,* (New York: St. Martin's Press, 1979) p. 57.

important supply route to the Soviet Union. Further, it was now also open for Polish refugees to come to Iran, including some 900 Polish Jewish children, mostly orphans, who had survived bombings, disease and starvation.

The story of how more than 100,000 Polish refugees, Christian and Jewish, wound up in Iran has its roots at the beginning of the war on Sept. 1, 1939, when Polish Jewish families fled to the Soviet Union after Germany invaded their country. When Germany invaded the Soviet Union in June 1941, Poles had to move deeper inside the Soviet Union, where even more children were separated from their families and placed in Soviet orphanages.

After the Soviets invaded and annexed eastern Poland and the Germans occupied western Poland, the Soviets began a campaign of mass arrests of Christian Poles, whom they sent to Siberian camps and Soviet Central Asia from early 1940 to mid-1941. In August 1941, the Soviets released Polish POWs, Jewish and Christian, who had fled both German and Soviet invasions and allowed the creation of a Polish Army in the Soviet Union — Anders Army, named for its commander, Gen. Wladyslaw Anders. In March 1942, the British and Soviets agreed to evacuate Anders Army from the Soviet Union via Iran to go to Palestine.

By late summer 1942, around 116,000 Polish refugees and Anders Army personnel had made their way into Iran. Among them were 2,000 Jews, half of them children, mostly malnourished and in rags. The Jewish Agency for Palestine learned of the children's pending arrival in Iran and sent Zipporah Shertok (wife of Moshe Shertok, who eventually became Israel's second prime minister) to organize and to separate the Jewish children from the rest to have them repatriated to Palestine.[3]

The children were housed in camps around Iran, including in tents on the grounds of a former military barracks outside Tehran. For help, Mrs. Shertok contacted, among others, Elizabeth Kotler, the daughter of a St. Petersburg rabbi, who had fled the Russian Revolution with her merchant

---

3. Aryeh Levin, e-mail correspondence with author, October 2017.

husband Leo and first settled in Berlin where her father-in-law sent a convoy of German trucks to Iran during Reza Shah's modernization campaign. The couple resettled in Tehran when Hitler came to power. Mrs. Kotler, who was very much at home among the Iranian Jewish community, immediately got the wheels rolling to aid the refugees. Among those she approached was Habib's uncle Hajji Aziz.[4]

Aziz was one of the 12 founding members of Iran's Zionist movement in 1919. Iranian Jews' early Zionist activities were centered on religion and language, mainly the introduction of Hebrew classes and publications, but also raising money for the Zionist Congress, whose goal was to facilitate Jewish settlement in Palestine. Although Reza Shah suppressed the movement in 1926, it began to flourish again in Iran after a decade and a half.[5]

When the refugee crisis arose, assistance came from the American Jewish Joint Distribution Committee, the Hadassah Women's Zionist Organization in the U.S., and the Youth Immigration Department of the Jewish Agency, but Mrs. Kotler organized the Iranian Jewish community. Besides contributing money and other assistance to clothe, house and provide medical care for the young refugees in their own camp, the Tehran Home for Jewish Children, some Iranian Jews took children into their homes, pending their departure to Palestine. In January 1943, 716 of the Tehran Children, as they became known, were repatriated by land, then sea; 110 more were sent in August overland via Iraq. The remaining children stayed and were adopted by Iranian Jewish families.[6]

---

4. Aryeh Levin, email correspondence with author, October 2017.
5. Avi Davidi, "Zionist Activities in Twentieth-Century Iran," in *Esther's Children: A Portrait of Iranian Jews*, ed. Houman Sarshar (Beverly Hills: The Center for Iranian Jewish Oral History, 2002) p. 246.
6. "Tehran Children," United States Holocaust Memorial Museum, Washington, *Holocaust Encyclopedia* online.

"Prior to the arrival of Polish Jewish refugees and the subsequent appearance of Zionist activities in Iran, Iranian Jews' relationship with Israel was understood through the biblical tradition that denied the Jews the return to their homeland without the coming of the Messiah," writes Alessandra Cecolin in her book *Iranian Jews in Israel: Between Persian Cultural Identity and Israeli Nationalism.*

Iran was Habib's millennia-old homeland, a country that was finally embracing equality for Jews, opening doors for him. All this was happening while Jews were being sent to gas chambers in Europe, where decades earlier they had been killed in pogroms. His uncle Aziz had helped the children who had survived: They had lost everything. They needed a Jewish state where they could be safe.

My grandfather visited Palestine for the first time shortly before his second son Karmel, my father, was born on Jan. 24, 1943. The story goes that, smitten by Mount Carmel, he decided to name my father after the mountain range.

Meanwhile, business was good for Elga LLC, which had undergone a change in structure. After a dispute between Habib's brother John and Lotfollah Victory, the company purchased Victory's 20 percent share and divided it among the three youngest brothers. Sion, 21, took over the work involved with customs, Nejat, 23, was assigned to real estate, and 17-year-old Attollah, "Eddy," who was just finishing high school, had a role to be determined.

The brothers worked hard. "We took our business very seriously and worked from dawn to dusk," Davoud recalls. "We did not close our business on the Sabbath, except one day on Yom Kippur and a half-day before it. We just worked and worked. We took showers, I believe, no more than once every month. We shaved two or three times a week. We changed our coat and pants once every two or three months."

The work could require a special touch. Davoud drove one day to the Iranian port of Khorramshahr, where 10 trucks full of goods shipped from

Europe awaited him. En route back to Tehran, he was stopped by Russian and British soldiers who controlled the distribution of supplies. Davoud bribed the Russian soldiers with watches and the British with whiskey and money. Another time, when a major shipment of imports arrived at the Iran-Iraq border at Khanagin-Ghasr-e Shirin, the post office wouldn't transport the goods to Tehran. Davoud drove to the port, packed the parcels himself and tailgated the trucks back to Tehran.

Though their labors were constant, Davoud remembers, "We were happy." Prices rose for their watches and silks, and so did profits. "Sometimes, we had five to 10 bags of bank notes in the safe at home and waited to find time to deposit the money in the bank. We concealed part of it in the gable of the roof."

Another development enhanced business further. In 1943, John moved to New York. From there, he would send his brothers products that were in demand in Iran: ladies' combs, plates, glasses, forks, knives, jugs, socks, cotton, radios, sewing machines.

During the tumultuous war years, there were clear winners and losers. "The presence of Allied forces (in Iran) had an enormous impact on the distribution of supply, which led to famine in some areas and to increasing inflation in others," according to historian Nikki Keddie.[7] The war was "detrimental to lower classes and those on fixed incomes." The war prompted nomadic tribes to move again after being forced to settle under Reza Shah, and many impoverished peasants migrated to cities.[8]

"In 1942 through 1943, there were bread riots in Iran; hunger was widespread. Shortages of everything from tires and wheat to sugar and tea,

---

7. Nikki Keddie, *Roots of Revolution: An Interpretive History of Modern Iran*, (Yale University Press, 1981) p. 116.
8. Ali Madanipour, *Tehran: The Making of a Metropolis*, (Chichester, England: John Wiley & Sons Ltd, 1998) p. 28.

threatened the stability of the society and the very survival of some of its lower strata," historian Abbas Milani recounts in *Eminent Persians*.[9]

In barely a decade, between 1936 when Elga LLC was established and the end of World War II in 1945, my grandfather stood among what historian Ervand Abrahamian later called "old-time entrepreneurs who made their first million during the commercial boom of WWII."[10] This group went on to make additional millions in the following decades.

Shortly after the war, Habib sold the house his father-in-law Mirza bought for him and Nikkou Jan and bought a big house from a former Soviet diplomat, just across the street from Mirza's mansion. A water fountain adorned the front garden of the white stucco house, which the family called "Oscouee" after the diplomat's last name. Inside, a grand marble staircase led to bedrooms next to the house's piece de resistance, a bathroom that my father estimates as "the size of a Manhattan studio apartment," complete with a Swedish shower shooting water from all four walls.

The house was appointed with Persian rugs and paintings by 19th century Russian artist Ivan Aivazovsky, famous for marine scenes, all crowned by a chandelier hanging over the living room's Art Deco furniture and Steinway piano. "Oscouee" came with its own gasoline pump and pit for changing oil.

In 1945, Nourollah, Habib's younger brother, emigrated to the United States, joining John. When Iran lifted a ban on the import of secondhand clothes, John and Nourollah began sending used clothing to Tehran. After the war, affordable mass-produced clothing was in large supply in the United States — everything from corporate and career dress to athletic apparel and leisurewear. The changing lifestyles and consumption patterns

9. Abbas Milani, "From Rags to Riches to Revolution, The Iranian Economy, 1941–1979," *Eminent Persians: The Men and Women Who Made Modern Iran 1941-1979*, Vol. 2 (Syracuse: Syracuse University Press and Persian World Press, 2008), p 582.

10. Ervand Abrahamian, *Iran Between Two Revolutions*, (Princeton, New Jersey: Princeton University Press, 1982), p. 432.

in the United States created a surplus of gently used clothing. With more clothing donated to charitable organizations than could be re-sold in stores across America, organizations disposed of their overstock at bulk prices to commercial secondhand dealers.[11] Nourollah would buy it by the pound to send to Iran.

The brothers also had exclusive rights to import Singer sewing machines and Bulova watches to Iran.

After the war, my grandfather and Davoud became partners with a Muslim businessman, Hajji Mirza Attoallah Moghadam, who needed money to make large deals for the sale of cotton to Russia. They lent him 1.8 million tomans. Within a few months, Moghadam sold a large consignment of cotton to Russia and returned the money plus 1 million tomans in profits. In the 1950s, the three became partners in a venture called Hides, Wool & Cotton Joint Stock Co. They also invested in Gol Vegetable Oil Co. And a few years later they partnered in a textile manufacturing plant named Momtaz Co.

The switch from importing consumer goods to manufacturing started with Moghadam but expanded later with all the brothers.

In 1948, Habib's youngest brother Eddy, 24, was studying business administration at Massachusetts' Leicester Junior College. He was a short 25 miles from Leominster, which was nicknamed "Comb City" in the 1930s and later "Plastic City" as that industry grew. Leominster-based Viscoloid Co. supplied comb manufacturers with synthetic materials; celluloid and acetate celluloid supplanted increasingly scarce horn. The company also fabricated cuffs, combs and brushes.

Ubiquitous today, plastic was about to revolutionize the consumer goods industry. Plastics slowly entered quotidian 20th-century life, replacing expensive natural materials like ivory, tortoise-shell, agate, amber,

---

11. Scribd digital library, Secondhand Clothing Global Fashion, pp 232-237. https://www.scribd.com/document/79262409/Secondhand-Clothing-Global-Fashion.

malachite and horn. With this material capable of assuming infinite shapes, various textures, degrees of hardness, density, resilience and color by being molded or extruded at high volume and a modest cost to the manufacturer, the industry mass-produced items once reserved for the wealthy.

From 1940 to '45, wartime requirements accelerated demand for synthetic materials, which tripled in the United States.[12] They were used for military purposes like cockpit covers, mortar fuses and helmet liners.

Consumer plastics were another matter. Jeffrey Meikle in his book *American Plastic, A Cultural History*, notes: "Many postwar newcomers went out of business after littering the landscape with shoddy products. From teetering on being a fad in the '40s, the plastics industry took off in the United States in the '50s, and by 1960, annual production was 6 billion pounds, compared to 818 million pounds in 1945."[13]

The seven brothers laid a big bet on manufacturing plastic goods in Iran.

"In 1948, I visited a plastics factory for a class and found it interesting," Eddy told me over tea in his Los Angeles apartment. He sent a catalogue to Habib, Davoud and Sion.

"They told me to buy two machines," Eddy said. He bought two Reed-Prentice machines with two comb molds and a plastic bowl mold and sent them to Iran. Other machine purchases followed. "Every 15 seconds, they would make six combs."[14]

In 1948, Reed-Prentice, based in West Springfield, Massachusetts, manufactured two types of injection molding machines.[15] The process was simple. Raw plastic, in the form of pellets, was poured into a hopper that evenly

---

12. Jeffrey L. Meikle, *American Plastic, A Cultural History*, (New Brunswick, New Jersey: Rutgers University Press, 1995) p. 60.

13. Ibid, p. 6.

14. Attollah Elghanayan, interview with author in Los Angeles, April 2011.

15. The two available molds at the time were the 10D-6 and the 10D-8.

spread the material over a heated basin. The melted plastic was then injected into the mold, which was shut tight until it cooled and rapidly solidified.

Habib and Davoud set up the machines in a property in the Lalezar-No shopping district that they had purchased that year. They named their plastics manufacturing company Plasco. With John, Nourollah and Eddy in America, Davoud and Habib put younger brothers Sion and Nejat in charge of managing the factories. Sion "was in love with the machines," Davoud remembers, "and Nourollah loved buying them, especially old machines."

Soon Plasco Co. was also producing buttons, and the Lalezar-No factory was filling up with around 20 machines. This marked the first time plastic goods were being manufactured on such a large scale in the Middle East.

In Frank Capra's 1946 movie, *It's a Wonderful Life*, George Bailey turns down Sam Wainwright's proposal to get into plastics, on the ground floor: "I don't want any plastics, I don't want any ground floors."

My grandfather and his brothers did — and it turned out to be what Sam called the chance of a lifetime.

Gallery

Reza Shah, founder of the Pahlavi dynasty.

Habib's maternal uncle, Hajji Aziz, second left, with the other founders of Iran's Zionist movement in Tehran in 1919.

Lalezar Street in 1946, Tehran's most prominent retail thoroughfare was inspired by Paris' Champs-Elysées.

Habib, back row center, stands for a family photo c. 1925, flanked by his maternal uncles and mentors Hajji Aziz, center left, and Hajji Mirza Agha, center right. In the middle row are his mother's parents, Haim Saghi and Khorshid Khanoum. Nikkou Jan, Habib's first cousin, is seated bottom row, second right.

Habib, seated in the middle, surrounded by friends during his military
service c. 1928–1929.

Habib's brother Nourollah, back row third from left, graduated from Tejarat (business) high school in 1933. Nourollah's sons, Henry, Tom and Fred, went on to establish two real estate firms, Rockrose Development Corp. and TF Cornerstone. Their family was ranked 122 on Forbes List of Richest American Families in 2015.

Habib standing in the courtyard of his uncle Hajji Mirza Agha's Gilan-No Hotel in Tehran in 1935.

Habib and Nikkou Jan's wedding picture in Tehran in 1936.

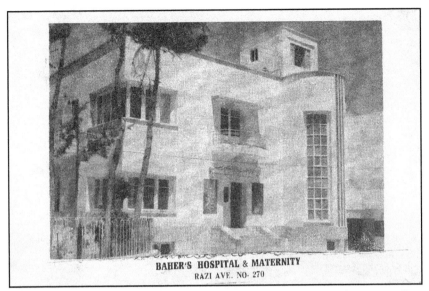

When they permanently moved to Shemiran in 1960, Habib donated their house at 270 Razi Ave. to Dr. Nassrolah Baher, the midwife Ghodsi Baher's husband, who transformed it into "Baher's Hospital and Maternity."

Nikkou Jan, Karmel, Fred and Habib in Tehran c. 1944-1945

PART II

Titan and the Symbol of Iran's Jews

CHAPTER 8

⌒

Roots and Uprootedness

Sitting in the back of the car en route to Tehran's Mehrabad airport, 11-year-old Karmel fiddled with the levers and button of his new camera, excited to take pictures of his journey — though fearful of leaving home. His mother Nikkou Jan had given him the camera during a big goodbye party at home on the eve of his departure in late August 1954; it would document his new life in America.

Friends and relatives in their cars and rented buses made a caravan-like procession from the house to the airport to bid Karmel bon voyage. Soon he would be starting Nyack Boys School in New York. His small consolation was that his older brother Fred, who had been sent to America a couple years earlier, would be in the same boarding school up the Hudson River from Manhattan.

At the airport, everyone hugged and blessed Karmel before he climbed the plane's steps accompanied by uncle Sion. Joining them was a family acquaintance whose brother would be Iran's finance minister in the 1970s.

On Aug. 31, they landed in Shannon, Ireland, where Sion was suddenly hospitalized. When he recovered and refused to get on another plane, the travelers purchased tickets to cross the Atlantic aboard the ocean liner RMS Mauretania.[1] Outside the ship's terminal at the Irish port of Cobh, they took pictures with Karmel's new camera before setting sail. During the five-day crossing, Karmel befriended a crew member who instructed him to ring his cabin bell for ice cream, which he did without hesitation more than once a day. On Sept. 16, the ship with its 1,360 passengers passed the Statue of Liberty under blue skies and docked on the west side of Manhattan. Davoud, John and Nourollah greeted them as they disembarked.

That September, my father, began a new life in a new country, starting a 13-year sojourn, spanning the Eisenhower, Kennedy and Johnson administrations, during which he attended a series of boarding schools in New York, Rhode Island and Massachusetts before going to the University of Vermont. Unlike his own father's childhood in Iran, he was shipped away to spend his formative years far from home and community. While my grandfather had remained in Iran to be groomed for business by his uncle, my father, uprooted from Iran, was becoming American.

Back in Tehran, Karmel had been a *sheytoon*, Farsi for a rascal. He'd sneak up behind Nikkou Jan with his toy gun to scare her. Once, he rambunctiously hid in a drainage ditch, again making her frantic until relatives found him.

Now, survival and loneliness would become his childhood companions. I gained some insight into what it was like for my father to be alone so far away from home when I read a 1987 *New York Times Magazine* article written by another former student at the Nyack Boys School, Michael Norman. "Before Nyack, I do not think I knew what loneliness was," he wrote. "Now, having again walked the grounds and re-entered the rooms of the great estate where I spent a year of my boyhood, I can easily summon to the surface the deep ache of that first night in my room as I looked out between the mullions into the darkness at the car lights creeping across the bridge," he continued. "Nothing dulled that ache, not puppets brought from home

---

1. Passenger manifest from Sept. 11, 1954, retrieved from ancestry.com.

and held close in bed, not the nurse with the soft hands in the infirmary, not even the infrequent notes from my mother on her scented letterhead.

"I must have sensed then that a certain break had taken place and that there was no way to close the distance between where I was and where I had been. Later, I was told, or more likely shown, that men were not supposed to want that distance closed. And by then I had already started on the road to independence and self-reliance, and in so doing insured forever the loneliness."[2]

After I showed my father the article, he told me: "I remember my first night there too. I felt like the writer. I cried at night, I felt lonely and missed home. I agree with what he says about the lessons of separation, independence and resiliency which have made me strong."

He said his parents sent Fred and him there "because they thought they were doing the right thing, thinking they were giving us a better education. They didn't know any better." That decision nevertheless became key to how we survived the revolution and my grandfather didn't. I asked if we could visit his school together so I could see for myself the place where my uprooted father had been replanted.

We drove there on a sticky summer day. The Nyack Boys School, founded in 1934 on the former estate of attorney J. DuPratt White, closed in 1972, and the same campus is now called The Summit School. Sitting in the car next to my then 72-year-old father dressed in his preppy khakis and salmon colored T-shirt, my heart ached for the 11-year-old boy who'd been sent across the ocean.

As we drove through Nyack, along avenues with vintage street lights, we saw the same convenience store where my father would buy candy, and we took in the grand New England and Victorian-style rooftops peeking out from behind stone walls. We passed the childhood home of the artist

---

2. Michael Norman, "About Men - The Road to Self-Reliance," *New York Times Magazine*, Dec. 13, 1987.

Edward Hopper, known for painting solitary figures. I thought of my father as almost the prototypical Hopper subject: the man who, sitting by himself in a cafe, in his apartment, anywhere really, feels most at home where loneliness is present.

We drove into the school entrance, down the driveway to what used to be called Bok House, just feet from the Hudson River. At 11, my father had left his family home for the Tudor style 22-room stone and stucco mansion that served as dining hall, study hall and dorm for the youngest students, where he shared a room with three other boys. The hilly estate had several other cream-colored dormitories for middle and high school kids.

The school instilled order, discipline and self-reliance. Karmel would wake up in his room on an upper floor, shower, then put on his gray slacks, navy jacket with red trim and striped tie before standing for inspection. Downstairs in the dining hall, he ate breakfast, where his favorite was hot biscuits with melted butter. Students sat with their own classmates, but he could say hello or wave to his brother and cousin in the dining hall.

Henry, one of Nourollah's sons who was also a student there, captained the football team, enhancing my father's status with the other boys. Like every student, once a week, he'd be separated from his classmates to join the grown-ups at headmaster and school founder John Karkos' table. Within three years, Karkos would leap to his death off the nearby Tappan Zee Bridge.[3] My dad remembers the entire town in a tizzy for weeks over his headmaster's suicide.

Communication with his parents was limited. There were no phone calls home. Friday nights after supper, his first chore was to write home; the letter was checked for spelling until it was flawless. Then the boys could all gather around the television and watch *The Adventures of Rin Tin Tin* and *The Adventures of Ozzie and Harriet*, both popular shows at the time.

---

3. "Head Master Dies in Leap in Hudson John B. Karkos, Founder of Nyack Boys School, Jumps From Tappan Zee Bridge," *The New York Times*, Aug. 8, 1957.

In these and other ways, he was absorbing and assimilating the prevailing mores and lifestyle of his new country. He swam at the YMCA on Tuesdays and Thursdays and otherwise left the campus on weekends to shop at the convenience store, see movies, have ice cream at Woolworth's, and visit the showroom where he fell in love with antique cars. My father and a couple of other Jewish kids also attended Saturday morning Shabbat services at the local synagogue.

Our trip to Nyack was bittersweet: I loved walking on the school campus, going inside the old store and the Y, seeing the building that housed the old synagogue and driving on Main Street. Yet, as I imagined my father buying candy, swimming in the pool, walking back to the campus from Shabbat services, I couldn't help being sad for the little boy 6,000 miles from home.

My father explained to me that my grandfather had pondered moving to the United States one year before sending him away but that in summer 1953, after visiting his brothers in New York, he had made up his mind to stay in Iran.[4]

That same summer Prime Minister Mohammed Mossadegh was overthrown in a coup orchestrated by Britain and the United States. It's not clear when in 1953, but Davoud writes, "One day in 1953, they came to our office . . . and seized all our commercial books, files and papers . . . and took it with them. They also took Habib and me with them but released us after several hours of interrogation. However they kept the books and files, and examined them thoroughly for 10 days. . . . One can only guess how heavy those 10 days hung on our heads. Finally after a lot of trouble, seeing the right people at the right places and spending money, we were able to get our files back. Only Habib and I know what we endured."

"This kind of treatment against us was repeated several times under various pretexts. A couple of times, they took us to SAVAK (the secret police

---

4. Passenger manifest from Ancestry.com shows he landed in New York on June 22, 1953.

and acronyn for "*Sazman-e Etelaat Va Amniat Keshvar*" or Organization of Intelligence and Security of the Country) too but could not find any evidence against us."

What mystified me and what I wanted to understand was why a man as rooted in Iran as my grandfather would uproot his own son and send him to America when he wouldn't move there himself despite the difficulties of doing business in Iran at times.

Did it have to do with the way he had learned to do business, emulating his mentor Hajji Mirza Agha, who had stayed in Iran while his partner Hajji Aziz went to Paris? Was he merely more attached in the 1950s to his Iranian lifestyle than his brothers' lifestyle in New York?

Once John and Nourollah's families had settled in Queens, Sion and Eddy also moved to New York. The only members of the family left in Tehran were their parents and sister Saltanat, along with Habib, Davoud, and Nejat. In spring 1952, my uncle Fred and his cousin Henry were turning 13, the same year Eddy was marrying Flora Nehurai. With the entire family planning to be in New York for the wedding, Habib and Nourollah decided to celebrate their sons' bar mitzvahs at the same time and place. Flush with postwar money, they booked the gilded grand ballroom at the Waldorf-Astoria for a black-tie affair with hundreds of guests dancing to a live band deep into the night.

Was that not something to want to come back to?

Or did life in Iran just fit his personality more? It was, after all, a good life. Contrast the Waldorf gathering, for instance with the party Habib threw for the bris of Sina, the son born in 1950, two years after a daughter, my aunt Mahnaz, was born.[5] For that party, Habib invited the up-and-coming "Iranian Edith Piaf," the 26-year-old singer Marzieh, to perform. The evening became legendary in the family, as the dark-haired, Rubenesque

---

5. Between Fred and Karmel, they had a daughter Guiti, who died when she was around 2 years old. Nikkou Jan also had several miscarriages until Mahnaz was born. After Sina, she lost twins, a boy and a girl, who were stillborn following a car accident in the snow on New Year's Eve.

Marzieh performed a song everyone knew, *Shabeh Mahtab* (*Moonlit Night*), for Habib, whose name appears in the refrain:

Tonight is a moonlit night and I want my Habib.
If my Habib is asleep, I still want my Habib;
Tell him I'm here.

Over the years, whenever Marzieh sang *Moonlit Night* in her throaty mezzo-soprano, Iranians identified the Habib she was singing about with my grandfather.

There were other things, more serious, that made him feel attached to Iran, such as his charitable work in the Jewish community. In 1948, with Davoud and Jewish friends, he had established the Ettehad Charitable and Cultural Association of Tehran to help poor students of their old Alliance School, to which they felt indebted.

Might his decision have been influenced by the unspoken but lingering anti-Semitism that he saw in the United States? Since the end of World War II, John and Nourollah had settled in Forest Hills Gardens, a high-end Queens community laid out in 1910 as a traditional medieval English village. (The house Nourollah and his wife Victoria lived in was at the corner of a street called Rockrose Place, a name their sons Henry, Fred and Tommy would borrow for their real estate firm Rockrose Development Corp.) Nourollah and John bought their houses with cash hoping no one would realize Iranians could also be Jews. At the time, restrictive covenants reserved the enclave to white Christians.[6]

Working around insidious anti-Semitism at that time took many forms. For example, since Jews were not allowed in social clubs, the Catskills became a self-segregated summer resort. My father attended Camp Dalmaqua there, except in the handful of summers he returned to Iran. His parents' infrequent visits to New York further fostered his independence.

There was, however, a special visit when my father turned 13 in winter 1956, when Habib flew with Nikkou Jan and Sina to celebrate Karmel's bar

---

6. Richard F. Shepard, "Memories of my Queens," *The New York Times*, Sept. 3, 1995.

mitzvah. In a home movie from the party, Habib, two months shy of 44, looks suave in a white tuxedo jacket, mingling with guests, a drink in one hand, a cigarette in the other, chatting with his brothers like the cast of a Rat Pack movie.

By 13, my father had a striking resemblance to the actor Sal Mineo, who had starred with James Dean in the 1955 movie *Rebel Without a Cause*. Seeing the movie, he had made up his mind to become an actor when he grew up; so, when his father asked him what he wanted for his bar mitzvah gift, he said he wanted the whole family to visit California where they could tour Hollywood studios.

That summer, they embarked on a two-week trip to the West Coast. Besides family members, they were accompanied by Ghodsi Baher, the midwife who helped deliver all of Nikkou Jan's children and had moved to America and become Fred and my father's legal guardian. Habib had rented an apartment for Mrs. Baher, my father and Fred in Forest Hills,[7] where she stayed to be in charge of the boys when they weren't in school. The petite, spry, red-haired woman became a second mother to my father.

During the family's visit to MGM's studios, Nikkou Jan spotted Charlton Heston sitting in costume for *The Ten Commandments*, studying his script.

"Look! It's Moses," she yelled. "My God, it's Moses."

The family stayed at the Ambassador Hotel, and at night, they'd dine at the Cocoanut Grove at a table reserved for them in front of the stage. One night, Nat King Cole, one of my father's favorite singers, was performing. As Cole started to sing *Nature Boy*, Nikkou Jan fell asleep, as she easily did. Back home in Tehran, Habib didn't always take her to big social events for this very reason. When he arrived at parties by himself, people assumed he didn't love her, or that he was embarrassed by her. Perhaps he didn't want her to be embarrassed. Regardless, they had a special bond. When she'd

---

7. Outside the Forest Hills Gardens, on 67th Avenue between Queens and Yellowstone Boulevards a block away from where I coincidentally lived between 2003 and 2010.

visit their children in America, Habib would write her letters that she kept in her purse. The house wasn't home without her, he'd say. Reading the letters over and over again, she'd smile.

Summer's end after the family's trip to Los Angeles brought my father's entry into middle school — at the Peekskill Military Academy, where the motto included the words "Stand Firm as an Oak." In the cool autumn breezes, leaves turned red, yellow and orange. Karmel loved the foliage, but the falling leaves were a reminder that summer's fun was gone, along with his family, who'd returned to Iran. As the lights went off in his new dorm room, he laid his head on his pillow, alone again.

On our drive back to Manhattan from Nyack, my heart still hadn't stopped aching for the uprooted boy. I had stood with him where he had learned to detach himself from his family. That ability to walk away, no matter how painful, would allow him to pick up and leave Iran for good in 1977, sparing us the violence of the Iranian Revolution. Right there, along the Hudson flowing past us, was where he learned to leave.

We had survived. We were in the car together.

CHAPTER 9

~

Moving to Shemiran

On summer afternoons, weeping willows lazily sway in a tickling breeze over pools fed by mountain streams. Winter turns the trees into bewitching brides, snowflakes forming delicate veils over their naked limbs. This is Shemiran, meaning the "cold place." Nestled on the foothills of the snow-capped Alborz Mountains, Tehran's Shemiran District once served as the summer residence of the Qajar kings, then the Pahlavis: Saadabad and Niavaran palaces are in Shemiran, too.

Made up of a dozen neighborhoods including Darband on the far northern edge, Shemiran is where Tehran's post-revolutionary upper-classes-turned-multimillionaires since 1979 reside today. In the 1950s and '60s, the area had none of today's luxury high-rises, high-end clothing stores, restaurants and cafes. Centuries-old, slim, towering trees hugged hushed, winding roads crowned by the mountain.

In the mid-1950s, Habib and Davoud purchased a property on Khalili Street from Mahmoud Khalili, the owner of Butane Gas, the liquid petroleum gas company he founded in 1953. An orchard where Nikkou Jan loved to pick fresh fruit stood to the right. To the left, stairs led to an old cream-colored brick house with a large terrace with mountain views. Their families took turns using it in the summer. Up the slope from the old house, a large rectangular swimming pool was fed by the cool Darband stream that also supplied water to the entire house.

As wealthy Iranians increasingly began making Shemiran their primary residence, Habib bought Davoud's share of the property in 1958 to move there permanently, marking the start of my grandfather's halcyon years. Here were the good days that led to even better ones.

Some of Habib's merchant friends, who had hired architect Houshang Seyhoon to design their homes, introduced my grandfather to the renowned modernist who had created Tehran's Central Railway Station and monuments honoring the poet Ferdowsi and the scientist Ibn Sina. Seyhoun built a new house on the land formerly occupied by the orchard (over Nikkou Jan's protests about this location) while the beige brick house that had been used in the summer became a guesthouse.

After studying fine arts at the Ecole Nationale Supérieure in Paris, Seyhoun wanted to modernize Iranians' homes while retaining traditional flourishes.[1] For Habib and Nikkou Jan, he designed a two-story mid-century style house with an open floor plan. On the house's front facade, a mosaic mural of tiny purple, yellow, white, orange and turquoise tiles forming an abstract design separated two large floor-to-ceiling sliding glass doors. The left one opened into the living room and the other into the master bedroom. Sitting as a child at the patio lunch table in front of the mural, I remember being mesmerized by the tiles — shiny, colorful flecks that tangoed with the sun.

Nikkou Jan kept the sliding door to the bedroom mostly open because she enjoyed having friends and family walk into the house through her bedroom, where she'd invite them to sit on the bed to chat and catch up. The second floor had a room each for the younger children, Sina and Mahnaz.

---

1. Houshang Seyhoun, phone interview with author, June 2013.

The front lawn, about an acre, had a patio where the family ate lunch and a small kidney-shaped swimming pool.

In keeping with the architecture's mid-century aesthetics, the home was sparsely decorated with light green-gray velvet couches; the bedroom painted a light gray. From their previous house, Nikkou Jan and Habib had brought the china, artwork, carpets and Steinway piano. In Shemiran, Nikkou Jan had a small storage space, an *anbar* in Farsi, where she stored jewelry, textiles, rugs, coins and everything she wanted to give her children and their husbands or wives. Wherever she went, she nearly always held in her hand the key to her *anbar*.

When they permanently moved to Shemiran in 1960, Habib donated their old house to Dr. Nassrolah Baher, husband of the midwife Ghodsi Baher, who transformed it into "Baher's Hospital and Maternity." Habib's uncle Mirza gave part of his own neighboring land to Baher, too. That hospital was eventually purchased by Dr. Johnnie Eyvazzadeh, who refurbished and modernized it.

Nikkou Jan wanted the official first night at Shemiran to be Sept. 9, 1960, the wedding day of her eldest son Fred who had just returned from studying in the U.S. She had prepared her bedroom for the newlyweds, and declared no one could sleep in the main house until their nuptials.

Fred and his fiancée Eliane had fallen in love immediately after meeting a few months earlier. Fred had studied business administration at Boston's Babson College and, en route home to Tehran that summer, stopped off in Paris with my father, who by then was attending Hatch Preparatory School in Rhode Island. Uncle Davoud had sent word to the Hotel Claridge, where they were staying on the Champs-Elysées, for Fred to meet a young woman named Eliane Cuenca, studying at the Sorbonne. She was the daughter of a French-Russian Jewish couple who had moved to Iran to manage Habib and Davoud's old school, the Alliance Israélite Universelle.

They celebrated their wedding, a 500-guest, black-tie affair, on the lawn in Shemiran. Organized by Nikkou Jan, it oozed opulence, with waiters serving dinner, singers entertaining — and a wedding cake shaped like the Eiffel Tower.

This house was Habib's paradise. It didn't matter where he was, in Europe on vacation, New York or Israel for business, he was always impatient to return home.

When Habib and Davoud bought the property, the gardener Mash-Hatam (omitting his last name to protect the remaining family in Iran) and his family lived in a house below the old orchard next to the front entrance gate. Besides groundskeeping and tending to the two swimming pools, Mash-Hatam kept a couple of cows down by his house. Every morning, he delivered fresh milk to the main house. During the dozen or more years Fred and my father were away in America, the two families, Habib's and Mash-Hatam's, became close. Habib even mentored Mash-Hatam's children.

Nikkou Jan and Habib made a huge deal of the Persian New Year celebration of *Nowrooz*, the first day of spring that marks the start of the Iranian calendar. The new year, based on the solstice, can come any hour of the night or day. A week before the celebrations, Nikkou Jan and the children's nanny Layla Khanoum fluttered about, preparing for the festivities. First was the annual spring cleaning to ensure every inch of the house was immaculate. Layla Khanoum, who colored her nails with henna, would wear all her gold bangles, to remind Habib what she wanted as a gift for the new year.

She was in charge of putting together the traditional and elaborate *Haft Seen* arrangement of seven elements all beginning with the Farsi letter "S," each with a symbol of its own: *sabzeh*, wheat, barley or lentil sprouts grown in a dish, for rebirth; *samanu*, a sweet pudding made from germinated wheat, for affluence; *senjed*, the dried fruit of the oleaster tree for love; *sir*, garlic, for health; *sib*, apples, for beauty; *somaq*, the dried red sumac berry, the color of sunrise; and *serkeh*, vinegar, for age and patience.

Traditional Iranian pastries, dried berries and nuts were placed on the table along with a mirror, for cleanness and honesty. There were decorated eggs for fertility, and a bowl of water with goldfish, along with rosewater, believed to have magical cleansing powers. The entire display was set off by a small flag of Iran to mark the national holiday. Mash-Hatam sent a huge basket of hyacinths up to the house. Everyone, including Layla Khanoum, Mash-Hatam and his wife and children, gathered around the big dining room table to eat the traditional dill rice with fish. After the meal, Layla Khanoum carried a large tray of burning *esfand* seeds, rue in English, like incense, over everyone's head to push out any evil that might have entered the house during the year.

There were "first of the year" presents. Habib would say, "We all have to get our first gifts from Nikkou Jan's hands because she is the good-luck charm." She also had to be the first person to enter the house in the new year; so, a few minutes before the year officially started, Nikkou Jan left the house, walked around the garden, knocked on the door, and walked in. She would hand out brand-new 5-toman or 10-toman bills, the first one always to Habib. After she finished, Habib would start giving out the big gifts. Layla Khanoum, of course, always got new gold bangles. Everyone else got money, and all the salaries were doubled that month for Vali the caretaker, Hamzeh the cook, Layla Khanoum and Mash-Hatam.

Occasionally on *Nowrooz* Day, the singer Marzieh, who had become a friend of the family, came to the house. Nikkou Jan invited her to sing *Shabeh Mahtab* and afterward gave Marzieh her first gift of the year. Marzieh, too, said Nikkou Jan's blessing would make it a prosperous year for her.

I remember a few cool mid-March nights in Shemiran where smoke from the small bonfires we built once a year, on the eve of the last Wednesday before *Nowrooz*, rose to the stars. The family gathered to jump over the flames, a purification practice, part of New Year festivities that left me spooked and in tears. I preferred warm summer days when we'd gather for lunch on the patio. In the afternoons, my cousin Shahrooz and I would take turns on his skateboard going down the tiny hill, from the patio to the gate. By the gate was a garage where my father kept a collection of antique cars. We'd sneak inside to play hide-and-seek among the cobwebs that had formed between them.

Shortly after the move to Shemiran, Mahnaz, Sina and Mash-Hatam's young children became inseparable, studying, eating and playing together. One of Mash-Hatam's daughters, Shamsi, and Mahnaz slept in the same room in the main house. Shamsi had good taste, Mahnaz remembers, and always wore stylish clothes. One time, an acquaintance who thought that Shamsi was one of Habib's daughters called to see if Habib would give Shamsi's hand to one of his sons. Habib's reply: "She is like my daughter. If you know a good Muslim boy who is interested, send him over to us."

Once Mahnaz grew to her mid-teens, Habib and Nikkou Jan sent her to Fryerning Finishing School in Essex, England, for two years. At the airport, before saying goodbye, Habib pulled Mahnaz aside to have a few words with her. "You are going there to study and to have a good time," he told her. Drawing her close, he held his finger up straight between their two faces and continued: "There are two things I want you to remember. Do not smoke and do not go out with boys."

When there was a school dance, Mahnaz would have fun buying a dress, getting ready, applying make-up and doing her hair, but once she got to the party and a boy would approach her, she would remember her father's admonition — and run to hide in the bathroom.

Habib was close to Mahnaz. When he missed her a lot, he visited her in England, even if only for a couple of days. He would sometimes bring her back with him for a week for holidays. In the plane they'd sit and talk.

"Mahnaz," he said during one of the trips, "I know you are a girl and the only daughter I have, but you have to remember one thing in life, you must always be *sangeh zireh asiab*," meaning no matter what life throws at you, you must be resilient.

Resilience was a trait the family would sorely need.

CHAPTER 10

The Business Empire

I've inherited nothing from my grandfather — neither money nor business acumen. Saving, investing, innovating, diversifying, expanding, growing, marketing, selling, all the things he excelled at are not in my DNA. And my father's tough love — perhaps reflecting that old "Firm as an Oak" school motto — meant that, after he paid for college, I would never benefit from any subsidies to make ends meet.

In the winter of 2001, tired of living from paycheck to paycheck, I set out to supplement my paltry magazine writing salary, by selling scarves and pillows. I taught myself to sew straight lines on a sewing machine, bought yards of colorful velvet fabric from New York's Garment District, and sat at the kitchen table to make my wares. Then, in mid-December, from my tiny apartment in Ridgewood, Queens, I schlepped a plastic folding table and bags full of my creations on the L and C trains to Manhattan. Setting out early in the morning to arrive shortly after sunrise, I claimed my space of prime Soho sidewalk in the hope that the scarves and pillows would be enticing enough to earn a spot under a few Christmas trees. Standing on the sidewalk shivering, I'd smile at New Yorkers and tourists who zigged-zagged between high-end shops and street vendors, checking off their holiday lists. After two blustery Saturdays ending long past the winter sun had set, I returned to my apartment with full bags.

That's when I focused my energy on finding a new job. A year later, I started to work as a photo editor first at The Associated Press and then in 2011, more than a decade after my Soho fiasco, at Bloomberg News, where the world I was born in and the world I'd chosen to make a living serendipitously merged. At the financial news organization, nearly every story taught me about business. And I saw more and more clearly how the pioneering business empire my grandfather and his brothers built contributed to nearly every economic indicator measuring growth: manufacturing, industrial production, construction spending, retail sales, durable goods orders and gross domestic product.

They successfully expanded and diversified their small family import business into a multimillion-dollar conglomerate with Habib serving as the public face. His ascent to business titan began when a powerful group of Iranian merchants opened its door to a Jew — just one.

In 1959, the Tehran Chamber of Commerce (in Farsi, *Otagheh Bazargani*) issued a communique stating that for the first time a Jew would be allowed to join the ranks of merchants who had banded together in the late 19th century to protect their businesses from foreign competition and government corruption. Whoever was elected would become part of a circle of businessmen with clout and connections.

Two men entered the race: my grandfather and Morad Aryeh, another successful entrepreneur who owned the largest tile manufacturing company in Iran. Aryeh was famous at the time for having written Mohammad Reza Shah a blank check when the king briefly fled to Rome in 1953; that was before he agreed to overthrow the popular democratically elected Prime Minister Mohammad Mossadegh in a coup orchestrated by the CIA and Britain's Secret Intelligence Service.

In his memoir, Davoud recounts receiving a call from Aryeh's brother, Raffi, asking Habib to withdraw from the race and campaign for Aryeh. "I told him that [former Chamber President Mirza Abdul Hossein] Nikpour wanted us to stay, so we would stay in the race, and so should he," Davoud wrote. "Whoever won the election would congratulate the other, and we would remain friends as before. He agreed."

After a campaign in which Habib and Davoud held meetings with whole-salers, businessmen and bankers, both Jewish and Muslim, Habib won by a wide margin.

The history of the Chamber of Commerce, which was established in 1884, explains the rocky relationship between the government and Iran's business class — a business class attempting to distance itself and be independent from the whims and harmful interference in the economy of successive autocratic rulers.

The state "had generally been seen by the rich as a parasitic nuisance. It operated independently of the will of the affluent classes, particularly the merchants, and often to their financial detriment," Abbas Milani explains in a chapter devoted to Nikpour in *Eminent Persians*.[1] In fact, successive governments' meddling in the business community's affairs strained rela-tions with merchants, who would eventually help bring down the monar-chy in 1979.

My grandfather gained visibility and contacts by being a member of the chamber and remained apolitical his entire life — a promise all the sons had made to their mother Khanoum Jan. But what Habib couldn't know in 1959 was that he'd eventually bear the brunt of government meddling into the economy and the shah's insecurities about free-market vagaries.

---

1. Abbas Milani, "Abdul-Hussein Nikpour," *Eminent Persians: The Men and Women Who Made Modern Iran 1941-1979*, Vol. 2 (Syracuse: Syracuse University Press and Persian World Press, 2008), p. 657.

The Business Empire

In 1935, Reza Shah's government became involved in selecting one-third of the members in the representative body of the chamber. The economic minister or his surrogate could also participate in group discussions and decision-making. In 1941, as the government's preferential treatment of its cronies grew, merchants who worked in the powerful bazaar protested, demanding that the government end its interference in the chamber's affairs.

Later, Nikpour, who served as chamber president for more than two decades, ran for the Senate along with another chamber member, Mehdi Namazi, to help further the merchant class' interests. The chamber functioned as an independent lobbying group with merchants, having a large say in economic policy until 1963.

A series of ministerial power plays led first to the creation of a separate Chamber of Industries and Mines and then, in 1970, to a merged Chamber of Commerce, Industries and Mines – again dominated by the government.[2]

But for the decade and a half between 1959 and 1975 – the year when, as we'll see, Habib's fortunes would turn amid historic change – the family's businesses expanded and diversified, contributing to the country's growth in a business-friendly environment supported by a king intent on furthering his father's ambitions to modernize Iran. The conglomerate employed an estimated 6,000 people. Habib was fully aware that his enterprises meant a modernizing transformation for the country. In the early stages of manufacturing, my father remembers standing outside the factory supervisor's mezzanine-level office as his father gave pep-talks to the factory workers to boost morale and galvanize their feelings that their work was part of something important and innovative.

---

2. "Chamber of Commerce, Industries and Mines of Persia" entry, *Encyclopaedia Iranica* online edition.

Here's a breakdown of a conglomerate that grew and diversified over the span of two-and-a-half decades.

Plastics

As the brothers acquired more machines and expanded the range of products, they moved the small Plasco Co. factory in Lalezar-No to the new industrial zone on Karaj Road in the late 1950s. Sion continued to be in charge of the factory. In 1960, as orders grew, the youngest brother Eddy returned from the U.S. to Iran and took charge of business correspondence and placed orders for raw materials and spare parts.

He also attended plastics shows in the United States, Germany, Japan and Italy to see what new plastic consumer goods were being made. He and John shipped samples to Tehran where molds were produced to manufacture the products. In the early 1960s, they faced strong competition from Leon Sarhadian & Partners, a five-man firm of engineers with whom Sion decided to partner. The new company was registered under the name PlascoKar (Joint Stock) Co. Gradually, they expanded the factory. Sion, assisted by Sarhadian, was managing director of PlascoKar factory and company. Sion also set up a chain of plastic retail stores throughout Tehran and a large shop in the bazaar for wholesale.

The business manufactured all sorts of affordable consumer goods never before made in Iran. Besides sets of melamine table services that were extremely popular mostly with people who couldn't afford fine china, the factory made baskets, light switches, plastic awnings, water hoses, sandals, plastic bags and toys — all to meet the everyday needs of a growing urban class. PlascoKar became the largest plastic and melamine manufacturing plant in Iran. Some 270 production machines used 50-60 tons of raw material per day.

The *Survey of U.S. Business Opportunities* called PlascoKar "the major plastics producer in the country," employing 500 and producing more than 10,000 tons of products. It added: "By 1975, 22 plastics manufacturing companies were operating in Iran of which only three had the capacity of more than 10,000 tons of plastic products per year. The total sales of domestic plastics manufacturers reached almost $60 million."[3]

Plastic was quickly becoming a universally-used commodity. And Iran was making the Middle East's best plastic products, with the potential for making Iran a major economic power in the region.

Refrigerators and Stoves

The brothers diversified their business to also manufacture larger durable goods. In 1958, they established Pars-America, the first refrigerator and stove manufacturing company in Iran. Until right after World War II, when Iran started importing refrigerators for homes, Iranian households purchased fresh food daily or stored perishables over big chunks of ice inside containers in their basements.

The brothers built a plant to manufacture refrigerators and stoves under license from General Steel, a Canadian manufacturer, and sold them in Iran under the General Steel name. At first, various parts arrived from abroad to be assembled in the factory. Subsequently, they were allowed to keep the General Steel name and build their own appliances, with their own engineering department. They took innovations in American-made refrigerators, for example, and applied them to their own products. For complicated technical assistance, they relied on Canadian or American manufacturers.[4]

---

3. *Survey of U.S. Business Opportunities* is a report by the Bureau of International Commerce focusing on foreign market opportunities for U.S. suppliers and made available by the Bureau's Office of International Marketing in cooperation with the U.S. Foreign Service-Department of State. Most reports are based on research conducted by overseas contractors under U.S. Foreign Service supervision or by economic and commercial officers of the Foreign Service or Department of Commerce.
4. Amir Victory, phone interviews with author, May 2011.

In 1958, they held 100 percent of the Iran market, before other companies, namely Arj and Azmayesh, gradually entered the market.

My grandfather and his brother in New York, Nourollah, were responsible for expanding the factory, while Amir Victory, son of Lotfollah Victory, moved to Tehran from New York in 1968 and eventually became president of Pars-America. By the end of 1978, Pars-America produced about 146,000 units a year. Its refrigerators were popular because they were 20 percent larger than their competitors' and cost 15 to 20 percent less. Also, their motors worked better than most amid Iran's tremendous voltage variation.

Habib took care of the financing with the banks, and was in charge of sales.

"Whatever you can make, I can sell," my grandfather would tell Victory.

Aluminum

Aluminum was growing as another industrial material that extended products to the masses, and the shah in the early 1960s asked the company to import an aluminum press to produce so-called profiles for Iran's building boom. These are metal bars used to build window and door frames.

In time, the aluminum plant, located inside the same facility as the appliance manufacturing plant, made about 200 tons of aluminum extrusions a year for use in other manufacturers' goods. Let's say a company wanted aluminum chairs for the garden: The factory would manufacture the tubes to make the chairs.

"We put some people in business, we helped them financially to set up workshops or smaller factories to make different aluminum products," Davoud remembered.

There were also industrial uses: When anybody needed anything of a special shape, the brothers would make it for them in their mold shop. In the early 1970s, they participated in an international exhibition in Iran. Their booth drew a special visitor, the shah, to its displays of refrigerators and freezers and even samples of large aluminum extrusions for goods ranging from lampposts to car parts.

"They're used in everything," Habib explained.

Noting that they were the pioneers of aluminum manufacturing in Iran, the shah asked that they produce the big extrusions for helicopters for a new factory the government planned to open.

The brothers' aluminum business also helped in building cultural institutions. After a fire at Tehran's Opera House, they produced custom metalwork and aluminum framing to complete the building's renovation by fall 1971 for the 2,500-year anniversary of King Cyrus' founding of the Persian Empire.[5]

Construction

By 1962, the brothers had completed construction of Iran's then tallest private-sector building in downtown Tehran. The Plasco Building, at 17 stories, towered over the capital; the government-built National Iranian Oil Co. building was the country's only other high-rise. The earthquake-proof structure, its facade designed to echo trends in modern Iranian art at the time, was innovative: Plasco combined office space with the country's first multiplex shopping center, a four-story mall. A rooftop restaurant had 360-degree views of the capital. In the mid- to late-1950s, Habib's younger brother Sion began buying shops on Ferdowsi and Eslambol Avenues. The brothers continued to acquire land behind those shops and built Plasco in that space, with the help of foreign engineers and Nourollah, who was living in New York.

By 1965, they had also built the Aluminum Building on Shah Avenue, where Habib and Davoud established their offices. They built a third building, only five stories high, on Manoucheri street, that they named General Steel.

---

5. Amir Afkhami, Skype conversation with author, March 3, 2015.

They remained active in the construction business, by establishing the Louleh Shomal Co. that manufactured PVC pipes for the building boom.

Real estate

Besides the structures they built, the brothers invested in commercial, residential and agricultural land throughout the country. Like many large family businesses, they decided in the late 1960s to divide the real estate holdings among themselves — putting prices on each property and drawing names out of a hat to see who got what.

Around 1975, Davoud sold the Plasco Building to Hojabr Yazdani, a Bahai rancher who had made his money in the meat market. Yazdani also wanted to buy the Aluminum Building from Habib, but Davoud wasn't able to persuade his brother to sell it. My father recalls Davoud asking him to help persuade Habib to do it and to buy a building in the United States with the proceeds, but Habib laughed off the idea of investing his money in New York real estate.

Mining

Sometime in the 1960s, Bama Co. in Isfahan needed a partner to develop a mine to extract lead and zinc ore. In exchange for 70,000 tomans, Bama made Habib and Davoud partners. Later they purchased a 30 percent share, then an additional 15 percent. The purchase allowed Bama to expand by importing machinery and equipment. The mine's capacity grew to 50 times what it had been when they bought in, and whatever was mined was purchased by Russians. The two brothers held a 45 percent interest in what's now Bama Mining and Industrial Co., a lead ore mine.

Other factories and partnership with Moghadam

Davoud and Habib continued their partnership with Muslim businessman Hajji Mirza Attoallah Moghadam to whom they had profitably lent money for the sale of cotton to Russia right after the war. Although their later ventures with him in textile and other manufacturing paled in comparison to the rest of their enterprises, they stayed partners, and he proved to be a loyal friend during the Revolution.

The country's rate of growth had gone from an average of 4.4 percent per year in 1962 to 33.9 percent in 1973 and 41.6 percent in 1975.[6] "The economy had taken giant strides improving the lives of nearly every strata of society," writes Milani.[7] Iranian businessmen had even set their sights on expanding their production to export their goods. A photograph taken in the early 1970s shows my grandfather and other industrialists who belonged to the Chamber of Commerce visiting the Great Wall during a visit to China to lay the groundwork for trade between the two nations.

6. Abbas Milani, "From Rags to Riches to Revolution, The Iranian Economy, 1941–1979," *Eminent Persians: The Men and Women Who Made Modern Iran 1941-1979*, Vol. 2 (Syracuse: Syracuse University Press and Persian World Press, 2008), p. 583.

7. Ibid, p. 581.

CHAPTER 11

⁓

Modernizers vs. Fundamentalists

It wasn't until I stumbled upon my grandfather's name in a footnote to one of Ruhollah Khomeini's speeches that I learned Khomeini not only already knew who he was in the 1960s, but that the Shiite cleric was teaching his followers that Habib Elghanian was part of what he believed was Iran's problem.[1] The chilling discovery was tucked away in an April 10, 1964, speech Khomeini delivered to students in Qom against Mohammad Reza Pahlavi's White Revolution, which was designed to build on his father's modernization campaign and turn Iran into a global economic power.

Started early in 1963, the White Revolution consisted of six points including the sale of state-owned enterprises to the private sector, profit-sharing in industry to empower the working class, the nationalization of forests and

---

1. *Anthology of Imam Khomeini's Speeches, Messages, Interviews, Decrees, Religious Permissions, and Letters*, published by the Institute for Compilation and Publication of Imam Khomeini's Works. p. 270.

a literacy corps to facilitate compulsory education. For Khomeini, the most reviled elements of the plan were electoral changes to allow women to vote and non-Muslims to hold office, and land reform meant to curtail the influence of landlords, clergy and the merchants in the bazaar.[2] The shah's government purchased land at low prices, mostly by force, from owners who lived entirely on rental income, often absentee landlords; the properties were divided into small parcels to give away to villagers and create a new base of support among peasants, effectively abolishing the landlord-serf relationship.

Instead of going through the parliament, the shah sidestepped the political process, choosing the populist route by putting the plan to a referendum. "The White Revolution merely marked the end of Western-style parliamentary democracy and the beginning of the absolute monarchy," Robert Graham writes in his book, *Iran: The Illusion of Power*.

When the shah called for the vote to pass the land reforms in January 1963, Khomeini fought it. His stance: The move would diminish the abundant, highly profitable real estate of the religious endowments controlled by Islamic scholars — including himself. Adding insult to injury for Khomeini, the referendum also would give women the right to vote. He advocated boycotting the polls.

The shah responded by ordering a surprise attack against the Faizieh school in Qom, where Khomeini taught. Army troops killed a dozen students, and many clergy fled. But Khomeini stayed — with his house door wide open. "If we all go from here, Islam will have no defenders in the country," he said.[3]

---

2. Abbas Milani, "From Rags to Riches to Revolution, The Iranian Economy, 1941-1979," *Eminent Persians: The Men and Women Who Made Modern Iran 1941-1979*, Vol. 2 (Syracuse: Syracuse University Press and Persian World Press, 2008), p. 584.

3. Marcus Eliason, "Khomeini Ran His Revolution from a French Village," The Associated Press, June 6, 1989.

In 1935, the Faizieh school became a gathering place for clergymen who opposed Reza Shah's introduction of Western clothing. The shah had rescinded his father's ban of the veil, allowing women to cover or not, and had moved on to other more substantive changes to secularize Iran. Khomeini pushed back at every step.

Khomeini's resistance to land reforms led to another round of riots in Tehran on June 4-5, 1963. Soldiers pitilessly punished the rioters, leaving hundreds dead and wounded.

Afterward, Khomeini was imprisoned and developed breathing problems. More street demonstrations — and the probability of even more upheaval — persuaded the shah to free him, but with a warning that he could not discuss the shah, Israel or his claim that Islam was in peril. Dismissing such restrictions, Khomeini kept making speeches.

Soon thereafter, he was under house arrest. Rumor had it that the shah had ordered Khomeini's execution. To preclude that, religious leaders met and gave Khomeini the title of imam — meaning "spiritual leader" and a word that carries substantial clout in Shiite tradition. Shiites believe the Muslim world's leadership passed from the Prophet Muhammad to his cousin and son-in-law Ali, the first imam, and then through Ali's descendants to the 12th imam, who will return at the end of time as a messiah.

Khomeini was imprisoned for a year in October 1963 after alleging that parliamentary elections had been rigged. Once he was free again, he denounced "the Americanization of Iran" in reaction to an increasingly cozy military relationship between Iran and the United States. Especially infuriating to him was a grant of diplomatic immunity to U.S. servicemen serving in Iran as part of a $200 million arms deal. It exempted the Americans from trial and punishment in Iran's court system. Khomeini derided that as an insult to Iranian sovereignty.

In his April 10, 1964, speech, the cleric explained to students gathered at his home how to combat the changes: "The objective is Islam. It is the country's independence; it is the proscription of Israel's agents; it is the unification of Muslim countries. The entire country's economy now lies in Israel's hands; that is to say it has been seized by Israeli agents. Hence, most of the major factories and enterprises are run by them: the television, the Arj factory, Pepsi Cola, etc." (1)

The footnote identifying these so-called "Israeli agents" read: "The Thabit Pasal and Elqaniyan [cq] families were among those mediators of world Zionism who resided in Iran . . ."[4]

Thabit Pasal is a reference to what was known as the Sabet Pasal Co. that belonged to several businessmen including Habib Sabet, a Bahai whose vast business interests included banking and broadcasting. He also distributed products from American companies including RCA, Squibb, Autolite, Phelps-Dodge and Pepsi-Cola. In 1958, he started Iran's first television station and opened a second in 1960.[5]

Bahaism was founded in the 19th century in Iran; its adherents are considered apostates from Islam. The seat of the Bahais' governing body is in Haifa, Israel, near the shrine and grave of Bab, the founder of the faith.

The shah's ties with the United States and Israel had developed from his lifelong suspicion of the Soviets and mistrust of communism. At the end of World War II, British and Soviet troops were scheduled to withdraw from Iran by March 1945. Yet that November, the Soviets had not completely withdrawn. Adding to the shah's woes, two autonomous republics within Iran with clear sympathies for communism and socialism were proclaimed: The Autonomous Republic of Azerbaijan and the Kurdish Republic of Mahabad. Both republics now depended on the Soviets for protection and

---

4. A note inside the footnote reads: See Dawlat va Hukumat dar Islam, pp. 264- 267.
5. "Habib Sabet Is Dead: An Iranian Altruist and Industrialist," *The New York Times* obituary, Feb. 20, 1990.

supplies. The formation of these republics threatened to balkanize Iran and push it into the Soviet sphere.

To persuade the Soviet forces to withdraw from Iran, Prime Minister Ahmad Qavam promised them oil concessions in northern Iran. But after the Soviet departure, the two republics collapsed and the Iranian parliament refused to ratify the oil agreement.

This crisis compounded the shah's concerns about Iran's security and drew him close to Israel, which he believed was a strong regional bastion against both communism and the Soviet-inspired, anti-monarchist tide of Arab nationalism.[6]

The U.S. had helped turn Iran's gendarmerie into a full paramilitary force, and the shah had turned to the Israeli intelligence service to help train Iran's security agency, SAVAK, but these developments had no connection with my grandfather's or Habib Sabet's personal achievements. Khomeini was promulgating racist conspiracy theories, pointing fingers at Iran's most famous Jewish and Bahai businessmen and calling them Israeli agents carrying out an Israeli plan to overtake Iran. For Khomeini, a successful Jew or Bahai had to have been working on Israel's behalf. To the cleric, my grandfather and Sabet were not Iranians. And he went further. In an early 1960s speech, Khomeini had said, "The shah takes so many of his cues from Israel that we wonder if he is not himself a Jew."

In the April 10, 1964, speech, Khomeini instructed the students to "make firm your ranks. . . . These are the agents of imperialism, and imperialism must be uprooted.

"Do your utmost to raise the banner of Islam in the universities, to promote religion, to build mosques, to perform prayers in congregation to let the act of prayer be seen by others. Religious unity is of the essence. It is

---

6. Robert Graham, *Iran: The Illusion of Power*, (New York: St. Martin's Press, 1979) p 63-64.

religious unity that makes this society so great and firm; if you like Iran to be independent, then be united in religion."

For Khomeini, whose speeches advocated isolationism and xenophobia, Iran had room for just one thing: his own religion and his co-religionists. And his hypocrisy toward Israel was clear: While he saw a Jewish state as an unwelcome development, he prescribed an Islamic Republic for predominantly Muslim Iran — with Iran's Jews as second-class citizens.

I don't know whether my grandfather was unaware of or just indifferent to what Khomeini said about him. After all, Khomeini was soon to become a marginalized figure. The shah exiled him to Turkey. Khomeini persisted with his public pronouncements, quickly straining the Turks' sense of hospitality. Next, he alighted in Najaf, Iraq, a place that is holy to Shiites because it houses the tomb of Imam Ali, the sect's founder. At home there, Khomeini made plans for his Islamic state. "We want a ruler," he said, "who would cut off the hand of his own son if he steals and would flog and stone his nearest relative if he fornicates."

Khomeini wanted to take modernity out of Iran instead of integrating Islam into a modernizing world. The 1964 speech laid out how he would isolate Iran, prevent the country from further developing and end minority participation in the nation's affairs.

At the same time, the shah, educated in Switzerland, continued pursuing his own design, aiming to Westernize and liberalize his country — but without allowing Iranians to play a more active role in politics.

Well before the White Revolution, Habib and his brothers had played major roles in modernizing Iran, but their identity complicated their actions. Their Plasco Building, for example, became a much-discussed landmark but also represented risk. Even before it was built, "many cautious Jews were warning them about building a high-rise, which would not only make them conspicuous but would cause envy among Muslims in general and the bazaaris in particular," according to Parviz Nazarian, whose company

Polban was in charge in 1959 of the huge job of excavating and compacting the land for laying the foundation of the building. [7]

Opinion about the building was split between Muslims who embraced modernization and considered Jews to be fellow countrymen and those nostalgic for the era when non-Muslims faced restrictions that prevented them from participating in Iran's economy and building houses taller than Muslims' homes. When the high-rise was completed in 1962, a Shiite cleric named Mahmoud Taleghani objected to the building, citing the long-ago rescinded rule about the height of buildings. Taleghani later recanted, but anti-Semitism was still pervasive.

A story I heard about the building is illustrative. "When I was a child back in the early 1960s," an Iranian-Jew, Fahriar Nikbakht, told me, "me and my brother were at the small fish market across from the Plasco Building, waiting for our father to finish his long haggling with the fish seller. This was the highlight of the transaction but a depressing hour for us who also had to keep smelling fish. It was dark when we finally tried to find a way between the crowd in order to get out, find a taxi and go home."

As he and his brother followed their dad outside, they saw a growing throng. "There were hundreds if not thousands of frenzied people shouting and talking. Something had happened. Finally, we were able to see a huge fire, seemingly engulfing the western side of the Plasco high-rise," he said. "We weaved through the crowd and emerged on the eastern side, found a taxi and got inside. The taxi driver, however, would not move; he was happily watching the fire. In the end, my father asked him angrily why he wasn't moving. The driver responded: 'Aghaa! I want to watch the Johood's building burn down.' That incident showed me as a child, how much people hated us. I might add, that the fire did not even affect the Plasco Building at

7. Parviz Nazarian, *My Walk Toward the Horizon: A Memoir by Parviz Nazarian* (Los Angeles: Ketab Corp., 2016).

all." As it turned out, an old movie house next door was ablaze, disappointing the cabbie.

Over half a century later, on Jan.19, 2017, I would wake up to a note from a CNN editor in London: "I know I am emailing you at a difficult time," she wrote. "The Plasco Building must have meant a lot to you and your family. It would be great if you can share your memories of your grandfather and what the building meant to you and your family."

A difficult time? I wondered what that meant as I quickly typed, "Plasco and Tehran" on my phone. The iconic building, which had been turned into small workshops for the garment industry, had caught fire after years of neglect. It collapsed in the early morning hours. Some 20 firefighters died trying to save the landmark, which by 2017 had been long dwarfed by the many new skyscrapers built by government cronies-turned-multimillionaires since the 1979 Islamic Revolution.

That morning, as I played back the videos of Iranians watching in horror as the Plasco Building went up in flames, I recalled Khomeini's speech and knew Iranian state media wouldn't mention my grandfather's name. In Iran, Habib Elghanian had indeed become the footnote to history that Khomeini had once yearned for.

CHAPTER 12

A Two-Sided Coin

I own a couple of artifacts from Iran that I keep in my home but recently realized belong in a museum rather than in a closet. Tucked inside a wicker box of souvenirs and old birthday gifts — charms, amulets and small gold coins my mother has given to me over the years — is a silver coin, slightly larger and thicker than a quarter. Engraved on one side is an image of the shah, encircled with the words, in Farsi, "Two thousand five hundred years Shahanshah Aryamehr, Mohammad Reza Pahlavi. Anjoman Kalimian. Iran." On the other side is a Menorah, a Hanukkah candelabrum, surrounded by the same words, in Hebrew. Both inscriptions are followed by the date, according to the Iranian or Jewish calendar. The rare coin was minted for the 2,500th anniversary celebration of King Cyrus' founding of the Persian Empire. Habib had contributed $40,000 to issue the coin as a symbol of the Jews' acceptance in Iran during the reign of the two rulers who had been benevolent to Iran's Jews: Mohammad Reza Shah Pahlavi and King Cyrus.

In October 1971, the shah hosted festivities in Persepolis in a grand tent city called the Golden City with a guest list that included heads of state and

prominent Iranians including those in the Jewish community. The celebrations to honor King Cyrus were meant to highlight Iran's history and to
showcase the country's progress. But it had a distinctive European flavor,
suggesting in many ways that, for the king, progress meant Iran could be
just as sophisticated as the West. A Parisian interior design firm planned the
tent city, inspired by "Field of the Cloth of Gold," the site of a 1520 meeting
between France's King Francis I and King Henry VIII of England. Maxim's
of Paris catered, Lanvin designed the royal family's outfits, Limoges created
the dinnerware, Porthault provided the linen, and Mercedes-Benz limou-
sines chauffeured the guests.

Khomeini ridiculed the event as the "Devil's Festival." Western media
described it as extravagant and decadent. Leaders came from around
the world, but those declining invitations included Britain's Queen
Elizabeth II, U.S. President Richard Nixon and French President Georges
Pompidou — bitterly disappointing the shah.

Guests including Habib received a large polished wooden box filled with
Iranian-made cigarettes and cigars. Since he no longer smoked, he gave
the box to my parents, who in turn gave it to me. Too large to be displayed
anywhere in my home, the box sits under sweaters in my closet. Its lid carries the emblem of the event, the Cylinder of Cyrus, at the center. Though
there is disagreement among historians about the cylinder's message as a
charter for human rights, the shah proclaimed the iconic pre-Islamic baked
clay relic from the 6th century B.C. the first declaration of human rights and
adopted the cylinder as the symbol of the commemoration.

Cyrus, who conquered Babylonia, an empire that included present-day
Jerusalem, described the rights of all his empire's inhabitants, saying that
while he was monarch, "I will never let anyone take possession of movable
and landed properties of the others by force or without compensation. . . .
I announce that everyone is free to choose a religion. People are free to
live in all regions and take up a job, provided that they never violate others' rights."

Cyrus even had encouraged Iran's Jews, who had deep roots in Persia, to return to Jerusalem. In 597 B.C., King Nebuchadnezzar II of Babylonia conquered Jerusalem, capturing some 10,000 Jews including King Jehoiachin of Judah. Jehoiachin's uncle, Zedekiah, whom Nebuchadnezzar appointed the new king of Judah, tried to break away, provoking Nebuchadnezzar to lay siege to Jerusalem again, destroying the Temple and carrying away more Jews. Cyrus, famous for building the largest empire the world had seen until then (spanning today's Turkey, Israel, Georgia and Arabia in the West to Kazakhstan, Kyrgyzstan, Pakistan and Oman in the East), conquered Babylonia and liberated the Jews, allowing them to resettle in Jerusalem and build the Second Temple. Following their liberation, only some Jews returned to Jerusalem. The Bible's Mordechai, the great grandson of one of Nebuchadnezzar's 10,000 captives, eventually became the leader of Iran's Jews.

Mordechai and his niece Esther became the Bible's most famous Persian Jews, their story commemorated during the Jewish holiday Purim. Their saga, according to the *Book of Esther*, began when Cyrus' son King Xerxes I named Haman prime minister. Haman decreed that anyone who walked past him should bow. Mordechai refused to bow to him or anyone but his own God. Infuriated, Haman asked the king to kill all the Jews.

Mordechai asked Esther, who was one of Xerxes' wives, to intervene on her people's behalf. She arranged to have the king's history book open to the page relating the story of how Mordechai had once saved his life. When Xerxes read the story, he decided he wanted to honor Mordechai. Esther revealed she was Jewish and that Haman was plotting to kill the Jews; she asked her husband to spare her people. Xerxes hanged Haman on the gallows built for Mordechai, and the Jews of Persia were saved.

As the appointed guardian of the coin and the cigarette box, I've come to realize that they represent something even more valuable than museum pieces. They symbolize how my grandfather identified himself. He didn't think of himself as Jewish without being Iranian. Being Iranian and Jewish were two sides of the same coin. My grandfather, who became Iran's best-known Jew, was the symbol of the community's "Golden Age."

What was amazing and what I imagine he was proud of was that, despite centuries of ostracism, Jewish assimilation during his lifetime had been swift. In 1940, 80 percent of Iran's Jews were poor. By 1979, just 10 percent remained poor while 80 percent were middle class and 10 percent belonged to the economic and industrial elite. Even though Iran's estimated 100,000 Jews represented just 0.3 percent of the population in 1979, two of the 18 members of the Royal Academy of Science were Jewish, as were 80 of the 4,000 university lecturers, and 600 of the 10,000 physicians.[1]

Iran's Jews had been able to successfully participate in their country's modernization during the Pahlavi era, in part thanks to the investment in education and training programs made possible by Iran's own Jewish philanthropists and by outside help from groups like the Joint Distribution Committee (JDC), the world's leading Jewish humanitarian assistance organization, and the Alliance Israélite.

Even though he only completed primary school, Habib focused much of his philanthropic activities on education and health.

Soon after the end of World War II, Habib, Davoud, their maternal uncle Hajji Aziz and six other wealthy Jews founded the Jewish Charitable and Cultural Association of Iran. Habib was vice president and Davoud treasurer.[2] The association first divided the Alliance school's budget deficit among the founding members and paid it off. Then they built a dining room that could seat up to 250 students to replace the existing hall that originally had room for 60. They ran the dining room with the American Joint Distribution

---

1. David Sitton, *Sephardi Communities Today* (Jerusalem: Council of Sephardi and Oriental Communities, 1985) p. 184-185.
2. Morteza Senehi was president and Mehdi Cohanim, secretary. The other founders were Habib Moradpour, Moussa Eliassian, Attollah Youmtoub, and Jamshid Kashfi.

Committee's help, before expanding even further by building a larger hall to seat 500 to 600 students.

The JDC, Davoud recollects, had all 2,300 students in the lower and upper schools medically evaluated. A doctor examined the children once a month. All needy children were given free meals. The JDC bore 70 percent of the cost and the Jewish Charitable and Cultural Association of Iran 30 percent.

"Warm lunch was served to the 1,200-1,300 students who attended classes in the upper school and the 500-600 students in the lower school," Davoud writes.

One of the Alliance alumni, Esagh Shaoul, wrote me after reading a *Washington Post* op-ed in which I mentioned the role of the Alliance schools in helping Jews: "He (Habib) was one of my great heroes. I was one of the many thousands of Jewish students in Ettehad School who had free lunch in the school every day provided by your grandfather. In the very noisy dining room where we ate, your grandfather always walked around smiling and made sure we all had enough to eat. This lunch was our main source of daily nourishment. As he had heard me play violin for the students on some occasions, he knew my name. So many times, he would approach me by name to ask if I had gotten enough to eat."

Davoud recalled that all the students who left the Alliance after 1950 were "healthy, wholesome and studious. They had a moral obligation to help the Alliance school or the Association when they grew up and held jobs. Many of them did."

Later on, more help for education came from outside groups including Otzar Hatorah, an association focused on Jewish religious education in Muslim countries in the Middle East and North Africa. It established a school where Hebrew, English and Farsi were taught. The Jewish Charitable and Cultural Association of Iran did some fundraising at the Hatorah's request, and bought a school named Ganj-e-Danesh headed by a Rabbi

Levy. Gradually the association bought one other school for Otzar Hatorah. Much later, in the 1970s, Habib had set his sights on opening a university in Tehran's Yousefabad neighborhood.

Being Jewish for Habib meant fulfilling a moral obligation to look out for the next generation while upholding the traditions and beliefs his fore-fathers fought to keep. Habib went to synagogue on major holidays like Rosh Hashana, Yom Kippur and Passover — very seldom on the Sabbath. Friday's Sabbath dinner was the night the whole family gathered at his parents' house.

Habib's favorite Jewish holiday was Sukkoth, which commemorates the 40 years the children of Israel wandered the desert after the exodus from slavery in Egypt and lived in temporary booth-like shelters called sukkah. Habib had a beautiful one to celebrate the holiday, with deep-purple hand-made curtains with floral embroidery.

"All the important folks from the bazaar and anyone who wanted atten-tion would come over, and Habib would serve everyone a glass of cognac or whiskey," my uncle Fred told me. "Davoud was there, too. Habib would sit near the entrance of the sukkah around a table with huge piles of fruit. That's where he would hold court. That was the real time where Muslims would make it a point to show up and pay their respects to him."

In 1959, the same year Habib was elected to the Chamber of Commerce, he also became the secular leader of the Jewish community, by dint of becoming the head of the Central Jewish Board of Tehran, the organization that managed the internal welfare of the Jews and their relationship with Israel. Until 1958, one man had served as the head of the Central Jewish Board of Tehran and the representative of Iran's Jews in parliament. Morad Aryeh, the same man who had competed with Habib to be elected to the Chamber, played both roles.

That year, the Israeli foreign ministry had sent Meir Ezri, an Iranian-born Israeli citizen, to Tehran to enhance Israeli-Iranian relations; he would serve as Israeli ambassador to Iran from 1958 until 1973. But when he arrived in Tehran, Aryeh didn't welcome the idea of an Israeli official or an Israeli Embassy in Iran; he refused to establish any contacts with the embassy. Ezri quoted him as saying, "There is no place for a Zionist movement or for an Israeli embassy."[3]

In his memoir, Ezri wrote, "As time passed the leadership of the Jewish community came to the conclusion that in tandem with the development of Iran-Israel relations, it would be preferable to be represented in the parliament by a Jew who supported Israel and could lobby Israel's interest in parliament." Jamshid Kashfi, a good friend of Habib's, was elected as parliamentary representative.

"The chairman (of the Central Jewish Board, or Anjoman) would henceforth perform the role of string-puller behind the scenes," Ezri wrote. "The one who could use his influence to get things done. The one chosen for this function was Habib Elghanian — a figure much admired in the community, a businessman and an industrialist who gained the esteem of non-Jews as well as Jews. He was always ready to help the needy — Jewish and non-Jewish alike, with his own money if necessary."

In his role as Anjoman chairman, Habib supported efforts to improve the status of Jewish women. In 1965, he backed efforts to reform inheritance laws for Jewish widows and daughters to have "substantial shares of their husband's or father's estates." The decision was binding on all the rabbis of Iran and paved the way for a court of law to be established for Iranian Jews to deal with marriages, funerals, inheritance and divorce.[4]

---

3. Abbas Milani, "Morad Aryeh," *Eminent Persians: The Men and Women Who Made Modern Iran 1941-1979, Vol. 2* (Syracuse: Syracuse University Press and Persian World Press, 2008), p. 609.

4. Meir Ezri, *The Legacy of Cyrus: My Iranian Mission*, (Israel, 2011), p. 489.

In 1976, the Anjoman established, with the help of the Hatef Women's Association, a retirement home for seniors, where Nikkou Jan became active.[5]

When I met Hechmat Kermanshahchi, a businessman and my grandfather's right-hand man at the Central Jewish Board, in his office in Los Angeles, he talked about what they accomplished at the board. Together, Habib and he established in 1965-66 the *Sandogh Melli*, the National Jewish Fund, to help Iran's poorest Jews.

"There were around 1,400 poor Jewish families in Tehran, and we would provide for them whatever they wanted. It was like a Social Security," he explained.

Of the 9,000 Jewish families in Tehran, about 5,640 families joined the *Sandogh Melli*, he said, each family contributing to the fund. The *Sandogh* replaced the old way of raising money.

"In the past, a respected member of the community, or an elderly person would take a handkerchief in his hand, raise it in the air in the bazaar to catch everyone's attention, and say, 'There is a girl who is getting married and she needs a dowry; give me money,'" said Kermanshahchi, who wanted to collect money in one place and distribute it to the subcommittees who could then give it to whoever needed help. "At the beginning of each month, Habib and I each paid 10,000 tomans to the eight employees we had working at the *Sandogh Melli* so that we didn't use the money we collected for poverty relief."

Kermanshahchi smiled, relating a memory: In the hallway outside Habib's office in his company's headquarters in the Aluminum Building was a waiting room with two dozen chairs where people lined up to ask him

---

5. Jack Mahfar, *From Laborer to Entrepreneur, Memoirs of Jack Mahfar: from Joubareh in Esfahan to Tehran and Geneva* (Cologny-Geneva: The Mahfar Cultural Foundation, 2013), p. 125.

for help. One day, Habib noticed a man who had been sitting in the same chair all morning and never got up to move to the front of the line.

"Sir, who are you?" Habib finally asked him in the afternoon. "I've noticed you've been sitting here since this morning. Come with me."

The man, holding a religious book in his hand, followed Habib into his office. Habib sat at his desk and the man, who still lived in the old run-down neighborhood, the *Mahalleh* where Habib grew up, got on his knees.

"Sir, what are you doing?" Habib asked. "Sit on a chair."

"No, it's disrespectful. I can't. I have to be on the floor," the man said.

"Sir, no. Please, I can't talk to you if you are sitting on the floor like that." The man grabbed Habib's hand and kissed it.

"I can't convince you to sit on a chair, can I?"

"No," the man insisted. He opened the book with a letter inside it.

Habib put on his glasses to read it. It was from Hakham Yedidiah Shofet, Iran's chief rabbi, who'd written it for the man and told him to take it to Habib. It said the man's daughter was getting married, and he didn't have any money.

"*Mobarakeh!* Congratulations! Who is the boy? Have you asked around about him? Is he a good guy?" Habib asked.

"I know him, he's good," the man replied.

"Very good."

Habib rang a bell and called Kamali, the office assistant. "Get him money for his daughter's wedding and tell Amir Victory to send a fridge to his house and two sets of melamine plates, one for the bride and groom's house and one for him. And give them extra cash to buy the groom a nice suit and a decent pair of shoes for the wedding."

The money for the wedding would come from the *Sandogh Melli*. The man kissed Habib's hand once more and left the Torah for him as a gift. Habib drew it close to his face. He told Kermanshahchi that when he opened it, he smelled a jasmine flower the man had left inside.[6]

---

6. Heshmat Kermanshahchi, interview with author in Los Angeles, April 2011.

Habib also did good deeds in stealth. When my father returned to Iran, he was driving his paternal grandfather Babai home on a rainy day. Noticing an old woman walking, they stopped to ask her if they could give her a ride. Drenched, she got in, and the three got to chatting. She told them about her son who was very sick. "He's getting treatment," she said, then went on: "A nice Jewish man is paying for it. He's the owner of the Plasco Building. And he also comes to visit to see how he's doing." This was the first time my father and Babai had heard about this. They turned to each other and smiled.

Habib's commitment to helping improve the lot of Iranian Jews and his devotion to Israel had deep roots. And so, when the Iranian government recognized Israel de facto in March 1950, Habib and the Jewish community embraced this development. For about a decade, however, the two countries' official ties remained largely informal to avoid inflaming the fierce opposition from the clergy, including Khomeini.

Israeli-Iranian relations were strengthened following Egyptian leader Gamal Abdel Nasser's revolution in July 1952. The ensuing arms deal between Egypt and the Soviet Union meant Israel needed a friend in the region, and the shah, worried about Soviet influence in the Middle East, needed to make friends with an American ally. Since the shah had aligned himself with the United States during the Cold War, Israel became a natural partner to help strengthen his ties with the U.S. Israel was also a good candidate because it could provide technical expertise in Iran's modernization efforts and be an oil client. Israel sent experts to Iran to train military officers but also sent students, and provided expertise in fields including agriculture, medicine and infrastructure which included finding new sources of water, paving roads and even helping rebuild the earthquake-torn region of Qazvin in 1962 where over 12,000 people were killed. Between 1958 and '67, Israel helped develop Iran's armed forces while Iran sold Israel increasing amounts of crude oil.

In 1961, the alliance was further cemented with Israeli Prime Minister David Ben-Gurion's visit to Tehran.[7]

"For Iranian Jews, support for Israel and Iranian patriotism were not incompatible as the national interests of Iran and Israel converged," Aryeh Levin, the chargé d'affaires of Israel's diplomatic mission to Tehran beginning in 1973, told me. Levin, who succeeded Ezri, had grown up in Iran after his father fled from communist Russia.[8] Habib, Levin explained, "believed as other Iranian Jews did that Israel was a fantastic development in the history of Jews."

In the 1960s, as Central Jewish Board president, Habib arranged the sale of land that belonged to the organization and bought former Prime Minister Ghavam al Saltaneh's house from his son. The house on Khak Street was leased to the Israelis as the Israeli Mission building.[9]

Iranian Jews "believed in the power and strength of the Jewish state, its influence backed by the United States, and in its important presence in the area," Levin said. "They had watched the wars between us and the Arabs and they considered us to be all powerful. It was the Six Day War in 1967 that did it."

The Six Day War, during which Israel defeated its Arab neighbors, revealed cracks in how traditional Iranian Muslims viewed Iranian Jews. Muslims identified with the Arab cause, supporting the Muslim countries, leading to an increase in anti-Jewish feelings. The following year, when Arab sports teams were boycotting Israeli teams, Iran decided to host the Israeli soccer team during the 1968 Asian Nations Cup. In a match between Israel and Hong Kong, Jews rooting for Israel were pelted with bottles.

---

7. "Israeli Relations with Iran" entry in *Encyclopaedia Iranica* online edition.

8. Aryeh Levin, email correspondence with author, October 2017.

9. Hechmat Kermanshahchi, conversations with author and Davoud Elghanian memoir p. 64.

When Israel and Iran both qualified for the finals, tensions rose. "On May 19, the day of the game, it was rumored — incorrectly — that Habib Elghanian, a rich Jewish industrialist who was unpopular with Islamic activists, had bought 15,000 tickets (the stadium held fewer than 30,000) to distribute to Jewish Iranians so that they could cheer for the visitors. Few Jews attended the game, however, preferring to watch it on television after the untoward turn of events at the Israel/Hong Kong game," a historian noted.[10]

"I remember this final game very well," my mother's cousin, Arsalan Gueola, a soccer fan, told me. "I, along with many others from Tehran Polytechnic didn't go to class that day to be able to watch the game at Amjadiyeh (stadium). From the moment the game started to the end, you could only hear, 'Iran, Iran,' everywhere." This included Shahpoor Gholamreza, the king's half-brother, who was at his special balcony and standing throughout the game. Many Iranian fans wore eye patches, making fun of the Israeli defense chief Moshe Dayan.

My uncle John, my mother's brother, told me Jews were frightened to express their support for Israel. He had attended one of the games with his father, who had kept his foot on my uncle's foot the entire game so he wouldn't forget that he was not allowed to cheer for Israel. Iran won the final game 2-1.

None of the rumors and tensions deterred or intimidated Habib and his brothers from doing work in Israel. After having built two of Tehran's tallest buildings, they set out to build one of Israel's tallest towers at the time. The same year as the Iran-Israel soccer final in 1968, the 23-story Shimshon Building was completed in Ramat Gan, towering over the city.

---

10. Houshang E. Chehabi, "Jews and Sport in Modern Iran," *The History of Contemporary Iranian Jews*, Volume 4, ed. Homa Sarshar, (Beverly Hills: The Center for Iranian Jewish Oral History, 2001) p. 17-18.

After seeing it during a trip to Israel, I went to visit a tiny synagogue and an adjoining kindergarten built in Nikkou Jan and Hajji Aziz's names. The kindergarten structure had fallen into disrepair but the synagogue was still functioning. Habib and his brothers also donated money for new hospital beds for the largest hospital in the Middle East, the Tel HaShomer Hospital.

Habib twice participated in the World Jewish Congress, a representative body based on the concept of the unity of the Jewish people, democratically organized and able to act on matters of common concern. The WJC was established in Geneva in August 1936, in reaction to the rise of Nazism and the growing wave of European anti-Semitism. Its highest decision-making body, the Plenary Assembly, meets every four years and elects an executive committee. Habib participated in two Plenary Assembly meetings, in Brussels in 1966 and in Jerusalem in 1975.

In 1975, he read this statement on the condition of Jews in Iran:

"The Jewish community of Iran is the oldest in the Diaspora. It antedates Cyrus the Great, founder of the Persian Empire, who 2,500 years ago encouraged our people to go and build the Second Temple in Jerusalem. The favorable position enjoyed by the Jewish community in Iran — despite complications and difficulties of a political, social, and religious nature in a Muslim country — is in the tradition of the founder of the Persian Empire and is proof of the shah's magnanimity, humane principles, and wisdom. In the past half-century, notably during the Second World War, this tradition was further manifested by the hospitality and assistance extended to Jewish refugees by the Iranian government and people.

"During this period Iran has progressed rapidly in the economic, cultural and social spheres, and our community has benefited from this progress as well. Since the establishment of the State of Israel, close to half of our community has settled here, in the spiritual and cultural center of the Jewish people. Nearly all the 80,000 Jews in Iran today live in the big cities, two-thirds of them in Tehran. They are to be found in the economic and industrial sectors and also in the professions. Their educational level is comparable with that of the most advanced Jewish communities in the Diaspora. . . .

"The Iranian Jewish community, along with certain other religious minorities, is expressly recognized under the Iranian Constitution, and its religious rights and autonomy are safeguarded. In accordance with the principle of proportional representation, we have a Jewish member of parliament. The links of the Jewish people with Iran are ancient and solid. The Books of Daniel, Ezra, and Esther were written in Persia, and numerous Talmudic schools were founded there. Iran, its inhabitants and its kings have always been referred to with great respect in Jewish religious writings, which is not the case with certain other ancient civilizations. For many centuries Jewish religious books were an important means of acquainting Judaism as well as Christianity with the civilization of Iran."

That perspective didn't preclude his donating money to help finish construction of Tehran's turquoise-domed Hosseinieh Ershad Mosque in 1967 when the Muslims' building fund ran out.

Still, anti-Semitism persisted, though with a change. Under the shah, it was no longer as religious and exclusionary as under Iran's previous rulers. Now, it had economic undertones and was anti-Israel.

Lotfollah Hay, then Iran's Jewish deputy in Parliament, remembers the joke tossed his way by Muslim members of a social club when he'd arrive to play cards: "Mr. Mousheh is coming." *Mousheh* was a sly reference to Moshe Dayan, but *moushe* in Farsi means mouse, a reference to Hay's diminutive frame. Hay would not let the nasty comments pass. "I would answer back when they'd say things like that."

Habib didn't have to respond to such comments. "They loved him," Hay said.[11]

Levin agreed that Habib was highly regarded, but with an inevitable asterisk.

---

11. Lotfollah Hay, interview with author in Los Angeles, April 2011.

"The Jew element was always there in the view of the authorities and the public, but his acceptance in the Chamber of Commerce — the first Jew to be admitted — was seen as a boost to the Jewish ego and, more than that, a step in the ladder on which to climb in the business world and obtain recognition of Jews as more fully-fledged citizens," Levin said. "With years and with Habib's outstanding contribution to the Chamber of Commerce in promoting Iranian business interests and contacts in the world, Habib's prestige and position advanced. Yet, he remained forever the *Jew*."

Was this Habib's fatal flaw: not seeing he was more of an outsider than he thought he was — that what he considered his two sides of the same coin was seen as a dual allegiance?

What I would soon learn was that despite Iran and Israel's good relations at the time, when Jews were allowed to visit Israel, his trips there were closely watched and carefully documented by the shah's secret police, SAVAK.

The old regime, supposedly friends of the Jews, was creating files that one day would fall into more dangerous hands.

CHAPTER 13

⁓

Dad Returns to Iran

While my grandfather's life grew ever more deeply rooted in Iran, the United States was slowly taking root inside my father. During winter breaks from school, he stayed in New York in the apartment in Forest Hills with his caretaker Ghodsi Baher, and he returned to Tehran only a handful of summers.

After Nyack Boys School and Peekskill Military Academy in New York, he attended Hatch Preparatory School, which billed itself as catering to prosperous families seeking "only the best for their sons." For his first two years at Hatch, starting in 1959, its campus was in Newport, Rhode Island, on an oceanside compound with Gilded Age baronial estates and sweeping views of the Atlantic; it moved to Winchendon, Massachusetts, in 1961.

"Many students wore vests and pocket watches passed down from their family," my father says, recalling the privileged American world that he'd entered. He was on the varsity tennis team with Henry Ford's great-grandson Walter Buhl Ford III, whose mother, he remembers, used to send a limousine to pick up his laundry.

The few Jews at the mostly WASP school were considered outsiders, he says. Nonetheless, with every year that passed, the landscape, culture, education and personal connections made my father more American. At Hatch, he made lifelong friends and he revered headmaster Bob Marr. After high school, my father studied business administration at the University of Vermont, enjoying college life. During winter holidays, when the campus emptied, he stayed behind to ski.

After 13 years in the northeastern U.S., steeped in Americana, he returned to Iran in 1967 at 24, moving into the old guest house in Shemiran. He barely could read and write Farsi, so his father got him a tutor, and soon afterward he started to work in the refrigerator business. His older brother Fred had returned to Iran a few years earlier and was working with their uncle Sion in the plastics business. After about a year, Habib bought out the dozen Plasco stores from his brothers and gave them to Fred and my father to run and expand. By 1977, the number of stores grew to 21.

Dad idolized his father, who would often call him around midday, saying he'd pick him up with his driver for a lunch at Shemiran. During the ride, they'd talk about business and life. "Those hours were really the most valuable times I had with him," he says, "as there was nobody to disturb us."

In one conversation, he told his father about plans he and Fred had for a store they had bought, their largest up to that point. It had tall ceilings, and they planned to add a balcony, where they'd move their head offices. It would allow them to save office rent while also putting them in position to monitor things on the spot.

No, Habib said firmly, it would detract from the look of the store.

But after living on his own in the United States all those years, my father had become independent, if not headstrong. He and Fred followed their plan – and in time Habib acknowledged they'd been right.

Habib did offer further advice — to expand the merchandise line beyond Plasco products, for instance — and also helped his sons set up a housewares import division. This included a large warehouse with its own manager and drivers to distribute the merchandise to stores and the bazaar.

After a while, my father kept the stores and Fred went on his own. Habib set up an electronics company for Fred headquartered in Shiraz in partnership with Jamshid Emanuel, the former head of the refrigerator manufacturing company. They made sockets and copper wires, among other things, for the booming building industry. Emanuel was stationed in Shiraz, and Fred remained in Tehran.

Habib liked to see people beyond his own family succeed. People knew this about him and they knew that if they really wanted to improve their lives, he'd do whatever he could to help them. "If a foreman was good, instead of keeping him in the role where he knew he could rely on him, he'd try to make something more out of him," Fred told me. On the other hand, if he couldn't help someone who came to him, he wouldn't give him the run-around and waste his time or theirs. Iranians generally hate saying "no" to anyone, and though Habib could be gracious and approachable, he also could be blunt. If someone was inefficient, he'd tell them exactly what he was unhappy about.

In the years his sons were away, Habib mentored the children of his gardener Mash-Hatam — daughter Shamsi and three sons — and all four worked for the company. When Shamsi finished school, Habib sent her to secretarial school. The year my father returned to Iran, she became Habib's secretary. Until Shamsi got married and left her father's house, the driver Gholam Reza drove Habib and Shamsi to work every morning from Shemiran.

All of Shamsi's brothers also worked for Habib. Parviz, the youngest, worked in one of the Plasco stores. Manoucher, the oldest brother, started at one of the stores as a cashier.

One day, Iraj, the middle son, told Habib: "I don't want to study anymore, I don't like to study. I only want to work."

My aunt Mahnaz, recalling the story, said Habib told him if he kept going to school and studied accounting, he could go to work for Habib and he'd pay him 400 tomans a month, a lot of money at that time.

Iraj was persistent. "Habib Agha, I just can't study. Your offer is really good, but please just let me start working full-time now." Relenting, Habib took Iraj to the factory, where he became a quick study and took over as manager of the button manufacturing department at PlascoKar.

Later, planning to get married, Iraj told Habib he wanted to go to Germany and bring over two machines to start his own plastics manufacturing company.

"You want to bring machines and compete with me?" Habib joked. Still, he gave him a loan, which Iraj paid off as the small factory he built thrived.

Iraj, Manoucher and Parviz became so successful that each owned an imported luxury car — BMW, Mercedes, Jaguar. Parviz teased my grandfather about his no-frills Paykan.

"You don't worry about me," he said, laughing. "Worry about yourself."

Habib knew Ahmad and Mahmood Khayami, the brothers who introduced the Paykan, the first Iranian-made car, in 1967. To support Iranian-made goods, Habib switched from his Peugeot to the white sedan.

Habib always sat in the front next to his driver, Gholam Reza, for whom he bought a house and his own car so he could commute back home every night. When Gholam Reza's daughter was born with a cleft palate, Habib paid for her to have reconstructive surgery in Israel and rented the family an apartment in Tel Aviv so they'd have a place to stay.

One more car-related story: In the late 1960s, Habib had bought Mahnaz a Jaguar which arrived in Iran in a shade of blue she hadn't ordered but didn't exchange. Once a year, the day after the New Year, Habib would borrow the turquoise Jaguar, when he would be invited to the king's palace for the *Salam*, when influential men, dressed in tuxedos, greeted the king and exchanged New Year's wishes. His automotive humility aside, he knew better than to arrive at the palace in his Paykan.

Dad Returns to Iran

Habib operated with Swiss-clock precision, my dad remembers. His routine was *"daftar, khouneh, bashga,"* office, house, social club. At 7:30 a.m., he was ready to get into the car next to Gholam Reza. By 8, he sat at his desk across from his brother on the Aluminum Building's 11th floor. He was back home between 1 and 3 p.m., when he liked family and friends to join Nikkou Jan and him for lunch. If the weather allowed, he'd swim in the pool; otherwise, a short siesta. He'd be back to work from 3 to 7 p.m.

Habib and Nikkou Jan almost never ate in. In the evenings, they'd meet for dinner at one of the *bashgas*, the social clubs they belonged to. There, Habib would play a few hands of poker and be in bed by 11. On Friday, the Iranian day off, friends and family met at a *bashga* for lunch, and Friday night Shabbat dinners were at his parents' house on Laleh Street.

Prominent folks of Habib's generation didn't go to restaurants. They dined at their social clubs. Habib belonged to three, and his favorite was the *Bashga Iran*, located on the road to Shemiran. Members and their guests parked their cars at the entrance, then walked into a two-acre garden dotted with old sycamores, cypresses and willows. The building that housed the small casino and salons was rustic, an old yellow-pink brick house in the corner of the garden. Inside, a roulette, a baccarat and a blackjack table each had its own croupier, and there were private tables for cards. On Friday afternoons, Habib's table was set for 20 guests, with open invitations to join him for lunch. Tables were set outside under the trees where fresh grilled kebab was served over saffron-topped rice. At night, sparkling strings of tiny white lights hanging from tree to tree illuminated the garden where they played cards under open tents.

In the winters, he'd go to *Bashga Asr*, Davoud's favorite club. When the *Bashga Asr* owners needed money, Davoud bought the land from them. The third one was *Bashga Tehran*, in the middle of the city, inside an old house with centuries-old handmade carvings and moldings, where prominent businessmen and politicians gathered.

My father worked during the day and caught up with friends and relatives in the evenings. In spring 1969, at a friend's party, he met my mother Helen.

She had graduated from the University of Tehran with a bachelor's degree in French literature and traveled to Europe. Her father, Lotfollah Gueola, was the son of Joseph Gueola, who was among the 25 men chosen in April 1920 for the Central (Tehran) branch of the Zionist Association; they later voted for 13 of the 25 to form the Central Committee to which Habib's Uncle Hajji Aziz was elected. Joseph owned a boot factory and crafted boots for Reza Khan and the military. He combined his talent for working with leather and his knowledge of Hebrew and scripture to restore ancient Torah scrolls he'd collect traveling across Iran, notably Isfahan. After Israel was founded in 1948, he traveled to the Jewish state to donate the Torah scrolls to the new country.[1]

When my grandfather Lotfollah turned 9 in 1928, his father took him to the factory to teach him the trade. Once, his father took him to measure King Reza Shah's feet for a new pair of boots. Because of his ties with the military, Lotfollah also served as a broker for merchants who wanted to do business with the army. In the early days of the plastics company, Habib had gone to Lotfollah for help selling plastic buttons for military uniforms.

A mere six months after meeting my mother, on Christmas Day 1969, my parents married and spent just a couple of hours at the party. Eager to show America to his bride, my dad had two tickets to New York for their honeymoon. He rented a car, and the two took a road trip across the United States.

Back home afterward, my parents frequented the parts of Tehran that were bustling and cosmopolitan: art galleries, cinemas, theaters, nightclubs and restaurants. Dressed in Europe's latest fashions, they proudly compared life in Tehran with European capitals. Not every corner of the city glittered. At the time, villagers from places outside the capital that were not benefitting from the economic boom were migrating to Tehran, hoping to improve their lives.

---

1. Arsalan Gueola, *Master Joseph Gueola*, self-published manuscript, p. 63-65.

Dad Returns to Iran

I was born in spring 1972, a time when the country was trying to join the ranks of the world's most prosperous nations. It seemed as though the shah's dream of transforming Iran into an economic powerhouse was just over the horizon.

Industrialization was taking root with some 5,651 factories in Iran that year. At a meeting of OPEC, the Organization of Petroleum Exporting Countries, in Kuwait in October 1973, the price of crude oil was increased 70 percent. Then on Dec. 23, the shah confidently announced a new increase in the price. Europe and the United States, forced to adjust to the quadrupling of oil prices, went into a recession while those exports increased Iran's per capita income, raising the quality of life for all Iranians. After the shah announced the hike in oil prices, he declared education would be free up to eighth grade along with free school milk and free higher education for those who wished to become government employees.

In August 1974 came a $69 billion investment program designed to show the world how great Iran envisioned itself becoming. The government spent the equivalent of $22 billion from March 1974 to March 1975, close to the total it had spent the three previous years. It scrapped its goal of growing 11.4 percent, an already high rate, and went for 25.9 percent.[2]

Stoked by the prospect of consolidating his power and his dynasty in a prosperous country, the shah had brushed aside concerns about future oil market unpredictability, inflation, and the lack of skilled labor and infrastructure.[3]

Soon after I was born, my grandfather bought my parents land in Zaferanieh, in the north of Tehran. Remembering grand homes in places like Newport, my father had clear ideas about what he wanted: "to build a really nice house and to live well." He hired a noted architect, Parviz Malek,

---

2. Robert Graham, *Iran: The Illusion of Power*, (New York: St. Martin's Press, 1979) p. 19.

3. Ibid.

to build one of the Petit Trianon-style homes that were popular with the wealthy in Tehran at the time.

When Habib saw the plans, "he thought it was too much," my father remembers. Habib had not forgotten that he'd grown up poor and had seen the backwardness of the country. Yes, he had participated in the industrial milestones and contributed to the leap in Iran's economy, but his mindset was much different from that of my father's generation, born rich and educated outside Iran.

My dad went ahead with his plans. Construction on the three-bedroom manse began in 1974. Back then, I spent many hours at my maternal grandparents, Mamanji and Babaji's home. Many of my memories of Tehran are with them in their house in Yousefabad: Mamanji teaching me to tell time, watching her make pizza and french fries, taking afternoon naps on cots in their large second-floor balcony, playing a memory game with cards or going on popsicle forays to the corner store with my aunt Moji, watching cartoons with my uncle John, driving home from preschool with my aunt Jeannette and telling her about my first crush, Bertrand.

I held on tight to those memories long after we moved to New York. Separated from Mamanji and Babaji, who stayed behind in Tehran, I felt starved for their love. After the Revolution, new laws forbade a Jewish couple to leave the country together. For decades, we could only talk on the phone, and every conversation with them was an occasion for reminiscing. Never fading, the longing created by our unfair separation etched those days into my DNA.

Many of my other memories of Tehran are from the trove of photographs my mother brought with her to New York where, years later, she gave me my first photo editing assignments. We spent many weekends around our dining room table putting together albums of our former life. I'd always known the boxes of photos she had brought from Iran were important to her: I had watched her take them out of the closet, look at each picture carefully, smile sometimes, but often cry, then put them back for the next virtual trip to what she says were the best days of her life.

Thirty years of her life in Iran sat in those boxes. At Woolworth's on Third Avenue, near where the Bloomberg Building in which I eventually worked as a photo editor now stands, we bought albums to preserve my childhood pictures from Tehran. Chronicling my early birthdays in albums was among my first "assignments," and thanks to her, I still have those images — captured on Kodak paper and crammed inside my bookshelves.

Our old selves still need to breathe. So, I occasionally take the albums out for air. In most of the pictures, I'm either in the arms of my maternal grandparents, my mother or my aunts. I wasn't Habib's first grandchild or a boy — he had four grandsons who were older, Fred's boys and Mahnaz's sons — so, I was not the special first grandchild as I was on my mother's side. I never had a special name for Habib or Nikkou Jan, like I did for Babaji and Mamanji.

I'm told, though, that right after I was born, Habib stopped by our place in the afternoons to see me. And there's a picture of the two of us during my third birthday party in spring 1975.

The photographer catches us in a moment when neither is posing for the camera. When I stare at that photo, I know I wasn't born to be carefree. Even on my birthday, sitting in front of a big cake with big plastic clowns, I'm returning my grandfather's signature warm, confident smile with my best anxious look.

The good times were soon to end.

Gallery

Family photo with Habib and Nikkou Jan, second right, with Habib's parents Khanoum Jan and Babai, seated at center.

Habib and Nikkou Jan with my father Karmel, center, Sina and Mahnaz.

Ayatollah Ruhollah Khomeini on June 9, 1963.

The 7 Elghanian brothers, back row, Nourollah, Nejat, Sion, Eddy, and front row, John, Davoud, Habib.

Shah Mohammad Reza Pahlavi reads a speech in the Throne Room of Golestan Palace, Tehran on Oct. 26, 1967, following his coronation ceremony. Empress Farah, left, and their son Crown Prince Reza Pahlavi, right, listen to the speech.

A street scene in Tehran on June 16, 1970.

Honor guards line up during ceremonies to mark the 2,500th anniversary of the founding of the Persian Empire at the Tomb of Cyrus the Great, at Pasargad, Iran, on Oct. 12, 1971.

The banqueting tent during the celebrations to mark the 2,500th anniversary of the founding of the Persian Empire at Persepolis on Oct. 15, 1971.

Gallery

A wooden box from the festivities in Persepolis with the Cylinder of Cyrus on the lid with Iran-made cigarettes and cigars inside.

Silver coin minted for the 2,500th year anniversary celebration of King Cyrus' founding of the Persian Empire.

During the celebrations to mark the 2,500th anniversary of the founding of the Persian Empire, the shah, second right, Crown Prince Reza Pahlavi, right, and Empress Farah, third right, watch a wreath laying ceremony in Pasargad on Oct. 12, 1971.

Habib with the singer Marzieh.

U.S. presidential national security adviser Henry Kissinger, fourth from right seated bottom row, and Iran's Prime Minister Amir-Abbas Hoveyda, fourth from right seated bottom row, watch a a belly dancer perform in a hotel in Tehran on May 12, 1972.

Habib shows the shah PlascoKar sample products at a pavilion.

Habib and other members of the Chamber of Commerce in front of the Great Wall in China in 1974 where they had travelled to lay the groundwork for trade between the two nations.

Moshe Dayan in Tehran flanked by Habib and Davoud.

At my birthday party in April 1975 at Bashga Asr in Tehran.

Habib in Sanandaj in 1975 with Nikkou Jan, with their daughter-in-law Sheryl, Sina's wife, and their grandson Barry.

Habib at the palace with other influential Iranians for the *Salam* to exchange Nowrooz, New Year's wishes with the shah.

Gallery

Firefighters battle a blaze that engulfed the iconic Plasco Building before it collapsed in Tehran on Jan. 19, 2017.

Dozens of firefighters were killed in the blaze.

Firefighters at the scene of the collapsed high-rise which caught fire after years of neglect.

PART III

Fatal Decisions

CHAPTER 14

～

Scapegoat

The year 1975 turned out to be the beginning of the end.

It was the year the monarchy began to unravel. The shah charged ahead with well-intentioned but overzealous efforts to modernize the country without being willing to modernize on the political level. It also was the year my grandfather got enmeshed in the king's two most combustible economic and political policies: his plan to fight inflation and the growing power of his secret police, SAVAK.

With the December 1973 quadrupling in the price of oil to nearly $12 a barrel, the world's second-largest petroleum exporter wasn't at all prepared to absorb the resulting raft of riches. In a November interview with Italian journalist Oriana Fallaci, the shah said the price of oil would increase. Referring to Western countries, he said: "You've increased the price of the wheat you sell us by 300 percent, and the same for sugar and cement. . . . You buy our crude oil and sell it back to us, refined as petrochemicals, at a hundred times the price you've paid us. You make us pay more, scandalously more, for everything, and it's only fair that, from now on, you should pay more for oil."[1]

With this windfall of oil income, the shah envisioned more factories, construction and improved infrastructure. As Western countries were forced to pay more, after already reeling from an earlier oil embargo by Arab states to punish the U.S. for its support of Israel in the Yom Kippur War, the West sank deeper into recession. But all that money pouring into Iran sent inflation surging and exposed an unprepared economy.

Virtually all construction materials had to be purchased from abroad, but when the cargo arrived in Iran, the ports had neither the manpower nor the technology to unload it. Shipments of imported building materials languished in the main ports of Khorramshahr and Bandar Abbas. Even if the cargo had been unloaded fast enough, a shortage of trucks and drivers slowed the delivery of goods into big cities, further delaying construction projects.

With demand for land for new construction also strong, real estate prices rose. Villagers from rural areas who had moved to Tehran to seek jobs faced high rents and low wages. Unskilled construction workers had to live in shantytowns.

The education system failed to produce enough skilled workers. Positions for jobs such as carpenters, welders, engineers and accountants couldn't be filled, provoking salary increases. A bilingual secretary could earn $1,200 a month, an engineer with a foreign degree could ask for $2,000, while a manager with a graduate degree could earn $4,500.[2]

Thanks to these increases in salaries, workers' buying power increased. But because production couldn't meet demand, shortages forced consumers

---

1. William D. Smith, "Price Quadruples for Iran Crude Oil," *The New York Times*, Dec. 12, 1973.
2. Robert Graham, *Iran: The Illusion of Power*, (New York: St. Martin's Press, 1979), p. 90.

to buy at black market prices. For example, the selling price of a four-door Paykan was 35 percent more than the list price. Consumer prices rose with the rising cost of labor and raw material, triggering a 38 percent inflation rate. Even food was expensive. Demand outpaced supply because the White Revolution's land reforms of the 1960s had focused more on land ownership than production.

At the same time, the middle class — both the educated middle class and the shopkeepers and small businessmen who were allied with the clergy — clamored to have more say in politics. But the king refused to allow more political participation. On March 2, 1975, he established a one-party system and founded the Resurgence Party, or *Rastakhiz* in Farsi, with compulsory enrollment and dues. The mandatory system, coupled with an increase in surveillance by the SAVAK, rankled Iranians.[3]

Rather than using other fiscal policies to cool down the economy, the government instituted price controls in July 1975 by rolling back the prices of some 16,000 items to January 1974 levels. The king sent out students from the *Rastakhiz* Youth party to check and decide, sometimes on their own, the proper price for a product.

The government's economic management was out of touch. Two years earlier, flush with petrodollars, the government had set out to build hospitals with some 20,000 extra beds, but when companies returned to the Ministry of Health with their proposals, the plans were rejected: too expensive. Still, after deeming these projects too costly, officials decided to get the hospitals built another way.[4] The king's twin sister, Ashraf, turned to my grandfather and the Jewish community to contribute to the project as a charitable cause.

---

3. Ibid., p. 96.
4. Ibid., p. 110.

On July 17, 1975, her office called the Anjoman office, inviting Habib and Heshmat Kermanshahchi, my grandfather's right-hand man at the Central Jewish Board, and several others to a meeting.

"At her office, one of her aides started to tell us that during the last few years, the country had flourished and everything had improved and that our community had benefited the most from all these improvements, which was correct to some extent," Kermanshahchi told me over tea in his Los Angeles office.

The aide said Princess Ashraf had three projects for them. One would be to build a heart disease hospital in Tehran — "the best medical center in the whole Middle East," he remembers the aide saying.

"We made the calculation that that would cost 300 million to 400 million tomans."

The aide went on to say Ashraf wanted them to also build a university and a factory for pasteurized milk in Hamadan.

The Central Jewish Board had done much charitable work, and Habib had helped support hospitals in the past. Aside from donating the land of his old house for a hospital on Sheykh Hadi Street, he was involved with an old hospital on Cyrus Street. In 1949-50, a Jewish charity called *Kanoun-e Kheyrkhah*, which managed a clinic and a hospital, asked the Jewish Charitable and Cultural Association (the charity that Habib had helped establish) for a piece of land on which they could build a hospital. The association purchased the land, for which it paid half, then held a charity night to pay for the other half.[5]

All told, Ashraf's three projects would amount to 700 million tomans, Kermanshahchi said. "In order to understand the magnitude of this devil demand, the total money we were collecting in the *Sandogh Melli*, the charitable fund for the community, was less than 100 million tomans per year. We were not that rich. It was not possible."

---

5. Davoud Elghanayan, *An Autobiography*, p. 77

In a culture where saying no is deemed offensive, Habib said no — and this to a princess so admired by Soviet dictator Joseph Stalin that he once asked her to relay to her brother that "if he had 10 like you, he would have no worries at all."[6]

The SAVAK had its eyes on Habib. One of his roles as Central Jewish Board chairman was to help facilitate the emigration of Jews to Israel. Jewish organizations invited Habib and prominent members of Iran's Jewish community to Israel to ask them to help encourage more migration there. Between Israel's inception in 1948 and 1951, 24,822 Iranian Jews moved there, followed by 27,660 from 1951 to 1955.[7]

Aryeh Levin describes their difficulties and eventual integration: "They were forced to start their lives from scratch, but, unlike many others, they did not make complaining a profession." Eventually joining the Israeli melting pot, some even became national leaders.[8]

By the 1970s, as Iran's Jews became increasingly integrated into Iranian society, emigration to Israel had dwindled. Getting Iranian Jews to leave Iran for Israel was difficult: Not only were they comfortable in their native country, but they would also have had to overcome language and cultural obstacles in their new one.

On Feb. 2, 1974, Habib and other Jewish leaders were invited by the Magbit, an organization that raises money to support immigration to Israel, to visit the country. On Jan. 4, 1975, the SAVAK added an account of the

---

6. Brian Murphy, "Ashraf Pahlavi, twin sister of Iran's late shah, dies at 96," *The Washington Post*, Jan. 8, 2016.

7. Alessandra Cecolin, *Iranian Jews in Israel: Between Persian Cultural Identity and Israeli Nationalism*, (London: I. B. Tauris & Co. Ltd, 2016), p. 2.

8. Aryeh Levin, "Habib Elghanayan: A Reflection of the Iranian Jewish Community," *The History of Contemporary Iranian Jews*, Volume 3, ed. Homa Sarshar, ((Beverly Hills: The Center for Iranian Jewish Oral History, 1999), p. 24.

previous year's trip to Habib's dossier. The SAVAK relied on informants, and this entry raises the possibility there might have been one in Habib's circle.

The entry spells out places visited and names of officials, including Israel's president, who met with the group. In a meeting with government ministers, it said, Habib and another businessman "gave their word that when they returned to Iran, they would make bigger efforts than made in the past to collect bigger donations from Iranian Jews to help Israel and will make efforts with a big campaign to get Jews who live in Iran to immigrate to Israel."

The SAVAK agent, code-named Tuesday, wrote this assessment in the file: "Mr. Elghanian, capitalist and famous Jewish businessman who has profited and continues to profit from the privileges of Iran more than any other Iranian, considers Israel to be his principal country and encourages Iranian Jews to invest in Israel and in this way helps Israel's economy and does not care about the country where he is born, where he was raised and where he has profited enormously; he considers himself attached to Israel."[9]

Tuesday's assessment is corroborated by an agent code-named, imaginatively enough, Wednesday. The SAVAK suspected all prominent Iranian Jews of having treasonable dual loyalties.

Three days after my grandfather said no to Ashraf's office, in the early hours of July 27, 1975, three SAVAK agents parked their car outside the house of Habib's late parents, Khanoum Jan and Babai, in central Tehran. In the dark, the three walked past the small fountain in the garden and climbed the circular steps leading up to the main house. Standing on the landing, they knocked on the door.

Habib's niece Aziz, his sister Saltanat's daughter, who lived there alone, sat up, wondering who it could be past midnight. Half-asleep, she turned on the

---

9. Author correspondence with investigator Serge Klarsfeld, who forwarded copies of documents he obtained from authorities in Iran. The reference to Habib's visit to Israel has this citation: No. 21-250/60512, dated Jan. 4, 1975, and 21-250/113022.

light and walked to the door. As she turned the knob, the men forced their way in. One spotted the phone just inside the entrance and disconnected the line.

"Where is Habib Elghanian?"one agent demanded.

"This is his father's house," Aziz replied.

"Where does he live? We have some business with him," the agent said.

"Khalili Street, in Darband, Shemiran."

When the agents realized their intelligence was wrong, one stayed behind to ensure Aziz wouldn't inform Habib they were coming for him. Days earlier, a couple of other industrialists had fled Iran after getting wind that the government might be coming for them. The SAVAK couldn't afford to let another big fish slip through their net.

Two agents drove to Khalili Street. At the dead end, one got out of the car in front of the black gate and rang the bell.

Vali, the caretaker who lived in the old gardener Mash-Hatam's house since he had died and his family moved out, got out of bed to see who was outside.

"We want to talk to Mr. Elghanian," the agent said through the gate.

Vali, a short wiry man in his 30s, sprinted to the main house and knocked on the sliding glass door of the master bedroom where Habib and Nikkou Jan were asleep.

Habib got up and slid the door open.

"Vali, *chieh*? What's the matter?"

"There are two people here for you."

"What? Well, tell them to come in," Habib said as he put on his robe.

Vali ran back down to get them and walked them up the driveway to the main house. The two men stepped inside the bedroom from the yard.

"We have instructions here that say we have to take you," one of the agents said, waving the papers.

"I beg you, please," Nikkou Jan implored, "tell us what's going on or wait until the morning so we can figure out what this is all about. Why are you taking him in the middle of the night? Where are you taking him?"

"No *khanoum*, ma'am. He must come with us now."

"Don't worry, everything will be alright," Habib reassured her.

He put on a suit, and the men escorted him down to the car. As soon as they were out of earshot, Nikkou Jan, tears streaming down her cheeks, turned to Vali.

"*Boro* Vali. Go, take the car and follow them."

Vali jumped in the white Paykan, caught up to them before they made it out onto the main avenue.

When the agents realized Vali was in the car behind them, they stopped. "Let's go, Mr. Elghanian. Tell your guy there he can't follow us," one of the agents said before escorting him to his Paykan.

"Vali, please, don't worry," Habib told him. "Go back home. I will go take care of what these men want, and I'll come back."

In the meantime, Nikkou Jan called my father and Fred, both of whom rushed to Shemiran.

What kind of place have I come back to, my father wondered as his mother recounted how the men had whisked away his father in the middle of the night.

Dad called uncle Davoud to tell him what had happened. "Please find out where they took our father," he said.

By morning it became clear that, while the government's intelligence may have been sloppy, its media operation was ready to roll.

That very day at 7 a.m., the radio news blared about "Habib Elghanian arrested for price gouging." Uncle Davoud went out looking for his brother, but there were no signs of Habib at the local police station. At SAVAK head-quarters, they denied any knowledge of his whereabouts. Davoud went to the office and began contacting every government office he could.

That day the *Ettelaat* newspaper's front-page[10] headline read, "Elghanian Arrested." Next to his photograph were the charges: 1. Price Gouging. 2. Market Manipulation. 3. Lack of Conformity with Approved Prices.

---

10. *Ettelaat* newspaper dated 5 Mordad 1354 - July 27, 1975.

Underneath, it said: "The Commission of Public Protection will investigate the price gouging charges against Elghanian, the well-known millionaire owner of Plasco. Two others arrested on charges of bread and fruit price gouging."

Page 2 carried a photo of the shutdown Plasco flagship store my father owned.

The caption said: "Habib Elghanian accused of price gouging and interference with ordered prices was arrested. This morning, the Plasco store located in the Plasco Building and owned by his son shut down for price gouging. Business closed for violation of the Rules and Regulations of the Trade Guild affixed in front of the door."

The story began:

"The government fight against price gouging escalated to a new stage following the arrests of Habib Elghanian, the well-known industrialist," and the two others, who were named.

Three Plasco stores in different parts of Tehran were closed, the article noted, quoting a government official. And, it said, "the investigation made clear that Habib Elghanian was himself the maker of the products and had ordered the inflated prices and had refused to produce invoices for the cost of the goods sold in the stores; he was deemed responsible for being a major instigator of price gouging."

A sidebar was headlined, "Who is Elghanian?":

"Habib Elghanian is one of the largest factory owners in the country who started his activities producing different products 22 years ago," that story began, and it proceeded to outline his extensive holdings in real estate and the aluminum, construction and other industries and his membership in the Chamber of Commerce and other leadership positions.

A second sidebar was headlined, "The Fight Against Price Gouging Does Not Distinguish Between Small and Big."

Noting the arrest of "a billionaire industrialist and two regular guild directors," it quoted a government spokesman as saying that "whoever, and at whatever position, does not follow his Majesty's order will be open to prosecution. The industrialists in Iran owe their country. The owners of industry in Iran have benefited greatly from a secure business environment, which is the biggest factor in their success, and has enabled them to rapidly increase their investments by millions and billions."

In the first two weeks of what became known as the shah's anti-profiteering campaign to fight inflation, 7,750 people from the merchant class were arrested, a move that infuriated them. In the end, they would make the shah pay.

That first day of the campaign was a summer day with temperatures reaching 100 degrees. Davoud didn't know who else to call about his brother. At 6 p.m., the phone rang in the office. Habib was calling.

"I'm with the SAVAK," he told Davoud. "They are going to take me to exile. We are first coming to the office, then over to Sanandaj." The capital of Iran's Kurdistan province, Sanandaj lies 530 miles west of Tehran.

When Habib walked into the office accompanied by SAVAK agents, Davoud bolted from behind his desk to talk to his brother, but the agents held him back and instructed the two not to speak.

As soon as they left, Davoud called SAVAK head Nematollah Nasiri.

"What is going on, Mr. Nasiri?"

"Pretend your brother is on a three-month-long vacation, Davoud Khan," Nasiri said. "The weather in Sanandaj is as nice as in Shemiran, so he's lucky that way. Nothing can be done about this."

To divert attention from the government's own ineptitude in cooling down the overheated economy and to let Iranians think he was fighting inflation, the shah had devised the campaign to punish businessmen involved in making consumer goods. Instead of taking responsibility for their own failed economic policies amid simmering tensions, the shah and Prime Minister Amir-Abbas Hoveyda scapegoated the very people whose enterprises had contributed to bringing Iran into the ranks of industrialized nations.

Scapegoat

In his book *Eminent Persians*, historian Abbas Milani explains the roots of this wrong-headed campaign: "Two paradoxes tempered the unfettered growth of the private sector in this period. First was the shah's 'statist' proclivities. During Hoveyda's 13-year tenure as prime minister, he encouraged this tendency in the shah. Both men distrusted the market mechanism, particularly when it came to politically sensitive issues like price control and fighting inflation." The government actions killed confidence in Iran's economy, Milani says. "What happened to Habib Elghanian, the most prominent Jewish businessman of his generation, was a dire warning to all industrialists and an early indication that further investment in Iran might not be warranted."[11]

Others, too, saw through the government's moves. The king's anti-profiteering campaign "was a crude effort to brand the entrepreneur and the tradesman as the chief culprit of higher prices," writes Robert Graham, the *Financial Times* reporter in Iran at the time. In his book, *Iran: The Illusion of Power*, he adds: "Some considered it significant that the bigger names prosecuted in the anti-profiteering or prices campaigns were often outsiders — members of the Bahai sect like Sabet, or Jews like Elghanian."[12]

(A summons had been served in absentia on Habib Sabet, a Bahai, and the other ranking businessman Khomeini had assailed along with my grandfather in his April 10, 1964, speech as Israeli agents — an interesting confluence of targets for Khomeini and the shah. The Ministry of Commerce's Price Stabilization Committee had also arrested Hassan Khosrowshahi, whose family produced Vitana biscuits and other confections, and Mohammed Vahabzadeh, who sold BMWs.)

---

11. Abbas Milani, "From Rags to Riches to Revolution, The Iranian Economy, 1941-1979," *Eminent Persians: The Men and Women Who Made Modern Iran 1941-1979*, Vol. 2 (Syracuse: Syracuse University Press and Persian World Press, 2008), p. 586.
12. Robert Graham, *Iran: The Illusion of Power*, (New York: St. Martin's Press, 1979) p. 97.

Among the shah's inner circle, his closest confidant Assadollah Alam, also the minister of court, found Habib's arrest absurd. The law forbids a store from inflating prices but, he noted in his journal, "What does the director of the company have to do with that sale?"[13]

The day after their father was taken away to exile in Sanandaj, my father and Fred flew there to visit him. He was under police surveillance in a small motel, required to report to the local police station every morning. When members of Sanandaj's Jewish community heard that Habib was there, they saw him almost daily when he didn't have visitors from Tehran.

"I'm comfortable here. Please don't worry about me," he reassured my father. He expressed no anger. The following day, Davoud went to visit, and on the third day, Mahnaz and Nikkou Jan. He told everyone the same thing: Don't worry about me.

On Monday July 28, the day after Habib's arrest, a follow up front-page story was headlined: "Worldwide Reaction to Elghanian's Arrest."[14]

The story said Habib "announced through a statement last night his willingness to obey the decree issued by his majesty and his cooperation with the government in fighting against price gouging. In his statement, he had declared his readiness to distribute his merchandise at a discount, taking into consideration the cost of production and a minimum of profit margin imposed by the government. Elghanian has declared himself aligned with the government in fighting against price gouging and has declared himself to be fully cooperative with the government."

Countering the government line, the noted Iranian satirist Hadi Khorsandi wrote a humor column in *Ettelaat*.

"The arrest of Habib Elghanian for price gouging has become a big headache for all of us," he deadpanned. "Today, I went to buy bread. The baker

---

13. Assadollah Alam, *Yadashtaye Alam [Alam Diaries]* ed. Alinaghi Alikhani, vol. 5, (Bethesda: Ibex, 1993) p. 192.
14. *Ettelaat* newspaper dated 6 Mordad 1354 - July 28, 1975.

was charging inflated prices. I asked him, 'Mister baker, why are you over-charging?' He replied, 'No, I swear to God, mister. Who dares to charge high prices? Had I done that, I would have been arrested just like Mr. Elghanian.'"

Getting the same answer after objecting to overcharges when he goes to buy fruit and other products, the satirist has a suggestion for the government: Either everyone should be put in jail or Elghanian should be released.

Khorsandi was having fun, offering pointed commentary the same way then-popular American satirical columnists Art Buchwald or Russell Baker might have.

My grandfather's trusted colleague at the Anjoman, Hechmat Kermanshahchi, flew to Sanandaj to visit Habib.

"I stayed with him for about a week," he recalled. "Fortunately, there was a Jewish community there. There were three young men who befriended Habib from the first week he arrived. ... They were taking care of him and they wouldn't leave him for a minute."

Habib's days were free after he'd sign in at the police station, he said. "I took him some books. He laughed, he said he hadn't read a book in years and this was the first time he'd have time to read."

Other visitors followed, including Jamshid Kashvi, a childhood friend who had served as the Jewish delegate to the lower house of the Iranian legislature, the Majlis, from 1963 to 1967, and Musa Khan Neydavoud, a classical Persian musician Habib knew growing up in the *Mahalleh*, who entertained his old friend.

Back in Tehran, Davoud worked with close Jewish friends to investigate the details of his brother's case. They included Kermanshahchi; Moussa Kermanian, a businessman and Zionist organizer; Yousef Cohen, an attorney and Jewish delegate to the Majlis from 1975 to1979; Lotfollah Hay, the Jewish delegate to the Majlis from 1967 to 1975; Meir Ezri, the Israeli ambassador to Iran until 1973; Kashvi; and a dozen others.

They found out how the case had been built against Habib.

"The government had sent out students to stores to check prices," Kermanshahchi told me, "and had found a product in one of your father Karmel's Plasco stores they said was too expensive. That was the charge against your grandfather."

And that's how in 1975 my grandfather was scapegoated and exiled, ensnared in the wrongheaded and disingenuous move to address inflation, which would help bring an end to the monarchy a mere four years later.

CHAPTER 15

~

Not So Fast

The group Davoud assembled to help investigate his brother's case mobilized that summer to use their contacts and influence to bring Habib home.

Lotfollah Hay, the Jewish delegate in Parliament and a childhood friend of Prime Minister Hoveyda from their school days in Lebanon, met the prime minister to protest Habib's arrest.[1] Another friend, Yousef Cohen, sent his lawyer to court in Tehran with Habib's case. The court, which was surprisingly independent, issued its verdict in October: It sent a telegram to Sanandaj saying Habib was innocent and could go home.

The day Habib was to return to Tehran, Nikkou Jan planned a big party at the house. She and my dad, Fred and Mahnaz went to the airport to greet him, but he wasn't to be seen. Recalling the day, Mahnaz says she later realized, "Uncle Davoud knew something but he was scared to tell Nikkou Jan."

Indeed, he did. In his memoir, Davoud wrote: "Brother Habib was supposed to come home by airplane. I had learned the evening before, that as

---

1. Lotfollah Hay, interview with author in Los Angeles, April 2011.

soon as he would disembark the plane, they would take him directly for further inquiries." In the morning, at the airport, Davoud saw a car pull next to the plane when it landed from Sanandaj, and Habib was whisked away. Afterward, other passengers disembarked.

"We were so excited. We saw everyone get off the plane except Papa," Mahnaz recalled.

"Coming home with an innocent verdict made the government look bad," Kermanshahchi told me. "They had claimed he was profiteering, and now a court in Tehran issued a verdict that this man was innocent, that the government was wrong. They couldn't have any of that."

A friend was able to get permission for Davoud to visit his brother who was held in a jail in Tehran.

"I don't want to see anyone," Habib told the warden. He was furious. He'd been punished not once, but twice.

"Please tell him that his brother Davoud wants to see him for five minutes." Habib acquiesced.

"We've been doing so much to get you free, brother," Davoud told him.

"Just don't do anything for a while until we can figure something out," Habib suggested.

Davoud agreed, then tried persuading Habib to see Nikkou Jan and the children. It's clear from a footnote in Davoud's memoir that my grandfather didn't really understand at the time that he was being scapegoated. "Habib was mostly mad at his children, particularly Karmel," Davoud writes. "Habib's exile and imprisonment resulted mostly from the work of Plasco branches which they alleged were engaged in profiteering. Brother Habib could have said that he was not the managing director and that he had nothing to do with the branches. But if he had said that, they would have arrested Karmel immediately. He agreed to pay for his son so that he would be left alone. Even then, it was quite possible that they would have arrested Habib on another pretext. Habib's children thought it was all our fault but later realized it was no one's fault."

The next day, the family went to visit. Mahnaz and Nikkou Jan brought him clothes and candy. They met over tea in the visiting room that had a couch, chairs, a radio and table. Later, friends could visit, and Davoud would go every two days to brief him about business.

One day Majid Alam, a relative of Minister of Court Assadolah Alam, told Davoud to see Houshang Ansari, the finance minister. With the help of a friend, Davoud got an appointment. (It was Ansari's brother who had travelled in the 1950s with my father and his uncle to New York.)

"You may say whatever you want to say. I know your brother is innocent," Ansari told Davoud. "They had to catch someone for starters. Regretfully, they caught him. Moreover, you people have done a great deal of service to the development of Iran's economy. However, nothing can be done for now, and you have to put up with it until the right time comes. I suggest that you do not spend a penny. The more you spend, the worse it gets, not better."

Ansari asked for both Davoud's home and office numbers and suggested he wait for his call. "When I get the opportunity, I will speak to the shah," Ansari told Davoud, who the next day told Habib about the meeting.

On Thursday, Jan. 22, 1976, nearly six months after the ordeal began on that scorching Sunday in July, Davoud's home phone rang at 6:30 a.m.

"Your brother will be released today," Ansari said. "The order has been issued. Go at 10 a.m. and arrange for his release."

When Davoud arrived at the prison, the warden was surprised. He hadn't received any orders. As the two were talking, Habib's release orders arrived. They left the prison at 3 in the afternoon.

"Ansari has instructed you to keep a low profile in public, and you must keep quiet for a few days," Davoud explained to Habib as they drove to Davoud's house where the rest of his family waited for them. At Habib's own house, Davoud instructed them, "there should not be much coming and going" for a few weeks. That would allow Habib to reappear in public slowly.

Aryeh Levin, the chargé d' affaires of Israel's diplomatic mission to Tehran, and Habib's longtime friend, went to visit him a couple of days after his release. While the two were chatting, the phone rang, and it was Hoveyda.

"Everything will be fine now," the prime minister assured Habib. "Now you'll be able to return to your normal life."

Habib was glowing, but Levin was concerned.[2]

"What are you going to do now?" Levin asked him when he got off the phone. "Don't you think this would be the time to pick up and leave, at least for a little while, until the dust settles? Don't you think your imprisonment after this campaign against speculators, with a finger pointed at Elghanian the Jew, is a sign of worse things to come?"

"There is nothing to be upset about," Habib replied. "Everything will be fine. Hoveyda said so."

It baffled Levin that Habib felt as integrated as he did, that he had that inbred feeling that no harm could befall him in his own country.

Two months later, in March 1976, Habib was invited again to *Nowrooz* ceremonies at the palace, to exchange New Year's greetings with the shah.

"When the shah came to Habib, he asked him if his factories were running well," Davoud reports in his memoir.

Habib replied: "Your majesty, we want to import a 5,000-ton machine for heavy aluminum material, but the import permit is not being granted."

The shah turned to his secretary, who made a note.

That was all it took. When the office reopened after the New Year's holiday, they received a letter from the Chamber of Commerce, inviting them to talk about the machine, which could make parts for a range of products, from helicopters to lampposts. In May, brother Nourollah, who had ordered the machine, came to Tehran from New York to supervise the construction

---

2. Aryeh Levin, "Habib Elghanayan: A Reflection of the Iranian Jewish Community," *The History of Contemporary Iranian Jews*, Volume 3, ed. Homa Sarshar, (Beverly Hills: The Center for Iranian Jewish Oral History, 1999) p. 19-21.

of the 4,000-square-meter hall they had to build to house the "monster machine," as Davoud named it.

So, Habib continued to expand his empire even as other industrialists, having lost faith in Iran, were transferring their money out of the country. And more trouble was brewing as the government struggled to address inflation with new but still ineffective policies.

"Discovering that the war on the rich entrepreneurs did not end inflation, the regime took aim on shopkeepers and small businessmen. The central government imposed strict price controls on many basic commodities," writes Ervand Abrahamian, who best sums up what led to the shah's fall in his book *Iran Between Two Revolutions*.

"By early 1976," he continues, "every bazaar family had at least one member who had directly suffered from the anti-profiteering campaign. . . . Not for the first time, the bazaar community increasingly turned to its traditional ally, the clergy, for help and protection. The shah was disgruntling the bazaar whose alliance with the mullahs would fuel the revolution."[3]

Generous state investments in industry from 1963 to '77 — helping manufacturing's share of the GNP rise from 11 to 17 percent, and industrial growth jump from 5 to 20 percent — reflected the shah's modernization on the socio-economic level, expanding the ranks of the middle class and the industrial working class. But the shah, Abrahamian argues, failed to modernize politically. "Thus by 1977, the gulf between the developing socio-economic system and the underdeveloped political system was so wide that an economic crisis was able to bring down the whole regime," he writes.

"Making matters worse, as critics often pointed out, substantial sums were squandered on palaces and other extravagances of royalty, bureaucratic consumption, outright corruption, nuclear installations and ultra-sophisticated weapons too expensive even for many NATO countries."

---

3. Ervand Abrahamian, *Iran Between Two Revolutions*, (Princeton, New Jersey: Princeton University Press, 1982) p. 497- 498.

Although GNP kept growing – up 14 percent in 1972-73 and 30 percent in 1973-1974 – the shah had made a slew of enemies. These included the middle class and technocrats, leftists – Marxists, Islamic socialists, the Mujahedin and secularist socialists – and unskilled male migrants, mostly conservative and uneducated, who had moved to the cities during the construction boom. They hated watching the shah and his family get richer faster than they were. Why should the king and his family live extravagantly off proceeds of the sale of Iranian oil while they worked hard without getting rich?

Besides these groups, another unwittingly contributed to the looming revolution: the business elite who historian Abbas Milani says made "no serious efforts to save their own investments and the regime."

Members of the entrepreneurial class, to which Habib belonged, did nothing to stop the revolution, he writes. They packed up and left with what they could liquidate. They didn't push back to save what they had built. They didn't fight for laws, organize, build bridges, negotiate and otherwise stand up to preserve the modernization they had wrought.

The quid pro quo between the king and the economic elite was that the shah would create a business-friendly environment and the businessmen would stay out of politics.[4]

With so much government interference in the economy, even the Chamber of Commerce couldn't safeguard the interests of the merchants and industrialists.

"Qassem Lajevardi, a senator and industrialist, made a speech on the Senate floor expressing the industrialists' displeasure with the shah's economic policies," Milani writes in *The Shah*. "He talked about the dangers of price controls and arresting businessmen – industrialists will invest only if

---

4. Abbas Milani, "From Rags to Riches to Revolution, The Iranian Economy, 1941-1979," *Eminent Persians: The Men and Women Who Made Modern Iran 1941-1979*, Vol. 2 (Syracuse: Syracuse University Press and Persian World Press, 2008), p 582.

they are allowed to make a fair profit. A massive flight of capital had already started."[5]

On Jan. 24, 1976, two days after his father was released from jail, my dad turned 33. Appalled by the government's actions, he was among those who decided to leave Iran. He was ready to leave everything behind: family, friends, the stores, even the grand house his father was building for us, which was nearing completion.

At the end of the week, he went to see his parents and told them about his decision to leave Iran for good. Habib cried. "My dream was always that after school, you'd come back and stay in Iran," he said. "Everything I built is for you, your brothers and sister."

In May 1976, we moved into our new house in Zaferanieh, until my father could sell it along with his stores and leave.

I remember our home there very well. The house made of large limestone bricks had white arched windows and balconies and sat on top of a hill with a northern view of the mountains. A black gate opened onto a driveway that bracketed large steps leading to the house. A massive wooden front door opened onto an entrance hall crowned by a large chandelier. Cream-colored walls set off white hand-made wall carvings, and a wooden staircase led up to our rooms.

My bedroom walls were a pastel green, with white and navy lacquered furniture. It was at the back of the house and overlooked the path to the pool around the corner a dozen yards away. The house had two other bedrooms, my brother's and parents'. The master bedroom had a fireplace, French furniture, a green chandelier and arched windows that opened onto a balcony.

On the ground floor was a big formal dining room, but it remained empty; my mother never bothered to furnish it because she knew we would be leaving. I remember peeking into this room because I loved its deep turquoise walls and high white ceiling. We spent most of our time in our den, a cozy

5. Abbas Milani, *The Shah* (New York: Palgrave McMillan, 2012), p. 336 -337.

room where I'd sit for hours watching television variety shows and learning by heart Farsi pop songs by Satar and Shamaeezadeh.

Outside, on a landing of the wide stairs that led up to the house was a small area where we had put a table and chairs and sometimes ate breakfast. Nearby, in a large cage, we kept dozens of pigeons, and I worried about the one with brown and white feathers who stood apart from the gray ones. Being different, I thought, put him in some sort of danger. Violets were planted near the table, and I remember caressing the velvety petals, careful not to break them.

That fall, I started nursery school at the Lycée Razi. My aunt Jeannette, my mom's sister, worked as the school's assistant principal, and my aunt Moji, 10 years older than me, attended high school there, too. While I was painting pictures and creating tiny sheep out of cotton balls, my mother, who was pregnant with my brother, was putting the finishing touches on parts of the house we used most.

One day, when my mother and I were napping, she woke up asking me to call my grandparents. Her water had broken. An ambulance soon arrived to take my mother to the hospital while Mamanji and Babaji came to take me to their home.

I was back home for my brother's bris. Both my grandmothers fussed over him while dressing him in a little white outfit. In one of my favorite pictures from that day, Nikkou Jan is holding Shahram. She's smiling as she walks down the stairs with Mamanji next to her. My aunt Mahnaz and I follow them with my aunt Eliane, Fred's wife, and two other cousins, just a little older than me, right behind. In our den, where the ceremony was held, my father held Shahram, surrounded by Habib and the other men of the family, along with the rabbi. In the photos from that day, my father is the only one who looks happy.

Habib looks preoccupied, tired and sad. I can only imagine that it was with a heavy heart that he stood there so soon after his ordeal, looking at his son and grandson, knowing our family would be going away.

My dad remembers everyone thought he was crazy to leave everything behind. Surely their disbelief made my mom even more reluctant and sad to leave for a world so different from what she was accustomed to in Iran.

Images of that time before we left live vividly in my memory. The pool area behind the house included a gazebo where my parents hosted friends and relatives during the spring and summer before my brother turned 1.

In one set of pictures, my father, hair slicked back after a swim, is lounging in his swim trunks in a pool chair. He looks happy. I'm standing in my orange clogs, wearing a sleeveless yellow terry cloth summer dress decorated with three ducks in a bowl. When I look back at myself staring sideways into the camera, holding a notebook and pen I always carried around to doodle in, it's hard not to think how those pictures foreshadowed how I'd one day be chronicling that time in our life.

My father left Tehran a little before us to prepare our home in New York, a three-bedroom apartment overlooking the East River. We arrived there in August 1977, on a hot, humid, rainy day, and when we got off the elevator on the 31st floor, I remember looking out the window of the dining room and seeing nothing. The rain and humidity were so thick, everything was white — for days.

As we were settling into our new life, the 5,000-ton machine my grandfather and his brothers had imported from America arrived at the port in Khorramshahr. But the same infrastructure problems that plagued Iran two years earlier persisted. The machine couldn't be released because the bridges en route to Tehran couldn't support its weight. The Ministry of Roads informed Davoud and Habib it didn't have the budget to reinforce the bridges. To bring it to Tehran, Habib and Davoud gave money to the government to fortify the bridges. By October that year, the machine was starting to make samples.

Around this time, the government again took a strong hand in the economy, setting up a company to purchase 50 percent shares of every Iranian factory, part of the shah's plan to force industrialists to sell half their companies' shares to workers. Successful factories like Pars-America and PlascoKar were soon the targets of government officials.

"They estimated the value of Pars-America at 57 million to 60 million tomans," Davoud notes in his memoir. "When we saw this, we doubled the company's capital and injected 57 million to 60 million tomans in the company. The plant kept working. We prepared to take the share of Pars-America to the stock exchange so that it could be quoted there and could increase its value."

While they were busy setting up sales offices and hiring personnel for securing orders from government organizations, rumblings of the revolution grew louder by the day.

As tension built within the middle class and as more of the entrepreneurial class liquidated assets and bailed, unfounded conspiracy theories about Iran's secretive Freemasons circulated in the bazaars. "Although the vast majority of the upper class was Muslim, some senior officials had joined the court-connected Freemason Lodge in Tehran, and a few, notably (Hojabr) Yazdani, (Habib) Elghanian and (Morad) Aryeh, came from Bahai and Jewish backgrounds," Abrahamian writes. "This provided fuel for rumors often heard in the bazaars that the whole upper class represented an international conspiracy hatched by Zionists, Bahais centered in Haifa, and British imperialists through the Freemason Lodge in London."[6]

Habib was a member of Iran's secretive Freemasons, but the anti-Semitic conspiracy theory ignored the fact that he had just been imprisoned by the king.

---

6. Ervand Abrahamian, *Iran Between Two Revolutions*, (Princeton, New Jersey: Princeton University Press, 1982) p 432.

The shah's list of opponents kept growing: Besides shopkeepers, the clergy and the poor in shantytowns, there were civil servants, intellectuals, academics and journalists who envisioned a state without a king.

His enemies were emboldened when, after Amnesty International called the shah "one of the worst human rights violators in the world," he agreed to allow the Red Cross into his prisons, permit foreign lawyers to observe trials and civilians to pick their own lawyers with open trials.

While Habib's 5,000-ton machine produced samples in the aluminum factory that October 1977, the machinery of Iran's political opposition revved louder. Dissidents held poetry readings in Tehran, and on the 10th night of the readings, the overflowing audience followed the writers into the streets where they clashed with the police. Protests continued and those who were arrested were either released or given light sentences — which emboldened seminary students in Qom.[7]

In the meantime, Habib soldiered on as if wearing noise-canceling headphones.

---

7. Ibid., p 156–158.

CHAPTER 16

~

Losing His Lucky Charm

May 19, 1978, was a crisp spring Friday in Tehran, perfect for the weekly outdoor family lunch at the *Bashga Asr* country club. Mahnaz, who had married a decade earlier, called Nikkou Jan in the morning from her apartment in Vanak, a neighborhood south of Shemiran. She'd be taking her sons to the park, she told her mother, then added, "Be ready by noon and I'll come get you so we can go to the *Bashga* together."

Home from the park, Mahnaz was drawing the boys' bath when Layla Khanoum, the nanny, knocked on the bathroom door.

"Vali is on the phone," she said. The caretaker at Shemiran was calling to say that Nikkou Jan was nauseous and not feeling well.

"Finish giving the boys their bath," Mahnaz said. "I'll run over to see if Vahid is home so he can come to Shemiran with me." Vahid Shakib, a doctor, lived next door.

When Mahnaz and Vahid arrived, Vali was dutifully standing by an extremely pale Nikkou Jan, who was lying on a folding bed in the foyer. "I feel terrible," she said. As the doctor examined her, Habib arrived home to get ready for lunch.

"There's something wrong with her heart," Vahid said after a quick examination. "She's very sick. We need to get her to the hospital immediately."

As the ambulance took off, Mahnaz followed with her father. At the hospital, she ran to the stretcher, but Vahid pushed her out of the way and rolled Nikkou Jan in. Mahnaz and Habib ran behind them. It was only a few minutes later when Vahid came into the hallway where Habib was pacing.

"We couldn't save her," he told them both.

Nikkou Jan had suffered two heart attacks in the ambulance. In a family where the women lived well into their 80s, Nikkou Jan had died at 57.[1]

With his fist, Habib alternately beat his cheek and chest. "*Hallah chejouri misheh? Hallah chejouri misheh?* What'll happen to us?" he wailed. He grabbed his shirt, pulled it open and tore one side. Mahnaz recognized that her father's gesture was a traditional religious expression of a torn heart.

She felt herself shrink as she watched her father come unglued. Her heart pounding, she stood motionless, facing a world and a future without her mother. Already she was coping with her husband Mortezah Moreh suffering from multiple sclerosis.

The previous week, she had taken Nikkou Jan, who was diabetic, to two doctors after her mother had complained about pain in her left arm. Somehow, they failed to do a thorough cardiac exam. Nikkou Jan, for her part, never took care of her diabetes.

Habib was crying when Davoud arrived at the hospital with his wife Aghdas and their cousin Fereshteh. Vali had called *Bashga Asr* to ask them to let the rest of the family members arriving for lunch know they'd taken Nikkou Jan to the hospital.

Davoud put his arm around his brother's shoulders. "Let's all go back to Shemiran," he suggested. On the drive back, Habib pulled at his cheek with

---

1. Even though Nikkou Jan died on May 19, 1978, and Habib was executed the following year on May 9, the traditional Jewish ceremony marking the one-year anniversary of her death fell on May 9 according to the Jewish calendar.

his fingers. "*Bakhd azam gozasht, bakhd azam gozasht.* My luck has left me," he sobbed.

As relatives and friends came to offer condolences, Mahnaz greeted them while squeezing in her fist the key to Nikkou Jan's basement, where she stored her valuables. Her mother rarely went anywhere without that key, and holding it felt as if she was holding her hand.

Habib's oldest brother, John, who was in New York, broke the news to my father, who caught the next flight to Tehran with John's oldest son, Joe. When they arrived in Shemiran, hundreds of people filled the house. Dad spotted his father, inconsolable, in the center of a swarming cloud of familiar faces. In tears, they embraced.

The funeral service was held in Tehran, and then Nikkou Jan's body was transported to Giliard, an ancient Jewish cemetery where three generations of Elghanians were buried in a family plot. Habib arranged for buses to pick up everyone who wanted to make the hourlong trip. About 15 buses, 50 to 60 cars, and two truckloads of flowers headed east toward Giliard, a small village on a hill with mountains to the north watching over the cemetery's tombstones all arranged in the traditional east-west direction. Some 1,500 people followed Nikkou Jan's coffin.

Rabbi Hakham Yedidiah Shofet recited prayers and hymns, with the family joining in with the Kaddish as the coffin was lowered into the ground. "What's going to happen to us without you, Nikkha?" Habib repeated, tears streaming down his cheeks.

Mahnaz, Nikkou Jan's sisters, and other female relatives and friends threw flowers and poured rosewater on her coffin — a traditional gesture for a sweet afterlife. With the afternoon sun still beating down on them, Habib, Fred, Dad, uncles, and close male cousins and friends took turns shoveling dirt over her coffin.

Habib had instructed the cemetery workers to place the two truckloads of flowers on all of Giliard's tombstones. By the time the mourners filed back into their cars and buses, the cemetery lay under a fragrant blanket of blossoms.

For Nikkou Jan's shiva, the house was full. "For seven days, they came and went from morning till night," Davoud remembers. The last day of the shiva was held at the synagogue, attended by an estimated 2,000 to 2,500 people, many of them Muslim. Condolence letters and telegrams that Habib received included one from the shah's wife. After the synagogue service, Habib hosted a meal at the house, and when the last guests left, he sat down and asked for a *falloudeh*, a rosewater-flavored granita, to quench his thirst.

Seconds after the drink was placed on the table in front of him, the glass shattered.

* * *

By the time Nikkou Jan died in spring 1978, she, like most Iranians, had witnessed the early signs of turmoil directed against the shah's rule.

The opposition was roughly divided among those who wanted a democracy, those who wanted a theocracy, and Marxist groups, some of which were armed.

The secular National Front of Iran was headed by Karim Sanjabi, the former education minister under Prime Minister Mohammad Mosaddegh, the group's founder in 1949. The National Front was revived in late 1977 by Sanjabi, Mossadegh's Deputy Minister of Labor Shapour Bakhtiar, and Nation Party of Iran head Dariush Forouhar. Their platform was to reestablish a constitutional monarchy, free political prisoners, foster freedom of speech, and hold free and fair elections.

Islamist members of the National Front had splintered off to create the Freedom Movement of Iran. This group, which also supported the Constitution, was led by Mehdi Bazargan and Ayatollah Mahmoud Taleghani, who would later show some sympathy toward the Jewish community.

Other Islamist groups supported Ayatollah Khomeini, who was still living in exile in 1977. Among these were an armed group, the Mujahedeen of the Islamic Revolution Organization. Religious merchants from the bazaar who were traditionally allied with the clergy created the Coalition of Islamic Societies. There was also the Combatant Clergy Association that included Morteza Motahhari, Ayatollah Mohammad Beheshti, Mohammad-Javad Bahonar and Akbar Hashemi Rafsanjani.

The Marxists included the Tudeh Party of Iran, who were illegal and heavily suppressed by the SAVAK. The Marxists also had two armed groups: The Organization of Iranian People's Fedai Guerrillas and the breakaway Iranian People's Fedai Guerrillas.

The early stages of the revolution were led by the shah's pro-democracy opponents, National Front of Iran and Freedom Movement of Iran.

On Jan. 7, 1978, protests spiraled out of control when an editorial in *Ettelaat* newspaper criticized Khomeini, falsely accusing him of being a British agent, a closet homosexual and an alcoholic. To protest the article, 4,000 students and religious leaders demonstrated in Qom. In clashes with police, between 10 and 72 demonstrators died.[2]

That first protest in the holy city set off a cycle of demonstrations that spread across Iran every 40 days, with pious Muslims marching in the streets to mark the deaths of the marchers in the previous protest. Each new observance brought new clashes and new deaths. Roughly 10,000 people marched in each commemoration until June.

On June 6, in an attempt to appease the demonstrators, the shah ordered the arrest of Nematollah Nasiri, the head of SAVAK.

While these developments played out, our family tried to look forward from Nikkou Jan's death. Habib wanted to gather friends and family members from both the United States and Iran for a European vacation

---

2. Facts from the history of the revolution come from Ervand Abrahamian, *Iran Between Two Revolutions*, (Princeton, New Jersey: Princeton University Press, 1982).

in August. We all met in London first, where one of my few recollections was a visit to Madame Tussauds wax museum. The following week, we flew to Monte Carlo where about 30 family members and friends stayed at the Loews Hotel near the Casino de Paris.

"Dad's trip to Monte Carlo was to try to relax and forget things. He did seem relaxed," my father told me years later. "He loved swimming and gambling, and both were handily available to him there. He was enjoying himself, but he was missing Nikkou Jan, and he left early for Iran, as usual, to attend to business."

Habib was eager to return to the factories, and perhaps immersing himself in work was the best way to cope with Nikkou Jan's death. Being away too long from home always made him antsy, even more so now that the new 5,000-ton aluminum machine was ensconced in the space they'd built for it in the factory at Karaj.

At the end of our stay in Monte Carlo, my father returned home to New York while my mother, our Haitian-American babysitter Jackie, my brother Shahram and I flew to Tehran to visit my mother's parents. I was ecstatic. Mamanji and I had a repertoire of songs we'd sing together, some well-known French ones like "En passant par la Lorraine," which she'd sing rolling her r's, and some made-up songs like "You're My Sherry-Brandy." We could enjoy all the same things we used to before I moved to New York. My aunt Moji took me for popsicles again and played endless hours of cards with me. Mamanji was still making her signature bean dish for Thursday lunch, and Babaji cooked up fresh kebabs over white rice on Friday afternoons. It was a real treat staying with them that August — but what had started to unravel in Iran in 1975 was getting worse three years later.

Earlier, on Aug. 6, the shah had pledged free elections by June 1979. Yet, the following week on Aug. 12, more demonstrators died in Isfahan. To control the growing unrest, the government declared martial law and banned demonstrations. A week later, Cinema Rex in the city of Abadan went up in flames, killing 477 people. The regime and the opposition blamed each other, but the public concluded that the SAVAK had set the theater ablaze to frame the Islamists who hated movie theaters. The next day, 10,000 relatives and sympathizers gathered for a mass funeral and march, shouting, "Burn the shah" and "the shah is the guilty one."

As the grown-ups watched the news on television, Jackie, with her own memories of fleeing Haiti under the Duvalier regime's Tonton Macoute secret police, was more scared than anyone. Already sick from too much Persian food, she worried she might never make it back to her children and grandchildren in the United States.

The shah, meanwhile, tried to appease the opposition. On Aug. 27, the prime minister was replaced, casinos owned by the Pahlavi family closed, the imperial calendar that had replaced the Islamic calendar in 1971, anger-ing the clergy, was abolished[3] and all the country's political parties were given the right to be active.

My mom had a gnawing feeling this would be the last time she'd be in Iran. So she made up her mind to visit all the places she loved — her alma mater, the University of Tehran; the bazaar; Darvazeh Dolat, her childhood neigh-borhood where she lived in the 1950s; Sar e Pol e Tajrish, a large promenade with a shopping area and restaurants with views of the Alborz Mountains; our old apartment building on Abbas Abad; even her old hairdresser.

"I tried to see everything," she told me years later on one of our walks in New York. "I knew I would never come back. I said bye to all the doors and walls."

On Sept. 4, for the Eid al-Fitr holiday that marks the end of Ramadan, hundreds of thousands of Khomeini's supporters, led by Bazargan, the religious intellectual and pro-democracy activist, marched south from Gheytarieh, a district in northeast Tehran, to the center of the capital. Young, unskilled male workers living in city slums, many from traditional rural

---

3. The imperial calendar started from 599 B.C., a date based on the coronation of King Cyrus whose 2,500th anniversary the shah celebrated in 1971.

backgrounds, joined the street protests. During the march, they were joined by other revolutionaries. When they arrived in the center of Tehran, they gave flowers to the soldiers, asking them why they kill their own brothers.

Three days later, a Thursday, we were gathered around the dining room table eating Mamanji's *loubia* bean dish. Suddenly, my grandfather Habib walked in, without any of his usual small talk. He held four airline tickets, one each for my mom, Jackie, Shahram and me, and instructed us to be ready at 5 the next morning to go to the airport. He said we had to beat the morning traffic because a big demonstration was planned. No one said a word.

That Friday morning, Sept. 8, 1978, my grandfather's driver Gholam Reza picked us up. I sat in the back of the car thinking only about how much I was going to miss Mamanji and Babaji. The sun had just started to rise. At the airport, I remember running, running, trying to keep up, holding my mom's hand, then Jackie's hand, letting go, then catching up again. My mom told me years later: "I cried when we got on the plane. Why did I have to leave my country like that?"

It's unclear what my grandfather knew when he barged into our lunch that day, but as it turned out we left Tehran on a pivotal day in the Iranian Revolution. It became known as Black Friday. As we flew back to New York, a huge religious demonstration was about to kick off in Jaleh Square to protest the shah's regime. The soldiers ordered the crowd to disperse; the order was ignored. The military opened fire. Black Friday is thought to have marked the point of no return for the revolution, further radicalizing the protest movement, uniting the various opponents of the shah and mobilizing the masses. Initially, the opposition claimed — and Western journalists erroneously reported — that the Iranian army massacred thousands of protesters. The clerical leadership announced that "thousands have been massacred by Zionist troops." The real death toll: 84, according to "Figures for the Dead of the Revolution," quoted by historian Ervand Abrahamian.

Some of the wounded were taken to the Jewish hospital on Cyrus Street. Dr. Kamran Beroukhim, the young Jewish doctor who had overseen the hospital's renovations thanks to my grandfather's effort to keep the old hospital operating, sat in his car as his driver inched his way to the center of town through heavy traffic.[4] The hospital director had called Beroukhim "and started crying that they are bringing all the injured here. Bring as many people as possible and just come and help." The streets near the legislature, the Majlis, were blocked off and cars were banned beyond that point. Beroukhim got out of the car to walk and saw the army shooting people, aiming at their legs. He finally made his way to the hospital and began to stabilize the wounded before calling in more doctors. Then they called more ambulances to transfer patients to another hospital where they performed 70 to 80 surgeries to save injured protesters.

Even though unfounded rumors circulated afterward that Israeli soldiers had helped the shah's army, the young Jewish doctor became known among some members of the clergy, including Mahmoud Taleghani, for having helped the injured revolutionaries in the hospital my grandfather and Kermanshahchi had fought to save years earlier.

Whatever the number of casualties, the day was a public-relations disaster: The appearance that great numbers had been killed alienated much of the rest of the Iranian people and the shah's allies abroad.

On Sept. 24, the Iraqi government banned Khomeini's political activities in Iraq where he had been living in exile since the mid-1960s. Khomeini had refused to tone down his rhetoric. After being denied entry to Kuwait, he settled on Oct. 10 in the Parisian suburb Neauphle-le-Château in a house rented for him by opponents of the shah living in France.

---

4. This was the Kheyrkha Clinic when it first opened in 1942. It was turned into the Cyrus the Great Hospital and now called the Sapir Hospital and Charity Center and continues to treat all Iranians. In 1977, when the head of the nursing department asked that the by-laws prevent asking patients their religion, Habib was the first to applaud her suggestion.

Losing His Lucky Charm

By mid-October, more people were killed in Iran, this time in the main mosque in the city of Kerman. A succession of strikes quickly spread, crippling almost all the bazaars, universities, high schools, oil installations, newspapers, banks, railways, state and private factories as well as government ministries, customs and postal facilities. The working class and the middle class had banded together.[5] The bank clerks, oil workers and government employees were not only demanding higher salaries but the disbanding of the SAVAK, the end of martial law, the release of political prisoners and Khomeini's return to Iran.

Toward the end of October, my grandfather flew to the United States, mostly for business — mainly meetings in Forest Hills with his brothers Nourollah and John — and for a general check-up at the Mayo Clinic.

"Why are you in such a rush to return to Iran?" John asked him.

Brushing aside concern about the tensions back home, Habib replied that the business needed his presence in Tehran, and the Jewish community needed him, too. Besides, he added, "What would anyone want from me after everything I've done for Iran?"

My dad remembers how secure his father felt. In early November, Habib came to our apartment in Manhattan to celebrate my brother's second birthday. In Tehran, on Nov. 4, when students inside Tehran University tried pulling down the shah's statue, troops fired on them, killing some 30 students. Mourners took to the streets the next day attacking banks, luxury hotels, foreign airline offices, even burning down a part of the British Embassy after escorting workers out.[6] While most of our family had left Iran, Davoud and his wife, Fred and his wife, Mahnaz and her two sons, along with Amir were still there. Habib's older sister, Saltanat, her daughter Aziz, and some other members of the family remained in Tehran, too.

---

5. Ervand Abrahamian, *Iran Between Two Revolutions*, (Princeton, New Jersey: Princeton University Press, 1982) p. 518.

6. Ibid.

As Iran further devolved into revolution, the shah's attempts at concilia-tion kept failing. To appease the mobs, military hardliners decided to allow them to destroy whatever they wanted: Thousands of shops, banks, restau-rants and other public buildings were damaged. Prime Minister Sharif-Emami resigned. The shah went on television to say: "I heard the voice of your revolution . . . As shah of Iran as well as an Iranian citizen, I cannot but approve your revolution." Advisers pressed him to arrest former Prime Minister Amir-Abbas Hoveyda and use him as a scapegoat.

Back in New York, Nourollah and John, along with my father and his brother Sina, each repeatedly begged Habib not to go back at this dangerous moment. The most important thing, they emphasized, was to get Mahnaz out and that they could do that without him going back.

"I have to go back to Iran. Mahnaz is alone," he kept saying. "How can I just leave my life there and stay here? I haven't done anything wrong in Iran. I built buildings, I built factories, I helped Iran develop, I employ so many people, I haven't done anything bad to Iran that anyone would want to get me for anything. Nobody needs to worry about me."

The shah was tap-dancing, prevaricating, scapegoating. Hoveyda, who had served him faithfully as prime minister for 13 years, was jailed on Nov. 7. In September, it had been the shah who persuaded Iraq to expel Khomeini to get him as far away from Iran as possible and got the French to give him asylum; he settled in a Paris suburb. As The Associated Press' Marcus Eliason, in Paris from 1978 to 1980, recalled: "It was a mistake. Neauphle-le-Château meant access to international telephones and the world media, and these were to play a critical role in the revolution."

Eliason further reported: "Khomeini's message, delivered in a calm, low monotone, never changed: The shah must be tried by Islamic judges as a mass murderer; America was corrupt, Western influence destructive . . . Everything Khomeini said in his daily homily was tape-recorded and played over the phone to supporters in Iran who would rerecord the speech and circulate it clandestinely . . . Bearded mullahs manned the phones while

Westernized Iranian intellectuals sought out reporters to tell them about the liberal, Islam-based constitutional democracy that would arise once the shah was gone."[7]

The shah pardoned more than 1,000 political prisoners, including Ayatollahs Taleghani and Montazeri, ended media censorship, set up a commission to investigate the Pahlavi Foundation and dissolved the *Rastakhiz* party. He also declared that all exiles including Khomeini could return to Iran.

But the opposition was unwilling to compromise. From Paris, Khomeini said that if the shah had really heard the voice of the people, he'd know he should step down. Anyone who was with the government was betraying Islam, Khomeini said while encouraging more protests.[8] He called for an Islamic government. In early November, National Front leader Karim Sanjabi, and Liberation Movement head Mehdi Bazargan visited Khomeini in Paris and publicly allied themselves with him. Sanjabi was arrested upon his return to Tehran, leading to more protest strikes.

Earlier that summer, my grandfather had traveled with two other members of the Jewish community to Israel, where they met with Prime Minister Menachem Begin, who warned the delegation that the Islamists were accruing more power and chances were good that the shah could be dethroned. Begin told them they needed to get as many Jews out of Iran as possible, for their safety. The delegation's response: The shah would remain in power, and the Jews would be all right.[9]

---

7. Marcus Eliason, "Khomeini Ran His Revolution from a French Village," The Associated Press, June 6, 1989.

8. Ervand Abrahamian, *Iran Between Two Revolutions*, (Princeton, New Jersey: Princeton University Press, 1982) p. 51.

9. "Editor's Note: When Jewish Communities Lose Their Voices," *The Jerusalem Post*, David Horovitz, Feb. 29, 2008.

Aryeh Levin, who was present at the meeting, recalled efforts to keep Habib from returning to Iran from Israel. He said that during the trip from Tehran to Tel Aviv, the historian Habib Levy tried to persuade him to stay. "Habib said he could not imagine what would become of all the unfortunates who had no one to turn to. He was the captain of the ship and would go down last," Levin said.[10]

Undeterred by the entreaties of those who loved him, oblivious or in denial about the relentless march toward a tumultuous government overthrow, my grandfather just wanted to go home.

The last effort came in New York, before his final flight to Iran in November. His daughter-in-law Sheryl, Sina's American wife, drove him to John F. Kennedy International Airport. In her best broken Farsi, she pleaded with him to allow her to take him back to her house.

He shook his head. "*Khodahafes*, Sheryl joon. Goodbye."

---

10. Aryeh Levin, "Habib Elghanayan: A Reflection of the Iranian Jewish Community," *The History of Contemporary Iranian Jews, Volume 3*, ed. Homa Sarshar, (Beverly Hills: The Center for Iranian Jewish Oral History, 1999) p. 25.

CHAPTER 17

⁓

'A Very Gloomy Picture'

I shivered with anticipation inside the air-conditioned reading room at the Central Zionist Archives' building in Jerusalem, as I examined the files that turned up in my search.[1] Now open to the public, the archives hold a trove of papers belonging to, among others, the World Jewish Congress, the Jewish Agency and the Jewish National Fund. I'd come here hoping to exhume any details and insights on my grandfather's life. As I carefully turned the pages, a handwritten note caught my eye. Picking it up, gently shaking it awake from its long slumber, I was stunned that the piece of paper had been so meticulously conserved.

I ran my index finger over my grandfather's name, written on graph paper with what must have been a blue fountain pen.

"Honorary President: Habib Elghanian," it said, followed by his home and office phone numbers.

---

1. Armand Kaplan, Reports by Armand Kaplan on visits to Tehran - 1978, (Jerusalem: Central Zionist Archives) C10\2203.

The note was tucked inside a 23-page typed memo called, "My recent visit to Tehran (Iran) — November 22-26, 1978," written by Armand Kaplan, director of International Affairs at the World Jewish Congress, for the group's president and other WJC officials to assess imminent dangers faced by the Iranian Jewish community. The memo, archived for posterity, was marked, "CONFIDENTIAL NOT FOR PUBLICATION."

Seeing Kaplan's name under the letterhead of the *Congrès Juif Mondial* (French for World Jewish Congress) reminded me of another Frenchman: Adolphe Crémieux, the head of the Alliance Israélite Universelle. In the late 19th century, Crémieux had urged Iran's ruler to allow him to open schools in Jewish quarters across Iran to help ensure Jewish integration into Iranian society. And here, as the shah's power was crumbling, Kaplan, also a French Jew concerned about the Iranian Jewish community, had gone to Iran to evaluate their safety.

Sitting in the reading room in Jerusalem, I realized that Crémieux and Kaplan's concern, nearly a century apart, reflected the tenuous nature of our standing in Iran. It was at that moment, in my late 30s, that the Iranian girl living in exile all those years, carrying around the heartbreak and darkness that Iran had represented for me, disappeared. As I stared at Kaplan's name and thought of Crémieux, I felt safe and strong. I thought about what it means to be Jewish, upholding the age-old tradition of being our brothers' keeper. I remembered why I had a French education and all the notions of *liberté, égalité, fraternité,* instilled in me at the Lycée. I thought about home, New York, where I am free to be who I am, where I became who I am. I thought about working in a country with a free media without fear of being accused of dual allegiances and free to criticize whatever I don't like about the United States or Israel without having any of it be cause for hate, or life-threatening.

Kaplan had flown to Tehran on a discreet four-day fact-finding mission to check on the Jewish community. He came to assess what help Iran's Jews would need if the shah's regime collapsed and Jews were no longer welcome in Iran. His mission, as he explained, was also to show "the Iranian Jewish community that world Jewry is behind them, watching the situation very carefully and ready to act in case of need."

Before going to Tehran, Kaplan flew from Paris to Jerusalem to get briefed. In Israel, he heard an assessment that his trip to Tehran would corroborate. The sad picture he was offered was not only of the possible fate of the Jews if the shah fell, but of the community's own disorder: weak leadership, unwillingness of middle-class Jews to leave, and rich Jews who had liquidated their assets and left, leaving the rest of the community to fend for itself.

"There is unfortunately no real leadership in that Jewish community with whom you could talk and deal in a responsible way," Yehudah Dominitz, an official at the Israeli Ministry of Foreign Affairs, told Kaplan.

By the time Kaplan arrived in Tehran, the Central Jewish Board had undergone several changes, beginning in 1974.

During a February 1974 trip by a dozen members of the Iranian Jewish community to Israel, Habib and Ebrahim Rad, also a manufacturer, had an argument about "the management methods" of the Central Jewish Board. In his autobiography, Jack Mahfar, another Iranian Jewish businessman on the trip, describes being asked to arbitrate the argument. After hearing the two debate until 1 o'clock in the morning, Mahfar said:

"Mr. Rad, You are addressing Hajji [Habib] — who believes he has kept the Association alive until today — as if he were a low-level employee."

Turning to Habib, Mahfar continued: "Mr. Elghanian! You have often worked with individuals in the Association who did not question your instructions and acted according to your wishes."

Neither, he told them, was prepared to accept the other's words fully, and he called on them to hold a meeting in Tehran, voice their positions, and let the association settle the dispute.[2]

---

2. Jack Mahfar, *From Laborer to Entrepreneur, Memoirs of Jack Mahfar: from Joubareh in Esfahan to Tehran and Geneva* (Cologny-Geneva: The Mahfar Cultural Foundation, 2013), p. 214-216.

They did. In fall 1974, the Jewish Central Board, the Jewish Association of Tehran changed its name to the Jewish Association of Iran, and amended Article 23 of its regulations to call for general elections every four years. In March 1975, 12 members were elected; Habib was given an honorary title of chairman.

The biggest change occurred in 1978, shortly before Kaplan's trip to Tehran. As the younger generation became more assimilated in Iranian society, a new group of young leftist and anti-Zionist Jews challenged the old guard's leadership. Accounts vary about how the changes in the leadership occurred. *Encyclopaedia Iranica*'s entry says: "In the revolutionary atmosphere of 1978, the radical intellectual Jews of Tehran demanded that the *Anjoman* [Farsi for association] be dissolved and new elections held. In the elections of March 1978 the old Jewish oligarchy, including Elqāniān [cq], was ousted from the Anjoman and replaced by the radical and moderate young intellectuals."[3]

Separately, the leftists and non-Zionist Jews founded the Organization of the Jewish Intellectual Youth of Iran in 1978.

When I visited his practice in Los Angeles, Kamran Beroukhim, the doctor my grandfather had reached out to rehabilitate the old hospital on Cyrus Street, told me how the old and the new guard worked together during the revolution. He said that Habib was aware that his ties with Israel could become a liability for the Jewish community and needed a plan.

As Beroukhim recalled, Habib and his trusted associate Hechmat Kermanshahchi contacted him asking what he thought they could do. Beroukhim suggested that the best thing they could do was to resign as Anjoman leaders. They agreed and asked Beroukhim to bring people into the organization who could protect the community in case the shah fell.

Beroukhim did so, and he explained: "The community decided to split up and go in two different directions. We wrote a letter saying the young group

---

3. Anjoman-e-Kalimian entry in *Encyclopaedia Iranica*.

of intellectuals were anti-Zionists. Habib wanted to split up this way so they [a new regime] wouldn't hurt the Jews. Habib and Kermanshahchi saved the community this way. They thought the revolution could go two ways: success or failure, so they played both sides."

Beroukhim had helped forge good relations with the revolutionaries after treating the injured demonstrators on Jaleh Square on Black Friday. Ayatollah Taleghani met with Beroukhim along with Yeshayaei Haroun and another young Jew, Houshang Melamed, to thank them for their help.[4]

Beroukhim told me what Habib said when he returned from his trip to America where he was visiting us: "At the time of the shah, I didn't do anything bad; he sent me away [to exile]. Now if I can help the community, I want to help them. I am an old man. This is the time I have to help the people."

Beroukhim begged him. "This is not good. You have to leave."

Habib said: "I don't care."

Habib's decision to stay was far from unique among Iran's Jews, as Kaplan was learning even before arriving in Tehran. In his notes, he recounts meeting in Jerusalem with Oded Oran, deputy director of the Israeli government's department dealing with the Iranian issues: "It is obvious that the Jews have to get out as quickly as possible. He (Oran) knows from past experience that even in such conditions, Jews don't leave."

In another meeting in Israel, Avraham Abir, an Iranian-Israeli businessman, told Kaplan, Jews "will only leave in case of a massacre or expulsion."

Kaplan landed at noon Nov. 22, 1978, in Tehran, where Jean-Claude Cousseran, the first secretary of the French Embassy, picked him up at the airport to accompany him to his hotel. "Nobody knows where the situation will lead and everything is possible," Cousseran explained in the car.

Cousseran also advised him to move cautiously, go as unnoticed as possible, speak as little as possible on the phone and avoid any confidential

---

4. Kamran Beroukhim, interview with author in Los Angeles, April 2011.

conversations. "He said the Iranian authorities are aware of my being in Tehran, and although there is no reason to be afraid, it is a courtesy to be watched by the SAVAK," Kaplan said. Cousseran also apprised him of the general 9 p.m. curfew.

Kaplan chronicled his trip nearly hour by hour. Shortly after his arrival, between 2 and 4 p.m., he met with Michael Schneider, Iran's director of the Jewish relief organization, the Joint Distribution Committee. Schneider gave him a breakdown of where Iran's Jews lived. Between January and November 1978, some 3,000 had gone to Israel, either temporarily or to settle, but emigration had been tapering off in recent months. Some 4,000 out of the 10,000 mostly rich Jews had liquidated their assets, taken their money out of Iran, and reinvested it elsewhere, settling mostly in the United States, Canada and Europe. The remaining Jews, poor and middle class, had stayed put.

Some 60,000 Jews lived in the capital, about 10,000 in Shiraz and 3,000-4,000 in Isfahan, with 20,000-25,000 in the provinces scattered in various cities or villages.

The largest segment, the middle class, couldn't sell their assets. "Muslims don't want to buy from them because they believe that in due course, they will get everything for free," Schneider explained to Kaplan. "Unfortunately, the very rich people care only for themselves."

As for the leadership, well, hardly any existed, Schneider said, corroborating what Kaplan had been told in Jerusalem.

That same day, between 4:15 and a little after 7, Schneider took Kaplan to see Moshe Gilboa, a minister at the Israeli Diplomatic Mission in Tehran. "Moshe, Schneider and I decided whom from the Jewish community I should meet." Gilboa recommended that Kaplan meet a dozen or so people who represented a cross-section of the Jews. The handwritten list I had found was the piece of paper on which Kaplan had written the names and phone numbers.

Under Gilboa's contact information is Habib's name, followed by Schneider's. Then comes Aziz Daneshrad, the new leader of the Jewish Community, and Yousef Cohen, the deputy in Parliament who represented the Jews, followed by other names.

"There is no doubt in his [Gilboa's] mind that if the opposition come to power, the Jewish position in the country will deteriorate gravely, especially if the religious elements dominate," Kaplan wrote. "He too stressed that the only solution possible is to get them out of the country, and every effort should be made in that direction. Of course, he would like them to go to Israel, and the Israeli government, the Jewish Agency and other Israeli bodies have and will do everything possible to receive them and integrate them properly in their economic society, but if they want to go somewhere else, they may do so.

"The only thing which is important and most needed is that they leave now or in the near future when there is still time, before they may be trapped; we would then have to fight to get them out one by one and in much more difficult conditions. Unfortunately, he said, Jews for the time being don't move."

After his meeting with Gilboa, Kaplan retired to his hotel where he watched Prime Minister Gholam-Reza Azhari's televised speech. Azhari explained the shah would reign but no longer govern, and that the country would move toward a constitutional monarchy. Azhari said the government was aware that it was unable to solve the huge political, economic and social problems facing Iran.

No doubt Habib watched the speech that night, too.

The next morning, Thursday, Nov. 23, Kaplan visited Schneider to make final appointments. The only notable person Kaplan said he couldn't meet was Chief Rabbi Yedidia Shofet. The rabbi's son told them that Shofet was sick.

"He was not so ill," Kaplan later discovered, "since he had to celebrate five weddings in the same day. It was clear that the chief rabbi was a little afraid to meet me." Perhaps Shofet didn't want to have any connections with Israel, thinking this would protect the Jews.

After lunch with U.S. Ambassador William Sullivan and his wife, Kaplan met Habib. Reading the account of the meeting, I couldn't help but think that my grandfather could have been celebrating Thanksgiving with us that Thursday.

"From 4:30 to 7:30 I met in a private house five Jews, namely honorary President Habib Elghanayan, who was the former President of the Iranian Jewish Community, an old distinguished gentleman; former Jewish Deputy of Parliament Lotfollah Hay, a very wealthy Jew; Dr. Aghai, a banker (whose bank in Tehran was destroyed during the Nov. 5 riots, not because he is Jewish, many banks were destroyed that day, Iranian and foreign)," Kaplan wrote in his memo. The host was Kamran, a businessman. Also present was Hamid Sabi.

After a few words of welcome, they asked the purpose of his visit. Kaplan said his presence there was an expression of solidarity of the WJC with the beleaguered Iranian Jewish community and an effort to study the situation in the country, how that was affecting Jews and what they might do.

In response, they noted that government censorship prevented them from getting news and a sense of the future. "They are in a state of shock or trauma," Kaplan wrote, "they believe sometimes that they are having a bad dream and that they will wake up and things will be different from what they are going through now."

But with "no future for the Jews" in Iran anymore, he said, "rescue is the vital issue."

He continued: "They are surrounded by an anti-Semitic atmosphere and the Iranian people are waiting with impatience to jump on them. They doubt that the shah and the army will be able to cope with the situation, and if the opposition comes to power, especially the fanatic religious elements, then they are badly off."

Kaplan's memo noted their complaints about anti-shah reporting on the BBC's Persian language service, "propaganda" that they said energized the opposition, and they condemned France's toleration of Khomeini.

Kaplan's hosts spoke of the need to implement the resettlement project that had been outlined in Israel to a visiting Iranian Jewish delegation the previous fall. But, he wrote, "At that time, things were possible, now they have become quite impossible to implement. Many of the plans elaborated in Israel were dropped en route because of a lack of leadership in Iran." Kaplan said there was plenty of blame to go around in the wake of the failure to act quickly in getting people out before the tumult escalated.

Reading Kaplan's account, I thought of what Levin had said about Iran's Jews and how difficult it was for them to uproot themselves to go to Israel and how everything they had achieved through hard work and perseverance "blocked off their view of reality." This was true of my grandfather too. "They simply could not bring themselves to admit the earth was shaking under their feet," Levin had noted.[5]

The following day, Kaplan and Gilboa met with Yousef Cohen, the Jewish member of Parliament. "The future of the Jews is black," Cohen told Kaplan. "90 percent of them would leave if their assets would be bought by a special foreign corporation created for this purpose, at reasonable prices."

"Rich Jews," Cohen continued, "don't help at all. They look only after their own security, physically and financially. World Jewry must help. Meeting outside Iran in January with World Jewish Congress leadership would be useful to consider needed action for the future. . . . The rescue operation is first priority. Work towards creating a strong community leadership is needed, but will take time."

---

5. Aryeh Levin, "Habib Elghanayan: A Reflection of the Iranian Jewish Community," *The History of Contemporary Iranian Jews*, Volume 3, ed. Homa Sarshar, (Beverly Hills: The Center for Iranian Jewish Oral History, 1999) p. 25.

"Mr. Cohen," Kaplan wrote, "lays strong hopes on the creation of that Corporation Fund."

In Kaplan's second meeting on Friday, he met with the new president of the Iranian Jewish community, Aziz Daneshrad, and Professor Bral, a physicist. "Before coming," Kaplan wrote, "I was warned to be careful when discussing with Daneshrad. He greeted me without great effusion."

Daneshrad also told Kaplan that the censorship prevented him from having a clear view of unfolding events. "The situation of the Jews is preoccupying," he said. "Roughly 70 percent will remain in the country at all costs. The Anjoman tries to help. Jews are indifferent, especially the rich people.... Also, former Jewish personalities don't want to assist the country in its effort."

Underlining the need to create a united Jewish community able to evaluate developments and prepare short- and long-term rescue plans, Kaplan wrote, "For those who want to remain despite the dangerous situation, hoping it will improve one day, I gave many examples where people hoped the same but became trapped."

Kaplan stressed that world Jewry would help but needed a proper Iranian Jewish representative body to work with. Who are the leaders? he asked, then summed up: "Discrimination between the Jewish community personalities should be stopped and instead, joint forces are most needed . . ."

He spelled out the priorities. At the top, a rescue operation in the provinces for small, mid-sized and large communities, then in Tehran for poor Jews, then the middle class. Priority No. 2: figuring out how to help the middle class liquidate their assets and properties. Lastly, conduct outside diplomatic and political work for the remaining Jews.

At the end of the meeting that Friday, Kaplan recounted, Daneshrad "promised solemnly that he will undertake every effort with the aim to create such a united Jewish community body . . . and understood that it is imperative . . . to enable world Jewry to work with a responsible Iranian Jewish Community and see to it that every action be implemented in the interest of the entire community."

Following meetings on Saturday, when he heard more complaints about weak leadership, Kaplan concluded his memo by noting a "very gloomy picture" for those wanting to aid Iran's Jews. "Without a responsible group there able to deal with us, advise us and consult with us . . . this job will be very difficult to implement." Kaplan flew out of Tehran on Nov. 26.

Four days later, on Nov. 30, Habib was no longer able to go to the airport with a plane ticket and leave Iran. He became *mamnoor khorooj*, forbidden to exit. Bank Melli employees had prepared and given to the newspapers a list of names of people who had sent money abroad. Though they had done nothing illegal, their names were published and the government barred the men on the list from leaving the country.

Two weeks after Kaplan left Iran, the Israeli airline El Al began to triple its flights to Tehran to evacuate Europeans and Iranians. The usual daily flight was augmented by two additional planes that flew into Tehran empty and flew out full.

Whether a last-ditch effort at self-preservation or somehow a show of genuine support, Jews displayed solidarity with the anti-shah movement. Street demonstrations against the shah continued, and Habib and Sabi worked in concert to urge Rabbi Shofet to join the revolutionaries. On Dec. 11, protest marches melded with the religious processions of Ashura, and some Jewish groups joined Muslims expressing their support for the oncoming revolution. Sabi called the chief rabbi's son, Rabbi David, to persuade his father to show his support. The rabbi at first refused, saying he loved the shah, but then relented. They told him to not be scared, that the younger group that supported the revolution were open-minded and wanted to help the community, Beroukhim said.

I shivered again thinking about the predicament everyone was in. I held on tight to the handwritten note in my hand, staring at Kaplan's characterization of my grandfather.

"Honorary President Habib Elghanayan, who was the former President of the Iranian Jewish Community, an old distinguished gentleman."

CHAPTER 18

⁓

Immovable

The air was growing thick with religious fervor. Calls of "*Allah - o - Akbar, Allah - o - Akbar*" — God is great — filled Tehran's evening sky.

On Dec. 2, 1978, heeding Ayatollah Mahmoud Taleghani's directives, hundreds of thousands of people shouted the words into the dark from rooftops on the first of 10 holy days of Ashura to mourn the martyrdom of Hussein, a Shiite Muslim hero and the grandson of the Prophet Muhammad. Both the National Front and Liberation Movement also mobilized their supporters by calling for strikes on the first and last day of Ashura. From Paris, Khomeini urged Iranians to make more sacrifices, win over soldiers to their ranks and get the clergy to convince villagers that Islam opposed big landlords and capitalists.

Revolutionaries took heed. Thousands dressed in white shrouds to show they were willing to die, and poured into the streets, violating the curfew; hundreds were killed by authorities. The government released Karim Sanjabi of the National Front and other political prisoners and allowed other processions in urban areas without any military or police present in the main streets. On Dec. 10, 500,000 people led by Taleghani and Sanjabi protested.

Immovable

The following day, four times as many people came out — an estimated 2 million — to march in the streets with Khomeini's representative in Tehran leading them. Some banners read "Death to the shah," "Hang the American puppet" and "Arms to the people." When the rally ended at Shahyad Square, the opposition's message was crystal clear. The shah had to step down and be replaced by Khomeini and an Islamic government. They also called for the protection of religious minorities and the revival of agricultural and social justice for the deprived masses.[1]

Habib knew it was time to get Mahnaz and her two boys out of Iran. Her husband Morteza was in Israel for multiple sclerosis treatment.

After lunch in Shemiran, Habib put three airplane tickets on the table for Mahnaz.

"Tomorrow morning, you're leaving with Shahab and Shahrooz. You'll go to Israel, and I'll let you know what to do from there," he said. "And you are not to take anything with you. They are checking suitcases and confiscating anything of value."

There was no arguing with her father. That night, Shamsi came over and went to her room. Mahnaz was packing.

"I know you're leaving tomorrow. I got your tickets for you," Shamsi said, offering to help.

"Papa told me to not take anything."

"So what?" Shamsi said. She reached for a gold necklace on Mahnaz's armoire and began to string her friend's rings on it. "You'll wear a turtleneck over it, no one will be paying attention," she said.

Next, Shamsi went down to the *anbar* where Nikkou Jan stored her valuables, returning with four boxes. Nikkou Jan had prepared four coin collections, one for each of her children. Shamsi promised Mahnaz she'd give Fred his, put one each in Shahab's and Shahrooz's backpacks, and hid the

---

1. Ervand Abrahamian, *Iran Between Two Revolutions*, (Princeton, New Jersey: Princeton University Press, 1982), p 522.

last one in Mahnaz's suitcase. After they finished packing, Shamsi stayed in Mahnaz's room — just like when they were kids.

In the morning, Mahnaz, Shamsi and the two boys came downstairs together. The family's black poodle Goochi followed them, barking. Habib was waiting in the foyer.

"You don't have anything with you, correct?"

"No," Mahnaz replied.

He told her to remove her diamond earrings and put them in the safe. Instead, she handed them, one by one, to her friend.

"Shamsi," she said, "if I ever come back, you give them back to me; if I don't, they're a gift to you."

"Very good idea," Habib said.

Then he said, "I have a very important meeting. I can't come to the airport."

His grandsons and daughter gave Habib a long hug. They embraced Shamsi, Vali and Layla Khanoum and got into the car. As it passed the black gate, the boys, on their knees in the back seat, waved goodbye. Goochi kept barking.

At the airport, they bypassed the main building where passengers had their bags and passports checked. Gholam Reza stopped the car close to the tarmac where Shamsi had instructed him — she had arranged every detail of their exit — and where another car waited. That car delivered them to the portable stairs leading up to an El Al plane.

In a short time, they were en route to Tel Aviv and safety.

With one major preoccupation out of the way, Habib moved on to the next: paying his workers to avoid disruption in the factories. He called Lotfollah Hay to ask him to go with him to get funds from the central bank, Bank Melli. "I'm scared of an uprising in the factory. I need to get money so I can give the workers their salaries," Habib said.

Such an errand could be a challenge since, by Dec. 20, barricades and molotov cocktails had become part of Tehran's landscape, populated by gangs of young revolutionaries, many from the shantytowns. The army rank-and-file, who were all conscripts, were no longer firing at them.

Immovable

Entering the bank together, Habib went to see Yousef Khoshkish, the governor of the bank, and Hay to see the director. They heard shots outside and everyone started to run. Hay looked out the window and saw the bank's entrance was blocked by a bus so that no one could go in or out. At first, he couldn't find Habib in the chaos, though they later got out.

Toward the end of December, Hay went to visit Habib in Shemiran. Except for Vali and Layla Khanoum, the house was empty and the quiet was only broken by the barking dog.

"Since the curfew, I come here alone; it's dark," Habib told his friend. "The dog's become blind, he barks a lot. And Nikkha is not here."

At night, he'd close the big metal gate, putting the car behind it, and go to his bedroom with a candle. Alone and scared, Habib wept.

Hay sighed, recalling that time. "Everything was dark for him. Life was dark. You have to understand, this man had once been the symbol of our society."

Soon after, Israeli Ambassador Yossef Harmelin arranged for Hay and his wife to get out of Iran. After picking up money at his office, Hay went to see Habib at the Aluminum Building.

He told him: "Whether you have a passport or not, I have influence, I can get you out."

Habib replied, "I was in prison once because the government attacked me. Now I don't want to give the government any excuses."

Hay insisted, "I assure you there will be no obstacle for leaving." He would ask Harmelin to make the arrangements for Habib — it didn't matter that he was on a list of people who were barred from leaving.

"They rehabilitated me, they gave me a 5,000-ton press," Habib said. "I have a responsibility to stay."

Getting out of his chair, Habib walked around his desk, kissed Hay and put his hand on his cheek.

"*Saateh Shalom,* — bon voyage, go in peace."

I sat in Hay's living room in Los Angeles listening to his account and fighting back tears. He tried to comfort me — one of several friends of my grandfather who articulated the many reasons he would stay. "Habib's personality didn't fit America," he said. "He was unhappy in America, he felt isolated."

"Also, he felt responsible for the company."[2]

Kamran Beroukhim confirmed Habib's attachment to his factories and his workers.

"I was begging him to go, and he said, 'I brought the biggest machine to Iran for the aluminum factory, I can't leave my people who are working for me, who are dependent on me.'"[3]

Aryeh Levin, the chargé d' affaires of Israel's diplomatic mission to Tehran, also discussed Habib's decision. "What Habib feared most, as he admitted to a close friend, was a strike paralyzing his factories, an additional loss of face in the upper echelons of power and among his own peers," Levin wrote in an essay. "Habib's attitude may be incomprehensible when we look at the dangers everyone knew he was running . . . However, after a lifetime of relentless work and extraordinary achievements, it was his position in Iranian society that was uppermost in his mind. He thought he could prevent a disruption in his enterprises if he stayed on and guided them through the crisis. He was confident of the revolutionaries' even-handed attitude toward his person in the framework of their national interests. In the worst case, it would be some property that would have to be given up."[4]

My uncle Fred, when I visited him in Ohio, elaborated further. "He would not have wanted to be anywhere else. Everything was there. He wanted to protect his wealth and he really believed things would get better.

---

2. Lotfollah Hay, interview with author in Los Angeles, April 2011.

3. Kamran Beroukhim, interview with author in Los Angeles, April 2011.

4. Aryeh Levin, "Habib Elghanayan: A Reflection of the Iranian Jewish Community," *The History of Contemporary Iranian Jews*, Volume 3, ed. Homa Sarshar, (Beverly Hills: The Center for Iranian Jewish Oral History, 1999) p. 15-27.

"He wanted to be in Iran where he was important and a force to be reckoned with," Fred said. "He believed there was no reason this great country would be handed to extremists."

Jewish community leaders set up an emergency meeting that included my grandfather and the Association of Iranian Jewish Intellectuals,[5] during which they drafted a statement declaring their solidarity with the revolutionaries, and on Dec. 23, it was presented to Ayatollah Taleghani.[6] By Dec. 25, the economy was at a standstill with a new series of general strikes.

Meanwhile, from Tel Aviv, Mahnaz and the boys flew to New York where her father regularly wrote her.

"Dec. 27, 1978

"Mahnaz joon,

"Since all the elementary schools are closed until further notice, even though there is nothing to worry about, I feel you should for the time being enroll Shahab and Shahrooz in school there, even a language school for now. In any event, please do not leave until further notice.

"Love, Papa."

Habib closely monitored developments in Tehran. Sanjabi wouldn't head a coalition government because the shah wanted to keep control of the Army. In early January, the shah appointed a younger, less experienced leader of the National Front, Shapour Bakhtiar, as prime minister, and he took office announcing that the king would soon go on holiday and promising to lift the martial law and hold free elections. The shah working with

---

5. Kamran Beroukhim, interview with author in Los Angeles, April 2011.

6. Alessandra Cecolin, *Iranian Jews in Israel: Between Persian Cultural Identity and Israeli Nationalism*, (London: I. B. Tauris & Co. Ltd, 2016) p. 54.

the opposition National Front may have given my grandfather some hope, as his next letter, written over a couple of days, indicates.

"Jan. 1, Jan. 2

"My dearest Mahnaz,

"*Ghorbanet gardam.* I love you. I hope you are good and healthy. I am good too. I have not been able to get in touch with you by phone so I have sent a Telex [from Dec. 27] via Uncle John. I am assuming you already know all the schools have been shut down here so for now it's better that you enroll the children in school there and stay in New York until we see what happens. Most of my friends agree that things will get better in a couple of weeks.

I don't know what you have decided to do yet. Do you accept to stay and live in America or do you want to come back to Tehran? I think it's best for you to stay in America for now without worrying one bit about me. I am very comfortable here and every night I see my friends so please be assured that there is not a single night that I am lonely. I want you to feel 100 percent reassured in that regard and think about yourself and your children. If you decide to live in America, please let me know so an apartment can be arranged for you. Let me know so I can take care of it no matter what.

"For now, there are strikes and we can't find gas or fuel to get past the next couple of days. The streets are very crowded and it's very difficult to get from one place to another. Today is Thursday [that would be Jan. 4] and I am supposed to go to Karaj for lunch at Fereydoun's house. Danny and Dariush [Fred's two sons] are there too and we are busy for now. I am waiting for a letter from you to tell me about everything and everyone so I also know what to do for the apartment. I hope you have enrolled the children in school. I need a separate letter for each of them so I can arrange to send the $1,000 per student that is allowed to be sent out. We can't send dollars anymore. It's hard even to get a dollar for 85 rials even though it had recently just been 70 rials, about 20 percent higher. This is the situation now.

"Please pay attention to what's going on on the radio and television. It's impossible for me to call you but I am hoping that you can call me. Make sure you call at 9 p.m. Tehran time so that I am home. I am waiting for your call and love you all,

"Papa."

Mahnaz was writing letters but he wasn't receiving them, and phone calls were almost impossible. New York long-distance operators could rarely get through to Tehran.

Habib also wrote to his grandsons:

"Jan. 2

"My dearest Shahab and Shahrooz,

"I love you. I hope you are both well and that you are having a good time with your mother. I hope you have started school and are studying now. I am waiting for letters from you. It would make me very happy. I am good too. I don't go back to the office in the afternoons anymore and stay at home.

"The situation here in Iran is slowly improving. Please do not worry about me at all. Danny and Dariush are here too for now and are joining me for lunch at home until they leave in a couple of days. Diane might go to Nice since schools are all closed for now until we see what happens.

"The two of you need to take very good care of your mother, don't upset her and make sure she is happy and comfortable. Say hi to your mother and tell her to write me every week. And the two of you please write me as well. And I expect the letters to be full of details. That's it for now.

"Goodbye to both of you. I love you,

"Papa."

A few days later, he wrote again. He continued to convey only hints of the tumult swirling around him.

"Jan. 8, 1979

"I am writing this letter from home.

"My dearest Mahnaz and dearest Shahab and Shahrooz,

"I love you. I hope you are all well and healthy and that the children are going to school. I am waiting for your call to get more news from you. We are all healthy here. The past few days, Eliane and Fereydoun along with Nemat [Habib's maternal cousin] and Fofo [Nemat's wife] are staying with me. I hope that you are with Karmel and Sina and their wives and children and are having a good time.

"Today is the first day I have not been to the office. Everything is closed including the banks and stores. There are demonstrations everywhere but it's nothing too important, until we see what, God willing, happens here. We are all waiting for news.

"I am waiting for your call to see what you have done about getting an apartment. Pari, [Nikkou Jan's sister] Leeza [her daughter] and the other little one are coming to America so I am giving them this letter to deliver to you. It would be so nice if you could live next to them. Pari and Leeza will tell you everything that's been going on here. I am sending you two suitcases with your fur coat. I am not sure if they are putting the cases in a freight or on the plane. We'll know tomorrow. If you need any money, you can get it from Sina and let me know the price of the apartment so I can figure out what to do because you know there is control of foreign currency and it's impossible to get foreign currency out, but in any case I'll do my best. Pari has two packages for Sina. When the containers arrive, tell him to call me.

"I'm ending this letter now and God willing, I'll continue to write you letters. I kiss everyone. Tell Shahab and Shahrooz to write me.

"Goodbye,

"Papa."

As Jewish families worked out how to respond to the developments, the future of Iran's Jews, as a group, continued to stir the Israeli government. Just the previous day, Israel's minister of education and culture, Zevulun Hammer, voiced concern, again raising the issue of their immigration to Israel. "That was, after all, the reason for establishing the state of Israel," he said. In response, according to declassified Israeli State Archive documents, Prime Minister Menachem Begin said that if the Jews of Iran had wanted to immigrate to Israel, "we would have brought them over in the thousands; however, that is not the case."

The week after Bakhtiar took office, he canceled billions of dollars' worth of arms contracts, ended oil sales to Israel and South Africa, arrested more former ministers, promised to break up the SAVAK, froze the Pahlavi Foundation's assets and set up a Regency Council to fill in for the king during his upcoming vacation. He also reiterated the shah's announcement that Khomeini was allowed to return to Iran, describing him as an Iranian Gandhi. He warned the rest of the opposition that undermining the creation of a constitutional government would be answered with a military dictatorship.

Moderate religious leaders threw their support behind Bakhtiar while Sanjabi, insistent about the shah's ouster, kicked Bakhtiar out of the National Front altogether. And Khomeini, unwilling to accept any government appointed by the shah, called for more strikes. Work stoppages and street battles became regular occurrences. On Jan. 13, some 2 million people marched in 30 cities, demanding Khomeini's return.

Hay was gone, and Kermanshahchi's plan was to fly out on Jan. 18. But just after midnight, on Jan. 16, a man named Bekhrat, in charge of public relations for the Jewish community, who had good friends among Muslims, called Kermanshahchi saying he'd received firm information that the shah would be leaving that day. He told him it was very dangerous to stay in Iran.

Kermanshahchi called Habib right away. "This country is not our place anymore," he told him. Habib voiced no reaction.

As predicted, the shah left that day, flying to Cairo.

Facing this undeniable new reality, Habib remained, convinced that his arrest by the shah's government would make the new regime his friend — or so Kermanshahchi told me in his Los Angeles office years later. "He thought that all he had done was good for the country, good for the people, he hadn't done anything wrong."

When I pressed for more, he sighed.

"The main reason was that he had prepared for himself a fantastic way of life according to his own desires," Kermanshahchi said, noting Habib's respected place in both Jewish and Muslim communities and the fact that he'd created businesses and raised a family in Iran.

"He didn't think there was any other place for him."

My grandfather continued writing Mahnaz letters.

Immovable

"Jan. 18, 1979

"Dearest Mahnaz,

"These days are very difficult but I'm hoping they will pass. I go to the office in the mornings but stay home in the afternoons. I wait for your call everyday but there is no news from you. Try to get in touch with me. Fred and Eliane are here with me during the day and we are planning to have them stay at night too in Shemiran. I am waiting for the address of your apartment so I can mail my letters directly there. Please send me pictures of the kids and you. I am waiting for a letter. I have a lot of work now so I am going to leave you.

"Papa."

On Jan. 19, after Khomeini called for a street "referendum" to oust Bakhtiar and the king, over a million people came out in Tehran. Two days later, Habib wrote again.

"Jan. 21, 1979

"My dearest Mahnaz,

"I love you and hope you and the kids are doing well. I am good but problems these days are numerous. Hoping things will be better in a couple of weeks. These nights, despite all the headaches I have, I am waiting for one of you to call me but why don't you call? I know it's difficult to make calls. From Iran, it's impossible, but yesterday Nasser called Amir from New York.

"The container I sent left Jan. 12 from Germany on the Democracy ship to America. I'm waiting for your phone call to find out if it has arrived. I am also waiting for the letter about the kids' school and I am hoping to send every month $1,000 for each of their schools.

I can send $3,000 for each child who is enrolled in school. Hajji Aziz [his paternal uncle] is also sitting in the office and sends his regards. Today, we cannot send out a single dollar until we see what happens. I have sent Sina 9 carpets that were supposed to go with Japan Airlines but are now going with Air France. Tell Sina to go to Air France to pick them up. They are addressed to his company Rugs and Riches.

"I am waiting for your new address and phone number so I can write you there directly. For now, Eliane and Fereydoun are staying with me at night so please don't worry about me being alone. Please kiss the kids for me. Tell Sina and Karmel to write me. And if they can also get letters from their children's schools, I can send them each $3,000. Make sure to give this letter to Sina and Karmel to read too because I don't have time to write them each individually. Say hello to Helen [my mother] and the kids [my brother and me], Sheryl [Sina's wife] and the kids and let me know as soon as Sheryl gives birth. Make sure you call me immediately to let me know.

"Love, Papa."

On Jan. 27-28, 28 people were killed protesting the closing of the airport to prevent Khomeini's return. At the end of January, Israeli Prime Minister Begin held a meeting with top officials from the Jewish Agency on how to get Jews out of Iran. Following that meeting, more El Al planes were sent to Iran, which brought approximately 1,500 Jews to Israel.

Davoud and his wife Aghdas left Iran when they heard rumors that Khomeini would be arriving the following day. On Jan. 30, without tickets, they drove to the airport. After being told they needed the Israeli ambassador's permission to board an El Al plane, they drove to the embassy. Yossef Harmelin, the ambassador, quickly made the call.

"Then," Davoud wrote in his memoir, "he said I should phone Habib from the embassy and ask him to go to the airport where he would be put onboard the plane, that he needed neither a passport nor a ticket. The ambassador knew Habib was prohibited from leaving the country."

Davoud called, but Habib replied: "No, you go with Aghdas. I'll stay. We'll talk on the phone every day. I bear the responsibility of a people and the responsibility of the whole family."

"I tried my best to convince him but he refused," Davoud wrote. He and his wife got out on one of the last El Al flights from Tehran — among 340 passengers crammed into a plane that was supposed to carry 270.

Two days later, on Feb. 1, Khomeini landed in Tehran, accompanied by his Paris entourage and foreign journalists.

"Throngs of supporters, 3 million in all, gushed out into the streets, watching him wave from a blue and white Chevy, as his car inched its way south to the Cemetery of the Martyrs," The Associated Press reported.

On the BBC, Khomeini proclaimed, "I will strike with my fists at the mouths of this government. From now on, it is I who will name the government."

Bakhtiar didn't want to believe it, saying, "He is free to speak but he is not free to act." He was soon proven wrong.

So many factors had converged to pave Khomeini's way to power. The army's morale was low, the middle and working classes had fought together against the shah, and many former government officials were out of the country or in prison. Months of clashes, rallies and strikes had left the state in tatters, allowing for local organizations called *Komiteh*, committees headed by local clergy, to pop up. Financial assistance would come from rich merchants in the bazaars, small store owners and mosques where the poor could get food and fuel. Some clergymen formed militias by recruiting young men mostly from slums. These became the fearsome Revolutionary Guards, *Pasdaran*. Records declassified decades afterward even reveal secret contacts between Khomeini and U.S. President Jimmy Carter, discussing the Iranian military's role if the ayatollah succeeded the shah.[7]

Khomeini appointed the Liberation Movement's leader Mehdi Bazargan to put together a provisional government. To circumvent Bakhtiar, a secret Revolutionary Council was set up to negotiate with Bakhtiar's chief of staff.

From Feb. 9 to 11, the revolutionaries were able to secure control of Tehran's machine guns and other weapons. Guerrillas supported cadets in a mutiny at a military base in Tehran. Police stations and the capital's main arms factory were attacked and looted, along with other government strongholds.

The Revolutionary Council had defeated Bakhtiar's government, making Khomeini Iran's new ruler.

On Feb. 13, a group of Iranian Jews went out to demonstrate to support him. Chief Rabbi Yedidiah Shofet and other Jewish leaders had met with Khomeini as soon as he returned to Iran. "They were received with respect, and the imam's office gave the meeting wide publicity. They (the delegation) made the point that Judaism and Zionism are totally distinct issues. Khomeini adopted the formula: 'We distinguish between Jews and Zionists.'"[8]

Khomeini's visitors were content with differentiating the good Jew who didn't support Israel from the bad Jew who did.

The Iranian Ministry of Foreign Affairs headed by Sanjabi took over the Israeli Embassy's building and demanded that all Israelis quickly leave Iran. On the weekend of Feb. 3-4, the remaining 34 Israelis went into hiding in three safe houses. They made it out on flights to evacuate American citizens.

---

7. Kambiz Fattahi, "Two Weeks in January: America's Secret Engagement with Khomeini," BBC Persian Service, June 3, 2016.

8. David Menashri, "The Pahlavi Monarchy and the Islamic Revolution," in *Esther's Children: A Portrait of Iranian Jews*, ed. Houman Sarshar (Beverly Hills: The Center for Iranian Jewish Oral History, 2002) p. 400.

Palestine Liberation Organization leader Yasser Arafat was the first foreign dignitary to visit the new Islamic Republic. On Feb. 17, Arafat met with then-Deputy Prime Minister Ebrahim Yazdi, who would become foreign minister. Iran announced an end to relations with Israel. On the 18th, Khomeini met with Arafat. The following day, Khomeini's son Ahmad along with Yazdi welcomed Arafat to the old building that belonged to the Central Jewish Board. The PLO took over the building. Standing on the balcony under the words "VIVA P.L.O." painted on the wall, Arafat raised his left arm flashing the victory symbol flanked by Ahmad Khomeini and Yazdi.[9]

To allay their fears that Khomeini intended to harm Iran's Jews, he sent an envoy, Shahriyar Rouhani to the U.S., who asked to meet with heads of Jewish organizations there.

In a March 12, 1979, memo to the board of the World Jewish Congress, Kaplan reported that Haroun Yeshayaei and Hamid Sabi formed a Jewish Revolutionary Committee aimed at total national integration with the new regime. "They have already expressed publicly their hostility to Israel and espouse openly the Palestinian cause," Kaplan wrote.[10]

While Khomeini kept up anti-capitalist and anti-Zionist tirades, Habib tried to keep his businesses afloat.

---

9. Philip Dopolous "Iranian Jews, Fearing Repression, Flee Islamic Republic," The Associated Press, May 19, 1979.

10. Armand Kaplan, "Tentative up-to-date position paper on Iran" dated March 12, 1979. (Jerusalem: Central Zionist Archives) C10\2203.

CHAPTER 19

Arrest and Prison

The day they came for my grandfather, he could have been at dinner with us in New York or with Davoud who had settled in London. He could have been sitting in Jerusalem or Tel Aviv having tea with a friend.

Instead, he sat at his desk across from his brother's empty chair in Tehran's Aluminum Building. It had been a month and a half since Davoud left on Jan. 30 on one of the last El Al flights out of the country. The hustle and bustle of the office had ground to a near halt since many of the company's Jewish office workers had also left Iran.

Every day, Habib read newspapers with front pages displaying photos of executed generals from the shah's regime. But he could not watch events in Iran unfold as the rest of us did — from the outside. Amidst the chaos, he still made and kept business appointments, maintaining some semblance of normalcy.

On the morning of Thursday, March 15, he and Amir Victory, the president of the refrigerator factory, went to an appointment together. Habib was back in his office by 11:30. Shamsi was at her desk when she heard a knock on the door.[1] Thursdays were half-days marking the start of the Muslim weekend. Neither Habib nor Shamsi expected anyone that afternoon.

When she opened the door, three armed men from the Mujahedeen Khalk stood there. The Mujahedeen were part of the radical Islamic Marxist movement devoted to overthrowing the shah, and in the early days of the Islamic Republic were close to the clerics, who had put them in charge of finding the addresses of capitalists, and going after them. They marched in and faced Habib.

"Mr. Elghanian, we need you to come with us to answer some questions," one of the men said as he held out handcuffs.

"No need for those, gentlemen," Habib said. "I will come with you."

Nearly four years earlier, SAVAK agents had whisked him away from his home in the middle of the night in front of Nikkou Jan. She was gone now, and the Mujahedeen were operating in broad daylight. Then, he had told his wife not to worry, that he would go see what the men wanted and come home. Now, to Shamsi, he said, "I'll be back in the afternoon."

The men rode the elevator down and walked out into a mild 50-degree day. Habib slipped into the car's back seat between two guards whose modus operandi was to cover their captive's head with a dark sack before driving off to Qasr prison, where many of the shah's civil and military officials were imprisoned and executed. So far, the new regime had targeted high-ranking members of the government or military. Just two days earlier, Gen. Nader Jahanbani, the deputy chief of the Air Force, was executed at Qasr, one of 20 people killed there over 10 days.

Between Feb. 11 and March 15, 74 people had been jailed, tried and executed in the country, 49 in Tehran. The first notable executions took place Feb. 15 in Khomeini's first headquarters at the Refah school. Among them were Army Maj. Gen. Manoucher Qhosrowdad and former SAVAK head

---

1. Author 2011 phone interview with Shamsi who asked that her last name be withheld.

Nematollah Nasiri. The following day, Gen. Reza Naji and Lt. Gen. Mehdi Rahimi were killed.

When Fred, who remained in Tehran, heard the news of his father's arrest, he tried to put it in perspective. He knew some detainees had been released, and Habib had been arrested and freed by the shah earlier.

News of Habib's detention quickly reached abroad. Armand Kaplan found out the following day and added an addendum to another memo on Iran's Jews that he was finishing to the Governing Board of the World Jewish Congress: "Last minute: Habib Elghanian's arrest."

Noting that Habib had been taken to "the sinister Qasr prison," he said, "It must be underlined that in this prison are concentrated all the personalities from the former regime who were arrested. Some of them were already 'tried' and executed. Thousands are still waiting to appear before the so-called court of justice, which is a mockery of justice. The arrest of Mr. Elghanian, who was considered, and rightly so, for decades as the real leader of the Iranian Jewish community, until the events which took place in Iran since August-September 1978, is considered by knowledgeable Jewish Iranian personalities as the first significant sign of action which may be directed against the Jews in the country.

"This arrest has already provoked a feeling of panic among the Jews there. Efforts underway by various means to approach Khomeini in order to obtain his personal intervention with the aim to get Elghanian's release. We may know shortly if those efforts have succeeded or not. No doubt we are facing a new stage of the situation."

Kaplan recalled how, during his trip to Iran, he had pleaded with Jewish citizens, including Habib, to leave while there was time. "We begged them . . . We were listened to, some even agreed with us, but others were reluctant hoping that things may turn better than feared. Elghanian was among the latter."

As news of his arrest spread, Habib was making friends in his cell in Qasr, a former palace converted into a prison in the early 20th century. The

revolutionaries had freed many of Mohammad Reza Shah's political prisoners from there to make room for their own prisoners.

Not one to sit around his cell paralyzed by fear, Habib talked with other
prisoners and his guards. Through one guard he befriended, he sent Amir
messages, checking on business, and expressing concern about Fred and
his wife, also about my father, Sina, and particularly Mahnaz. Appearing
always hopeful, he told Amir not to worry, to keep his mind on the job, to
keep the factory going.

"Whatever God wants will happen," he told Amir.

He wrote to Fred from Qasr:

"My dearest Fereydoun,

"I hope you and Eliane Jan are both good and healthy. Try to write me
a few words but also please arrange for two or three weeks' worth of
fruit, I don't need any more clothes. Tell Vali to go to the Manoucher
store in Tajrich Boulevard, get 10,000 tomans, take half for his salary
and give the other half to Eliane.

"*Ghorbaneh shoma,*

"Papa."

Under the note to Fred, he wrote a message for Vali, hoping he was well
and adding, "Tell Ahmad [Vali's son] he has to go to school until God willing I will come out. Kiss the children on my behalf."

He finished the letter with another message to Fred: "Dearest Fereydoun,
You can send me news about yourself, telegraphs to Qasr prison, or write
me letters."

Another prisoner, a writer and activist named Amir Hossein Ladan
who was at Qasr between March 11 and April 11, was in the same section
as Habib, where they kept prisoners temporarily. At the time, they were

holding more than 400 prisoners in a space with a capacity of 90.

According to Ladan, Mohamad Taghi Majidi, an imprisoned military tribunals chief under the shah, introduced him to a man he described as an "older, very calm gentleman." Ladan said he and my grandfather walked and talked one entire night in the hallway among the other prisoners.[2]

"Once or twice, he got sad. And I comforted and calmed him," Ladan recalled. My grandfather talked to Ladan about his family, his brothers, his companies, his buildings and his factories.

In the morning, the prisoners began complaining, kicking doors. They hadn't been fed dinner. Majidi, Habib and a few others asked the prisoners to quiet down, while Ladan went to the guards to tell them the prisoners were hungry.

One yelled, "*Goh khordan*, let them eat shit. These people are all against the revolution."

It was another guard, a very different one, who that spring paid a visit to one of Habib's lifelong friends, Mikail Loghman, the caretaker of the Beheshtieh Jewish cemetery. At first, opening his door, Loghman was afraid the bearded young man had come to arrest him.[3]

"Don't worry, Mr. Loghman. Close the door. I want to talk to you. I am Habib Elghanian's prison guard. I know him very well. My father worked for him and we've had help from this family. If we had a problem, we would go to him. He's helped a lot of people," the young man said.

"He told me to come to you, he gave me your address and asked if I could come and ask you to help release him as soon as possible, whatever you can do. He's lost a lot of weight; he isn't feeling well. I changed his cell so

2. A.H. Ladan, e-mail correspondence with author, May-June 2015. This account can also be found in his book, *Divine Right & Backwardness: The Struggle for Justice, Liberty & Democracy* (Orlando, Florida: DOF Center for Democracy).

3. Mikail Loghman's account as told to Mehrdad Cohen, interview with author in New York, March 2011.

that Ayatollah Khalkhali wouldn't see him. They want money. If you can get together the money, they could release him. Please do something as soon as possible."

Khomeini had appointed Ayatollah Sadegh Khalkhali to be the chief justice of the Revolutionary Tribunals. Nicknamed "the hanging judge," he was known for summary executions.

The guard went on, describing how Ayatollah Hossein Ali Montazeri's son, Abbas Mohammad Montazeri, toured the jail and stopped in front of Habib's cell.

"What's your name?" he asked.

"I'm Habib Elghanian."

"We went to your house. If you bring us some money, we will free you," Montazeri said.

Official and unofficial accounts differ about just how possible it was to buy one's way out of jail. In a May 12, 1979, *Kayhan* newspaper article, Khalkhali told reporters that Elghanian had offered 500 million tomans to delay his trial and that Khalkhali had refused the offer.[4] There is no corroborating evidence to support Khalkhali's claims.

Five days later, the prison guard returned to Loghman's office in the bazaar.

"What's going on, Loghman Khan? Mr. Elghanian is not doing well; he lost a lot of weight. He says, please tell Loghman to help me as soon as possible. They are executing someone new every day."

Just the previous day, he said, Khalkhali had gone from cell to cell and stopped with his bodyguards at the cell holding Habib and a colonel.

"What are you doing here?" Khalkhali demanded.

"Nothing," replied the colonel.

"No, you must have done something that they've arrested you."

---

4. *Kayhan*, 22 ordibehesht 1358 – May 12, 1979.

"I didn't hurt anybody," the colonel said. "I went to Mecca. I pray every day."

"Just tell me one thing, when you became a colonel, did you swear to the flag of Iran?" Khalkhali asked.

"It's a rule, we had to," the colonel said.

"That's it, that's your crime. Take him and execute him right away."

The colonel cried, "I have five kids."

"A lot of people have five kids. When you killed people, they had kids, too."

They took him and executed him next door.

In the meantime, Khalkhali turned his attention to Habib.

"Who is this guy?"

"He just works for customs. He has no power," the guard said.

Khalkhali started screaming, "How many times have I told you, don't mix the military with the private people. Let me finish off the generals first, then we'll get to the others."

Suddenly, something urgent arose, and Khalkhali was called on a walkie-talkie and left.

The guard told Loghman: "Mr. Elghanian was shaking. Please help him as soon as possible. I can't change his cell again."

By April, the pace of the executions had accelerated. Amir-Abbas Hoveyda, the former prime minister, was executed on April 7. On April 11, former Foreign Minister Abbas Ali Khalatbari faced the firing squad.

Charles Naas, the chargé d'affaires at the U.S. Embassy in Tehran at the time, frequently met with then Deputy Prime Minister Ebrahim Yazdi. Naas had instructions to plead for the life of Hoveyda and Khalatbari.[5]

"He was clearly an intelligent man," Naas said of Yazdi. "I might have been naive, but I felt that when he and I talked and agreed that something

---

5. Interview with Charles Naas by William Burr, Foundation for Iranian Studies Oral History (Bethesda, Maryland: May 13, 31 and July 26, 1988).

could be done that he would, in fact, extend his best efforts to do so. So, I felt quite comfortable with him in sort of day-to-day dealing . . ."

"But he was deeply committed to the revolution, deeply committed to Khomeini. The hatred they had for the previous regime was made clear to one at all times," Naas said. Mentioning his own pleading on behalf of Khalatbari and Hoveyda, he added, "I think he may have been somewhat sympathetic to these specific requests, but he made it very clear to me that the revolutionaries were going to in fact take their share of blood, that the people had been pent up so long, had been so badly treated over the years, that it was politically impossible for the regime to curb at that time the excesses that were going on. In fact, I think as I was talking to him, Khalatbari was shot."

Naas continued: "And with great emotion, as I was speaking, he went over to his desk and he pulled out a file, a fairly thick file, which he claimed had been seized in SAVAK headquarters, and I had no reason to disbelieve him. . . . And there was sort of the before picture and the after picture. And the after picture always showed the person dead, and it showed some of them clearly. I remember a terrible picture of a young lady naked from the waist up, there was a picture of her first, a sort of bright, attractive — I say bright, she looked bright — young lady. And the next picture of her was sort of a slab, naked from the waist up, with burn marks all over her body.

"And so Yazdi, with a considerable amount of passion in his voice, asked how I could expect mercy for the people who had committed such atrocities?"

That spring, a half-dozen or so efforts to free Habib from prison were undertaken from Tehran, New York, Washington, Paris and London. They included contacting a U.S. senator, Jewish organizations and Iranian officials.

My father, joined by his uncle Nourollah, met with Sen. Ted Kennedy in Washington, explaining Habib's situation. Though Kennedy was sympathetic, he said there was nothing he could do to help.

Lotfollah Hay attended meetings at the Alliance Israélite with its leader Edmond de Rothschild and Jacob Kaplan, chief rabbi of France.

Dan Mariaschin, who worked at the Anti-Defamation League during that period, described another effort to intervene. ADL officials met with Henry, Nourollah's son, and John, Habib's oldest brother, several times because they had heard Habib could face execution. Efforts were made to reach former U.S. Attorney General Ramsey Clark and civil liberties attorney Leonard Boudin. "We pressed as many buttons as we could," Mariaschin said.[6]

In Iran, Kamran Beroukhim and Hamid Sabi said they tried, too.

"On May 7, we had a letter written by our chief rabbi, Rabbi Shofet, to Taleghani explaining how Habib for years had supported the community, how charitable he was, how he was the most important person in our community, how everybody loved him and so on and so forth," Sabi said.[7] "Then Kamran took the letter to Mahdi Hadavi, the public prosecutor. And Taleghani wrote a note to Hadavi, saying he confirms the content of the letter and he would ask for his immediate release."

"We took the letter to Qasr prison," Beroukhim said.

"We called everyone we could," Sabi said.

Aziz Daneshrad and Haroun Yeshayaei tried too, meeting another ayatollah on April 28, getting him to write a letter to an appeals court that Yeshayaei delivered personally to Khalkhali in Qom.

Jews weren't the only ones pushing to get Habib released. Their Muslim partner in the textile and vegetable oil factories, Hajji Mirza Attoallah Moghadam was liaising between the *Komitehs* and the family to get Habib out of jail.[8]

---

6. Dan Mariaschin, phone interview with author, July 2012.

7. Hamid Sabi, phone interview with author in Beroukhim's Los Angeles office, April 2011.

8. Armand Kaplan, "Report on the Elghanian case" (Jerusalem: Central Zionist Archives) C10\2203

By May 8, nearly 200 executions had occurred following secret trials. Hassan Pakravan and Nasser Moghadam, the last two chiefs of SAVAK, were both executed on April 11.

Habib had had a phone conversation with Moghadam, the last SAVAK chief, according to Moghadam's son, who says he was in his father's office when Habib called him before his arrest.

"What do you think of the situation, Nasser Khan?" Habib asked.

"I obviously can't leave, but you, you must get out while you still can," Moghadam had advised.

Now, it was too late for that.

CHAPTER 20

~

Trial and Will

There are photographs from my grandfather's trial. He is in a small prison courtroom, sitting in a white chair, wearing a gray pinstripe wool suit and white buttoned-up shirt.

Outside, where family members of prisoners nervously waited for their loved ones' verdicts, there were no familiar voices. The authorities hadn't told Fred that Habib's trial would be held that day. They hadn't called any witnesses, either. Like the rest of the accused, Habib had to defend himself — without a lawyer.

Five others were tried that Tuesday afternoon. Four had worked for the SAVAK, and all were convicted and executed. The fifth, Rahim Ali Khorram, an acquaintance of Habib's, was a businessman with vast property holdings, including an amusement park. Khorram was accused of operating casinos and maintaining Filipino prostitutes. Among the outrageous assertions during testimony was that the amusement park had a secret morgue and cemetery.

When Khorram was sentenced to death, he walked out of the courtroom to talk to his son. "I am going to be executed," he told him. "I think Habib stands a better chance." Khorram's son later telephoned our family in London and relayed his father's comment.

The summary trials and executions were still going on despite the narrative Foreign Minister Ebrahim Yazdi had fed foreign journalists about fair trials in March. On the 16th of that month, *The New York Times* reported that Yazdi said the new revolutionary tribunals were supposed to be held under Sharia law. The previous summary trials and executions had occurred because the shah had fallen so quickly that the revolutionaries had been unprepared to run prisons and a legal system. The *Komitehs*, spontaneously established to bring vigilante order, believed that the shah's secret police were capable of regaining power; if they had not been afraid of a plot, Yazdi told the foreign reporter, they would have had open trials.[1]

Both Prime Minister Mehdi Bazargan and Yazdi said that they had talked Khomeini into issuing an order to stop the summary trials and executions.

This was all subterfuge.

In a two-night execution spree at Qasr in April, six men who had all served in the armed and security forces, many high-ranking officials under the shah, were killed. On May 8, the day before my grandfather's trial, one execution took place there and 20 at the prison at Evin.

In those chaotic days, it was really Sadegh Khalkhali who was in charge of these tribunals. In his memoir, Khalkhali, the first post-revolution religious judge and head of the Islamic Revolutionary Tribunals, said: "All the people that I condemned and who were executed in the early days of the establishment of the Revolutionary Tribunals and later in the Qasr prison were all corruptors on earth and, based on the Quran, their blood was a waste."

Habib sat on a white wooden chair surrounded by a reporter, photographer and state TV cameraman, along with the prosecutor Ayatollah

---

1. John Kifner, "Iranian Official Explains Trials and Their Suspension," *The New York Times*, March 17, 1979.

Azari-Qomi — who also served as judge — and four rows of prison guards and *Komiteh* members.

The young men who served as the new government's eyes and ears were known for their eagerness to participate in the firing squads. They were anointed by the men of God and happy to do their dirty work. Before a trial would get underway, they'd yell, "*Een poshteh divariyeh*," meaning, "This one will have his back to the wall," referring to the wall where they gunned them down.[2]

Habib sat behind the desk at Branch 3 of the Tehran Revolution Court as Azari-Qomi called the court to order with the reading of a text from the Quran.

Azari-Qomi read the indictment in the crowded courtroom:[3]

"In the name of Allah, Habib Elghanian, holder of ID Card #6108, resident of Tehran, literate, spy, Zionist capitalist is accused of the following:

"1. Friendship with the enemies of God and enemy of the friends of God.

"2. Spying for the Zionistic State of Israel.

"3. Gathering contributions for Israel for the sake of bombarding Palestine and Muslim Arab people.

"4. Investing money made from exploiting and destroying resources of Iran to help Israel, who incessantly combats, steals and affronts Islam and God.

"5. Corruption on Earth by means of destroying resources and helping in the destruction of an entire generation of Iranians.

---

2. Abbas, photographer who covered similar trials, during Skype conversation and e-mail correspondence with author, March 23, 2013.
3. *Ettelaat*, 20 ordibehesht 1358 - May 10, 1979.

"6. War on God and the Prophet of God.

"7. Obstructing God's way and obstructing the wellbeing of weak nations against the value of humanity and Islam.

"8. Corruptor on Earth (*Mofsed-e-Filarz*).

"9. Helping the daily and cruel massacre of our Palestinian brothers."

Historian Abbas Milani summarized these fabricated charges best by describing them as "an exercise in cruel absurdity. The court trafficked only in generalities and eschewed making any specific charges."[4]

According to Khalkhali's memoirs, a corrupter on earth was "a person who contributes to spreading and expanding corruption on earth. Corruption is what leads to the decline, destruction and the deviation of society from its nature. People who were executed had strived in spreading corruption and prostitution, circulating heroin, opium and licentious behavior, atheism, murder, betrayal, flattery, and, in sum, all these vile qualities. These people's problems were aggravated by the fact that they did not repent once they saw the people's revolution."

The New York Times' John Kifner wrote: "The major charges sound odd to the Western ear, but Mr. Yazdi says they must be understood in the Islamic cultural context."

Writing about Habib's case in 1980, Amnesty International said it was "the only instance known of a non-Muslim being charged with a Koran offense." In the prosecution, Amnesty International found numerous violations of The Universal Declaration of Human Rights, including arbitrary arrest and detention, being punished for a crime which did not constitute a criminal offense at the time it was committed, denial of the right to freedom

---

4. Abbas Milani, "Hadj Habib Elghanian," *Eminent Persians: The Men and Women Who Made Modern Iran 1941-1979, Vol. 2* (Syracuse: Syracuse University Press and Persian World Press, 2008), p. 620.

of religion, the right to be presumed innocent until found guilty by a competent and impartial tribunal in accordance with law, the right to defense through an attorney, the right to adequate time to prepare a defense, the right not to be compelled to testify against oneself or to confess to guilt, and the right to appeal.[5]

The trial was televised in Iran. "In May 1979, I remembered Habib Elghanian's pleasant smile with deepening sadness and horror as I watched his televised kangaroo court trial," Janet Tavakoli, an American finance expert married to an Iranian and living in Iran at the time, wrote in a 2006 book. "Facial bruises and swelling showed through heavy makeup. Bearded mullahs dressed in dark cloaks, spat questions at him. Before he could answer, a mullah answered the question for him and twisted it into an accusation. Elghanian had no defense counsel and seemed disoriented and unsteady in his chair.

"If this could happen to Habib Elghanian," she wrote, "any Iranian could be arrested for being a collaborator with the shah and any foreigner accused of being a Zionist spy."[6]

Without a lawyer, my grandfather spoke in his own defense immediately after hearing the charges. According to an *Ettelaat* newspaper account published May 10, he is reported to have said: "In the name of God Almighty and with the permission of the Head of the Islamic Republic and the Honorable Revolutionary Court of Iran, I, Habib Elghanian, respectfully submit that I am proud to be an Iranian and that I will die here. I have not paid a penny to Israel or to Zionism. If ever the court proves that I have given financial assistance to Zionism, I am prepared to be condemned to the most severe

---

5. Habib Elqanian (cq), One Person's Story, Human Rights and Democracy for Iran: A project of the Abdorrahman Boroumand Center. https://www.iranrights.org/memorial/story/-2861/habib-elqanian

6. Janet Tavakoli, *Dear Mr. Buffett: What an Investor Learns 1,269 Miles from Wall Street*, (Hoboken, New Jersey: John Wiley & Sons, Inc., 2009), p. 213.

punishment if the Court can show me my signature as proof. I have several brothers but I am only accountable for my own signature. I am an enemy of the enemies of God and a friend of the friends of God. I oppose the Zionistic government of Israel because I am an Iranian Jew."

Habib continued to try distancing himself from Israel.

"In Israel, there are two factions of Judaism, the Sephardic and the Ashkenazim, and 85 percent of the Israelis are Ashkenazim, most of them Europeans and Americans, and then, between 5 and 8 percent are Sephardim and I am among the Sephardic Jews," he said. "The majority section does not accept us; therefore, I am considered as one of the minority in Israel. How would I therefore help the majority section? I have not helped the Israeli Army. How is it possible for me to help the Israeli Army, which bombs our Palestinian brethren?" he asked. "I am prepared to fight with all my life and heart against Israel as I am an Iranian."

He continued: "I am proud to be the part owner of the factories of Plasco Melamine, Plastic Shomal and Pars-America group, manufac-turers of General Steel refrigerators and aluminum frames. I forcefully declare that in Iran from the poorest poor to the richest rich, you will not find a house that doesn't have a product manufactured through my effort in my search to serve the interests of this country, and of course, I also serve my own interests. During the 53 days that I've been imprisoned, I have paid the salaries of all my workers. The court should pay attention to the fact that the raw materials for my factory must be purchased abroad and these purchases are made by me. If I do not attend to these matters, the factory would be lost and this would bring about certain dangers to the economy. My only mistake was that in 20 years, I was a member of the Chamber of Commerce."

Azari-Qomi's retort: "Mr. Elghanian, you say you had no cooperation with Israel. First of all, the question arises that if you oppose Zionism how did you reflect that opposition so that your compatriots and fellow Jews would note this matter? You said you had no property outside of Iran.

Yesterday it was reported that you had bought several plots of land near Tel Aviv in Israel. What explanation do you have about this report?"

Habib responded: "I spoke to several of my Jewish friends and said, 'How many Jews live in Israel?' They said between three and three and a half million. I said, 'Why do the Israelis who have so much land and live so well and wear the best of ties, why do they fight and kill people?'"

"Did you send this message to the Israeli authorities?" Azari-Qomi pressed him.

"No, I only discussed the subject with my friends," Habib responded. "If you find one square meter of land in Israel in my name, you can cut off both my hands and later in the evening shoot me. Of course, I repeat again, if you can show me my signature."

"Your claim cannot be accepted," Azari-Qomi said. "We cannot verify this by asking for such documents in Israel, which is our enemy, but according to reports from SAVAK, we have evidence as SAVAK cooperated with the CIA and the Israelis and these reports were drawn up during the height of your power. According to SAVAK document No. 21996, dated the 3rd of the 4th month 1349 [1970], it is reported that Habib Elghanian purchased several plots of land in Israel at a price over $1,000,000. Elghanian has also transferred capital from Iran and the purchased land has increased in value. These reports were then confirmed by several SAVAK agents in coded letters. In these letters your encouragement for Iranian Jews to emigrate to Israel was confirmed."

During the trial, another document was produced as evidence of his connection with Israel. Azari-Qomi quoted from a letter from his SAVAK files: "We heard today in a very private manner from Habib Elghanian that he spoke to the head of the Jewish Agency in Tehran to ask him to remove Briskin, who is an Israeli Army colonel, and with whom the Jewish community are not very happy. The Jewish Agency agreed to have him removed."

Citing another SAVAK report, Azari-Qomi said: "After meeting with a group of people, you said during a speech you would arrange for the minting of $40,000 worth of coins on the occasion of the 2,500th anniversary of the Iranian monarchy, with the monarch's symbol on the one side and the symbol of Zionism on the other side."

"I have only traveled to Israel six or seven times, then only for an eye cure," Habib replied. He also said that he was in prison under the shah for profiteering in the chain of plastic shops and all his life he has been of service to many causes. He also said he considered the shah to be evil. "(Prime Minister) Hoveyda and I had had differences of opinion. Please forgive me," Habib said. "They exiled me to Sanandaj and after serving my sentence, I asked my family to meet me at the airport in Tehran but when I arrived Hoveyda's men arrested me again. And I was later sentenced to another 61 days in jail. After serving the second sentence, Hoveyda summoned me. It had been a mistake, he said. He asked me not to say anything about this."

Wrapped in his dark cloak, Azari-Qomi read what he called, "the proof of guilt":

"1. Clear and implicit confessions from the records.

"2. Sufficient proofs and documents on record including money payments to Israel with the purpose to reinforce the defense disposition of that country.

"3. Meetings arranged with the most cruel foes of God and of the Palestinian nation, for example Abba Eban and other leaders of the Zionist state of thieves.

"4. Acquisitions of lands and real estate of great value, which is consistent with the above . . ."

"For all these reasons, I require the death penalty for the accused and the confiscation of his estate and the estate of his entire family."

All that remained before facing the firing squad was writing his last wishes.

In *Day Break*, a 2005 Iranian feature movie filmed inside Qasr prison, we follow the main character, a man who's been sentenced to death and allowed to write his will. Before he is brought out to be killed, we see a guard escort him through a maze of dark hallways lit by dangling light bulbs, hallways perhaps similar to the ones Habib walked down. The man steps inside a white-tiled room with two small windows covered with bars. A piece of paper and pen sit on a small white desk.

In a similar room, Habib stared at the information he had to fill out on the prison letterhead: location, name, date. The first words fall off the dotted lines.

"Block 1

"From: Qasr Prison

"Date: May 8, 1979

"Written by: Habib Elghanian, Son of Babai

"I. Bring my son Fereydoun to my home in Shemiran, Khalili Street, Darband, Telephone 373787.

"II. Collect all rent from the building Mr. Pourrezi will deposit in Bank Ettebarat Naderi Street.

"III. The rent of Villa #36 must be collected and placed in a separate account for Mahnaz.

"IV. Take delivery of my body and bury me in the family section of Giliard if possible near my wife.

"V. Notify the family in America of my death by cable.

"VI. The result of Pars-America's accounts, Amir must notify to America, they should be settled in any way you see fit.

"VII. My watch and my glasses must be taken from prison and delivered to Amir Victory.

"VIII. Take care of Fereydoun and Eliane and don't let them become too depressed.

"IX. For the [illegible] Management Bank Ettebarat and public warehouses, get them and give them to Fereydoun.

"X. I say goodbye to Fereydoun and Eliane.

"XI. [illegible]

"XII. Take what is owed to me and give it to Karmel in return for his debt.

"XIII. Whatever wealth I have from any source must be divided between all the children.

"XIV. This is the way God wanted it, Praise the Lord.

"XV. For the year of Nikkha Khanoum, you must go to her gravesite.

"XVI. The backpay of Vali and [illegible] should be given at the end of the month.

"XVII. Any receivables I have must be collected and used against debts I have.

"XVIII. I say goodbye to Amir.

"XIX. For one year my death must be observed on each sabbath.

"One watch and all my belongings must be taken from the prison.

"I expect Amir to follow up on his work (and not let go).

"I say goodbye to all the family.

"I owe 2000 rials to [illegible] the representative to Parliament, this point Mr. Yousef Cohen and [illegible].

"I say goodbye to all my staff.

"Give my regards to all my staff. Give my regards to Miss Shamsi also."

Minutes later, he stood blindfolded in front of the firing squad in the prison yard, whispering his final prayer: "*Shema Israel, Adonai Eloheinu, Adonai Echad,*" or "Hear O Israel, the Lord our God, the Lord is One."

Gallery

Our house in Zaferanieh in November 1976.

With my father Karmel in Zaferanieh.

The last picture of Mahnaz with her father in Tehran in winter 1977.

Khomeini at his residence in Neauphle-le-Château, west of Paris, after his expulsion from Baghdad in 1978.

Gallery

Mourners carry on Sept. 11, 1978, the open casket of a demonstrator slain during clashes with the army on the first day of martial law the previous Friday in Tehran.

Demonstrators protest the shah's rule in Tehran on Oct. 9, 1978.

Rioters set fires on Tehran's main streets during anti-government demonstrations on Nov. 5, 1978. Many banks and movie theaters were burned and damaged.

Gallery

Habib in New York in late October, early November 1978 before insisting on returning to Iran.

Shrouded women demonstrate against the shah at Behesht-Zahra cemetery in Tehran on Nov. 23, 1978.

Demonstrators hold up a poster of Ayatollah Ruhollah Khomeini during an anti-shah demonstration in Tehran on Dec. 10, 1978.

A boy, fist raised in symbolic defiance, heads a huge crowd of Khomeini supporters across Tehran in an anti-shah demonstration estimated at over a million strong on Dec. 10, 1978. Behind him demonstrators carry a banner reading: "Everyone has the right to take part in the government of his country," and behind another reads: "We will destroy Yankee power in Iran."

Fires rage in the middle of a road in downtown Tehran on Dec. 28, 1978.

Passengers enter the departure lounge of Mehrabad airport in Tehran on Jan. 2, 1979.

A soldier bends to kiss the shah's feet on the tarmac of Mehrabad airport in Tehran on Jan. 16, 1979 as the king and his wife Farah leave the country.

More than a million supporters of an Islamic Republic assemble around the Shayad monument in Tehran on Jan. 19, 1979.

Followers form a human chain around Khomeini to protect him from the crowd massed near his residence in Neauphle-le-Château a few hours before leaving for Charles de Gaulle Airport on Jan. 31, 1979.

236

Khomeini sits in a chartered plane in Paris before taking off for Tehran on Feb. 1, 1979.

Khomeini waves to followers as he appears in the first floor window of his headquarters in Tehran on Feb. 2, 1979.

Palestinian Liberation Organization leader Yasser Arafat, the first foreign leader to vist the Islamic Republic of Iran, kisses Khomeini in Tehran on Feb. 18, 1979.

Blindfolded men are lined up against a wall as they face firing squads in Tehran's Qasr prison on March 11, 1979.

My grandfather defending
himself in court.

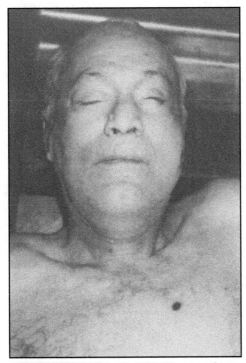

My grandfather in the morgue following his
execution.

PART IV

~

THE WATERSHED

CHAPTER 21

⌣

Burial and Escape

His body languished at the Qasr prison morgue. Dark bruises around his eyes and cheek, masked under makeup during his trial to hide signs of torture in prison, were unmistakable in the post-execution photograph. His face, haggard during the kangaroo-court trial, had ballooned, and his shoulders, once broad, appeared deflated. Placed on his naked torso, a piece of white paper had a Farsi notation handwritten in red ink: "Habib Elghanian Zionist."

Mikail Loghman, Habib's lifelong friend and Jewish cemetery director, drove to the morgue to get his friend. When he spotted Habib's corpse, the authorities refused to return his body for burial.

It was not uncommon in those days to be forced to pay for each of the firing squad bullets to get a body back. Families of executed men were strung along for days before a body was released. The revolution was a killing machine fueled by irrational, vengeful cruelty, its movements running counter to logic, decency and custom. And so, bodies waited in the morgue, only prolonging a family's anguish instead of allowing them to bury their loved one the following day, according to both Jewish and Muslim tradition.

"Sobbing relatives gathered at the Tehran city morgue shortly after dawn to collect the bodies," The Associated Press reported on May 8, the day before Habib was executed. "(Iranian) reporters only said one body was handed over, in a rough wooden coffin. Other family members were told to go home and wait to be contacted about claiming the corpses. Revolutionary guardsmen outside the morgue angrily told the victims' relatives that the executed were guilty of murder and deserved their punishment."[1]

On the morning of May 9, immediately after hearing the news of Habib's execution, Fred and Eliane went straight to Habib's sister Saltanat's house. Undaunted by government restrictions against marking her brother's death with religious ceremonies, Saltanat held the shiva, the seven-day grieving period that customarily starts right after burial. Although it would be days before the morgue finally released Habib's body, relatives and close friends dropped in to pay their respects, pray and eat the traditional *kuku sabzi*, a green herb omelet, after the end of the evening prayer. To stay inconspicuous, no one wore black or went every day.

During this time, *Pasdarans*, the young men recruited to form the Revolutionary Guards and to enforce the new government's Islamic codes and morality, were going house to house, feverishly looking for anything and anyone of value to them. On May 10, Fred and Eliane were already home when a half-dozen *Pasdarans* knocked on their door with orders to take over the property: the main two-story house, barn, riding arenas, pasture and horses. But without orders for what to do with its owners, the captors, young and inexperienced, and the captives were left to improvise.

---

1. The Associated Press, May 8, 1979.

Eliane asked the cook to prepare dinner for everyone. After the heavy meal of kebab and rice, Fred brought out a bottle of cognac. Eager to sample it, the ringleader rested his rifle against the wall. Fred filled glasses of cognac for himself, Eliane and the young men while they sat on the floor in the middle of the living room. The enforcers of Iran's new moral code, which strictly forbids drinking alcohol, enjoyed the digestif and small talk before falling asleep.

Waking up hungover and angry the next morning, the enforcers demanded to know where Fred kept the alcohol. They followed him to the cabinet, grabbed the bottles and poured everything into the toilet.

Still without a plan, they sat around the rest of the day until the evening when they again all reconvened for dinner and more small talk in the living room. After eating, one of the *Pasdarans* became suspicious that Eliane was hiding a weapon under her skirt and ordered her to put on a pair of pants. She changed into tight blue jeans.

The following morning, a Saturday, a car pulled into their driveway. It was Fred's uncle Nemat who after a few hours bribed the *Pasdarans* into letting him take Fred and Eliane. The guards were free to make up whatever story they wanted about their captives' escape.

Not wanting to put Nemat in any more danger but also afraid of getting arrested at the airport if they tried to leave the country, Fred and Eliane wandered Tehran, looking for hiding places. One of Fred's bridge partners kept them in his house for 24 hours until a hotel owner who knew Habib offered them a room.

In the meantime, between May 11 and 13, the authorities finally relinquished Habib's body to Loghman. A Jewish forensic pathologist, Dr. Nasser Mossanen, signed the death certificate, helping expedite his release. Loghman already had a hunch about what he was told: Habib Elghanian must be buried without any fanfare or ceremony. It wasn't as though many Jews would have attended his funeral. Any who did could easily be tagged a Zionist, and suffer the same fate.

"We don't know when it will be, but nobody will go to the funeral anyway," a middle-aged man told a *New York Times* reporter who visited a synagogue after Habib's execution. "We are scared." [2]

Loghman laid his friend's body in his hearse. As a sentimental gesture, for a final goodbye before taking him to the cemetery, he drove past the landmark Plasco and Aluminum buildings.

Just over a year earlier, hundreds had attended Nikkou Jan's funeral service in the big parlor at Beheshtieh. A caravan of cars and two trucks full of flowers made it to Giliard; that's where Habib wanted to be buried next to his wife, but it was not to be. After consulting with friends and other members of the community, Loghman decided to bury Habib at Beheshtieh in Tehran.

Loghman wrapped his friend's body in the customary white shroud without any of the ritual washing and purification meant to comfort the soul. Cleaning a bullet-riddled corpse risks creating tears in the skin, causing more bleeding and discomfort to the soul believed to still be present.

Around 7 p.m. — it's unclear if that same day but most likely the day after his release — eight male relatives of Habib's arrived for the burial at Beheshtieh. Quickly, they realized that with Loghman, they were one person short of forming the *minyan*, the 10 needed to say the prayers. A son-in-law of Saltanat ran out to get his son waiting in the car. Once all 10 were gathered, they lowered the body into the ground in a section of the cemetery for people who hadn't died of natural causes. Under the cloak of the cool spring night's darkness, they whispered the sacred prayer for the dead, the Kaddish:

---

2. John Kifner "Firing Squad Kills 2 Iran Businessmen, One Was Jewish Backer of Israel — First Private Citizens Shot," *The New York Times*, May 10, 1979.

Yitgaddal veyitqadash shemei raba be alma divera chireutei, . . . Oseh shalom bimeromav, hu yaasehshalom aleinu ve al kol Yisrael ve-i-m ru. Amen.

Covering the body with earth is the ultimate *mitzvah*, or good deed, because the dead can't express their gratitude. The men reached for the shovels, taking turns filling the hole, making sure not to leave the customary mound on fresh graves, or any other markings, for fear Habib's grave could be desecrated. When they finished, Loghman unlocked the gates, and the men raced to get home by the 9 p.m. curfew.

Fred and Eliane were still hiding at the hotel. They got in touch with Amir who gave them some promissory notes from individuals to whom Habib had lent money. If they could cash them, they would have money to live for a while. In the daytime, Fred and Eliane went around Tehran trying to collect these debts, the notes totaling $8,000.

The debtors would all be polite, but not many people wanted to pay. They were only able to cash about 20 percent of the notes. Amir supplemented this with money from the company.

Fred and Eliane made sure they were always back by the curfew and ate most of their meals at the hotel. Before leaving in the morning and after returning, they'd turn to the radio for that day's news. The television was useless to them, now mostly filled with religious programming.

In Washington, the State Department's country director for Iran, Henry Precht, drafted a long letter to the U.S. Embassy in Tehran, inquiring about the fate of Iran's Jews — and particularly about Fred and Eliane. [3]

"Are there any general or specific restrictions which would prevent relatives of Habib Elghanian from leaving Iran? Specifically, we have been asked about his son, Feridoun (cq) and daughter-in-law Eliani (cq) and nephew Faramarz. We would also appreciate embassy's recommendations whether a letter from a member of Congress urging that they be permitted to leave Iran would be useful."

---

3. Freedom of Information Act request by author.

While Fred and Eliane lay low and looked for an escape hatch, the French Nazi-hunter and human rights lawyer Serge Klarsfeld flew into Tehran from France on May 22 to investigate Habib's execution and to check on the safety of Iran's Jews. Once again, a French Jew. Adolphe Crémieux before Habib was born in the ghetto, Armand Kaplan while he was alive and in danger, and now Klarsfeld for his execution. It had always been French Jews who looked out for us.

Klarsfeld visited Fred and Eliane in their room.[4] He took down both their names on a notepad from the Intercontinental Hotel, where he was staying, and promised to make inquiries with government officials about their status. Written half in French, half in English, the note from his visit reads:

"*'Tout confisqué, mis dehors.'* Everything confiscated, thrown out of home.

"FEREYDOUN ELGHANAYAN

"Eliane Keunca [her maiden name]

"a letter from Mr. Hadavi to the Airport Passport Control *ou se trouvent les passports depuis mercredi 17 mai* (where their passports are being held since Wednesday, May 17)

"E. K. saw Amir Hosseiny *(mardi)* (Tuesday)

"3 children in France"

(That their children had been sent safely out of the country was in part thanks to advice they'd been given by Gen. Nader Jahanbani who, with Air

---

4. Serge Klarsfeld, correspondence and phone conversation with author, February 2011.

Force Maj. Gen. Manoucher Khosrodad, was a friend and fellow member of Tehran's equestrian set. Both generals were executed.)

Klarsfeld took notes as Eliane recounted that she'd seen an official of the Revolutionary Tribunal, Amir Hosseini, on the day Klarsfeld landed in Tehran. According to the note, they needed Mahdi Hadavi, the public prosecutor, to instruct the Airport Passport Control that held their passports to allow them to leave Iran.

Sitting across from the couple, Klarsfeld tried to reassure them they would make it out of Iran safely.

On May 24, Klarsfeld visited Foreign Minister Ebrahim Yazdi. When Klarsfeld protested Habib's execution, Yazdi told him: "Elghanian wasn't judged and condemned as a Jew, but because he was part of a criminal system. The shah was for the Iranian people what Hitler was for the Jews. You can see it in these photos of patriots tortured by the SAVAK I'm showing you."

Yazdi tried blaming Western media for focusing on the Israeli connections: "The charges of ties with Israel and Zionism were highlighted by Western media which we don't control, but they came, in reality, after his ties with the shah's criminal system," he told Klarsfeld.

Three of the nine charges were directly related to Israel: "*Spying for the Zionist government of the thieves Israel, . . .*" and "*Raising money and assisting Israel and its army that night and day bombards our Palestinian Muslim brothers, . . .*" and "*Investing money made from exploiting and destroying resources of Iran to help Israel develop, Israel who incessantly combats, steals and affronts Islam and God.*"

Klarsfeld also made inquiries regarding Fred and Eliane. The couple should have no problems leaving, Yazdi said. Later, Klarsfeld visited the office of the attorney general of the Revolutionary Tribunals, Mahdi Hadavi. Hadavi repeated the tired spiel about Western media being controlled by Jews. He showed Klarsfeld a recent issue of *Hustler*. (The new religious regime was "monitoring" the United States' most explicit mass circulation porn magazine.) That issue had an illustration of a donkey's body with a photo of Khomeini's head on it. Hadavi pointed to the editor's name, Lee Quarnstrom.

"That's not a Jewish name, it's Swedish," Klarsfeld had to explain.

Undaunted, Hadavi pointed to the word "Israel" on the page. All it said was, "Iran breaks relations with Israel."

Klarsfeld also met with Amir Hosseini, the Revolutionary Tribunal official Eliane visited on May 22. He asked Hosseini why the government wouldn't let Fred and Eliane leave the country.

"What's the hurry?" the official answered.

"Because the father was executed, their three children are in Europe, everything they own including their home has been confiscated," Klarsfeld replied.

"They'll leave when it'll be convenient for the country."

"So, can I tell the world that Jews are not allowed to leave Iran?"

"Not Jews, Zionists!"[5]

The prospect of leaving Iran through official channels was looking doubtful.

Behind the scenes, Davoud's son Moise, living in London, was working with a former poker buddy with connections in the Iranian government to help get his cousins out. Moise gave Amir instructions for Fred and Eliane to go meet the man at his home.

This guy is so cool. He is not afraid of anything, he is so confident. A real gangster type, Fred kept thinking about the man during their meeting.

He planned on getting them passports with fake names, but they had to be disguised. Fred grew a mustache, and Eliane had to look as plain as possible, which she could pull off easily since she didn't have any makeup

---

5. Serge Klarsfeld, "Ami des ennemis de Dieu et ennemi des amis de Dieux," *Tribune Juive*, Numéro 570, Juin 1979.

with her. She parted and combed her short hair flat to the side. Fred would become Fereydoon Sanatinia; and Eliane, Leyli Shokoofandeh.

While they waited for their passports, their driver retrieved two suitcases full of clothes after likely bribing the Guards to enter their confiscated home.

On June 19, with those two suitcases, first-class plane tickets, fake passports and birth certificates in their pockets, Fred and Eliane got into the car of the gangster's associate waiting outside the hotel to take the couple to Mehrabad airport. They made small talk with the driver as they glanced through the window at the streets of a city they were about to leave behind, streets they had spent weeks running around as they anxiously tried to cash promissory notes. On the changed streets, women wore tchadors and headscarves, their faces moist from the June sun.

When the car pulled into the airport they knew so well, the gangster was there to ensure the plane took off with them. Earlier, during their meeting, he had instructed them to only make eye contact, not talk to him, and focus their energy on looking confident. Since Fereydoon Sanatinia and Leyli Shokoofandeh were not a couple, they separated, each going through customs and security alone.[6]

When passengers were called for the Air France flight to Paris, each walked over to the tarmac. They climbed the stairs onto the aircraft. As she settled in her seat by the aisle, Eliane thought of her children's faces. Fred took his seat next to hers by the window.

Preparations for takeoff were underway. The airplane doors shut.

"*Mesdames et Messieurs*," the flight attendant began. "*Bienvenue à bord ce vol Air France à destination de Paris. La durée du vol sera environ 5 heures et 25 minutes.*"

---

6. The "gangster" remains a mystery man to this day. Seeking out his identity only leads to dead ends. Fred and Eliane can offer little about him, and Moise died of a massive heart attack in his sleep in 1998.

In about five and a half hours, they would be in France. As the wheels lifted, Fred reached for Eliane's hand and held it tight. He looked out the window thinking of his father in Beheshtieh and his mother in Giliard, not knowing if he'd ever set foot on his homeland's soil again. The pilot made the final announcement they were waiting for: They had crossed out of Iranian airspace. They were safe.

CHAPTER 22

Fallout

Habib's execution set off a cascade of reaction. Iranian newspapers celebrated the news, publishing photos of his corpse on front pages. International media, politicians and others swiftly condemned the rank injustice.

In the U.S., the execution was front-page news on May 10. The event was significant because the 198 others executed between Feb. 11 and May 8 had almost all been members of the shah's government, military or secret police. May 9 marked the first time a prominent civilian and a member of a minority group was put in front of a firing squad.

The Washington Post carried a front-page story: "Iran Executes Jew, Citing Ties to Israel."[1] *The New York Times'* A1 headline said: "Firing Squad Kills 2 Iran Businessmen, One Was a Jewish Backer of Israel — First Private Citizens Shot."[2] The other businessman was Ali Khorram. Inside the paper was one

---

1. William Branigin, "Iran Executes Jew, Citing Ties to Israel," *The Washington Post*, May 10, 1979.

2. John Kifner, "Firing Squad Kills 2 Iran Businessmen, One Was Jewish Backer of Israel — First Private Citizens Shot," *The New York Times*, May 10, 1979.

of the photos of Habib defending himself during the sham trial. *Los Angeles Times* readers woke to the front-page headline: "Iran Executes Jew as Spy for Israelis, Industrialist Is First Non-Moslem Condemned; 7 Others Also Killed."[3] While these papers had reporters in Tehran, other newsrooms across the United States, such as *The Philadelphia Inquirer, The Detroit Free Press, The Miami Herald* and *The Atlanta Constitution* – and even small newspapers from Erie, Pennsylvania, to Greensboro, North Carolina — picked up AP and UPI stories. European papers carried the news too.

Scathing editorials followed. On May 12, *The Boston Globe* wrote: "No one provided evidence that Elghanian passed on secrets, or that his loyalty to Israel was greater than his loyalty to Iran. No one linked him to anything more incriminating than meetings early in the 1960s with Israeli officials. He may have bought property in Israel. But under what code of justice could that be construed as a capital offense? Yet evidence has little bearing in the courts of the Ayatollah Khomeini. One can only wonder how Elghanian or anyone else could possibly defend himself against charges of 'being an enemy of the friends of God.'"[4]

A *Washington Post* editorial on May 14 expressed further outrage: "Of the two civilian victims, one was not only accused of 'economic imperialism,' that is of being successful. He was also accused of spying for Israel and raising funds for Israel to bomb Palestinians. What this seems to come down to was that he had met some Israeli figures in the early 1960s and had contributed to Israeli causes. In other words, he was murdered for being a Jew friendly to Zionism. In no other country in the world is this a capital offense.... Few would deny Iran's right to have a revolution. Many should protest the revolution's bloodthirstiness ..."

---

3. Doyle McManus, "Iran Executes Jew as Spy for Israelis: Industrialist Is First Non-Moslem Condemned; 7 Other Also Killed," *Los Angeles Times*, May 10, 1979.
4. "The Death of Habib Elghanian," Editorial, *Boston Globe*, May 12, 1979.

The Wall Street Journal editors wrote: "The event should not go unmarked even if it belongs in a growing category of world horrors about which the U.S. now seems powerless to do anything."

And as noted, Amnesty International said the case was "the only instance known" of a non-Muslim being charged with a Quran offense.

Upon hearing the news in Jerusalem, Israeli Prime Minister Menachem Begin described Habib as a "good Zionist and one who helped Israel," and he spoke in the Israeli parliament, the Knesset, urging the world not to remain silent following "the executions of this murderous regime."[5] Israeli Foreign Minister Moshe Dayan had an hourlong meeting in Paris with his French counterpart, Jean-Francois Poncet, asking the French to intervene on behalf of Iran's Jewish community. Dayan said the execution set a dangerous precedent and that the same accusation of ties with Israel could be used against practically all of Iran's remaining Jews.[6]

U.S. State Department spokesman Hodding Carter reiterated his country's criticism of the secret and summary nature of the trials and executions. He went on to say, "it is disturbing that Mr. Elghanian was a member of a minority community."[7]

While Western news organizations pilloried the Islamic Republic, an Iranian radio broadcast, citing protests in the Israeli parliament and media, justified the move: "The more clamorous this propaganda barrage becomes, the more it convinces the Iranian nation of the validity of its diagnosis, for it finds out more than before this alien spy was of great value to his overlords."[8]

---

5. William Branigin, "Iran Executes Jew, Citing Ties to Israel," *The Washington Post,* May 10, 1979.

6. "Iran - Dayan," Reuters, May 10, 1979.

7. William Branigin, "Iran Executes Jew, Citing Ties to Israel," *The Washington Post,* May 10, 1979.

8. Eliz Sanasarian, *Religious Minorities in Iran,* (Cambridge, U.K.: Cambridge University Press, 2006) p.

Such rhetoric frightened Iran's Jews. A confidential mid-May message from the U.S. Embassy in Tehran to the State Department[9] titled *Status of Jewish Community*, said: "The execution of Habib Elghanian last week created a great sense of anxiety within Iranian Jewish community and rumors spread like wildfire. A general feeling was that if a person of Elghanian's stature was not safe, then all Jews were in jeopardy. The alleged charges of supporting Zionism and sending money to Israel, local Jews feel, could be levied on a large number of Iranian Jews. The fears of the community were then further heightened by the arrest, at about the same time as the execution, of additional Jewish business figures in Tehran. The highest number of arrests that any of our sources has reported so far is 26 and the lowest is five."

Iranian Jewish author and journalist Roya Hakakian, a teenager in Iran at the time, described the mood: "On the morning of Elghanian's execution, ripples of fear shook the foundation of the community as a whole. Everyone was wondering who would be next."

"His strength strengthened the community for he had much influence among Jews and non-Jews alike. His confidence was not his alone. It was the confidence of a people," Hakakian added. "He assumed that the nation's gratitude rendered him immune against any malice."[10]

What also frightened Jews was seeing some Muslims celebrating the execution in the streets by passing out sweets.

In an attempt to head off further persecution of Jews, Kamran Beroukhim said, "We decided to go talk to Khomeini to calm everybody down, the Jews and the Muslims."

Beroukhim and three other members of the Association of Iranian Jewish Intellectuals — Aziz Daneshrad, Haroun Yeshayaei, Abdollah Zargarian — along with two rabbis, Uriel Davidi and Hakham Yedidia Shofet, took a van

---

9. Freedom of Information Act request by author.
10. Roya Hakakian, "How Iran Kept its Jews," *Tablet*, Dec. 30, 2014.

to Qom to visit Khomeini and express their solidarity with the revolution and get assurances from him of the Jewish community's safety. When they arrived at the imam's home, they were expecting crowds outside waiting to be blessed, but the place was empty. They followed the sound to a room filled with the usual gaggle of journalists, microphones and cameras. Khomeini's aides asked Davidi and Shofet to sit on each side of where the imam would be seated. Khomeini came in.

After preliminaries, the delegation said many had families in Israel whom they could not be forbidden to be in touch with. If they left to live there, it was because they were poor and had nothing here, they said, then reminded Khomeini that "freedom and respect were bestowed upon Jews in Islam. They asked him to emphasize this point to reduce discord."[11]

Then Khomeini spoke, saying Moses was a great prophet and "Iran's Jews had nothing to do with those bloodsucking Zionists."

Three days after Khomeini received the delegation, he issued an order to restrict the executions. On May 13, he announced that death sentences would henceforth be limited to any person "proven to have killed people" or "any person who has issued orders for the killing of people or who has committed torture resulting in death."

The AP reported that "there was speculation that the order was in response to fears of the Iranian Jewish community and foreign criticism resulting from the execution last Wednesday of millionaire Jewish businessman Habib Elghanian."[12]

Despite all the talk, at least nine more Jews were executed from 1979 to 1981: businessmen Isaac Senehi, Gorgi Lavi, Albert Danielpour, and Mansour Ghedoushim, newspaper editor Simon Farzami, hotel owners

---

11. Eliz Sanasarian, *Religious Minorities in Iran*, (Cambridge, U.K.: Cambridge University Press, 2006), p. 137.

12. "Khomeini Decrees Death Penalty for 'Killers' Only," The Associated Press, May 14, 1979.

Ebrahim Berookhim, Youssef Yadegar and Farajollah Hakimi, and architect and real estate developer Isaac Lahijani.

Prime Minister Mehdi Bazargan spoke out against the revolutionary courts: "As we stage a revolution against tyranny, we should not be tyrannical ourselves, we should be just the reverse."

Khalkhali, the chief of Iran's Central Revolutionary Court, defended the courts to foreign journalists. "These people tried by Iran's Islamic courts ruined an entire nation, caused misery, massacre and corruption. There cannot be any mercy for them," he said. He criticized "Western notions of judicial process" that include defense lawyers and protracted proceedings. He defended the tribunals, calling them as "humane as Nuremberg."

"Those who barred freedom, or those who helped the satanic regime in any way, are guilty as well as those who killed and tortured," he told reporters.[13]

Iranian media, the Islamic Republic's de facto propaganda tool, said that Iran's Jews hated Habib, calling him "a disgrace to the Jews in this country. He was an individual who wished to equate Jewry with Zionism. . . . The mass of information he kept sending to Israel, his actions to achieve Israel's designs, the colossal sum of foreign exchange and funds he kept transferring to Israel; these are only samples of his antinational actions; these were the acts used to crush our Palestinian brethren. The Iranian Jews hate to have a spy like [Elghanian] as their symbol."[14]

The reality was that thousands of Jews had emigrated to various countries between December 1978 and May 1979, and now panic had set in and

---

13. Roland Flamini, "Murder of Shah, Family Is Sought by Chief of Tribunal in Tehran," *Time-Life News Service*, May 14, 1979.

14. Eliz Sanasarian, *Religious Minorities in Iran*, (Cambridge, U.K.: Cambridge University Press, 2006), p. 112.

thousands more were preparing to obtain passports to leave.[15] Before and during the revolution, about 15,000 to 17,500 Jews headed for Los Angeles, 9,550 went to Israel, around 5,000 to Europe and 2,500 to New York. [16]

The Anti-Defamation League also sprang into action and arranged a meeting with the highest diplomatic representative of the Iranian government in Washington, Ali Aghah. Arnold Forster and other ADL officials, along with a handful of leaders of other Jewish groups, including the B'nai B'rith and the American Jewish Committee, met him at his residence. A memo Forster wrote on May 22 to ADL director Nate Perlmutter recounts the delegation's questions and Aghah's head-spinning answers.

Forster began by expressing the "deep concern of American Jews for the Iranian Jewish community," explained his pro-Zionist philosophy and purpose, and expressed outrage at Habib's execution. The delegation told Aghah that all those around the table had acted as Elghanian had, in making contributions to Israel, and that they had come for proof that Elghanian was a spy.

ADL Vice Chairman Max Kampelman quoted a comment by former U.S. Vice President Hubert Humphrey: "If you want to understand and gain the goodwill of Americans, please know that we judge a society by its treatment of its Jews." While the U.S. had no right to interfere in the internal affairs of other nations, Kampelman told Aghah, "We do have a right to judge. Let your leaders know the truth of Humphrey's words. Inestimable damage has been done by the execution of Elghanian."

The ADL's Ken Bialkin asked Aghah: If the Iranian government was capable of committing one "unspeakable outrage," could it not later perpetrate such murder on a mass basis? Bialkin went on to explain the reasons

---

15. Philip Dopoulos, "Iranian Jews, Fearing Repression, Flee Islamic Republic," The Associated Press, May 19, 1979.

16. Alessandra Cecolin, *Iranian Jews in Israel: Between Persian Cultural Identity and Israeli Nationalism*, (London: I. B. Tauris & Co. Ltd, 2016) p. 2.

for Zionism and Israel after 2,000 years of persecution, asking that Iran and Israel learn to live in peace together.

Referring to Habib's financial contributions to Israel, Paul Berger, a lawyer representing the American Jewish Congress, asserted that "making financial contributions to alleviate human suffering in Israel is a perfectly proper activity," and that spying is something else altogether.

Aghah replied that he understood the delegation's concern about the Iranian Jewish community. He then reminded them that Iran had welcomed Polish-Jewish refugees from Hitler and that he did sympathize with Iranian Jews who were not rich.

The rich Jew line was followed by another well-known canard about Jews controlling the media. "You know who runs the news media here. Your own Jewish people, some of them. Therefore, I don't talk to them anymore," Aghah said. "Elghanian was spying for another nation."

He noted that Beroukhim and five others of the Jewish community in Iran had met with Khomeini and that under Islamic law, the *dhimmis*, meaning Jews and Christians, were protected people. He concluded that "no Jew in Iran has been persecuted because of his love for Israel."

The delegation explained that spying charges were a major accusation and that "in American society it would require a full plenary trial with a presentation of facts, not generalizations."

Aghah responded with a non sequitur, saying that Israel had trained the shah's secret police.

The delegation pressed him on the Iranian government's definition of spying. The ADL's Abe Foxman reminded Aghah that sending money to Israel and visiting the country were allowed under the previous government and if that constituted his government's definition of spying, the present delegation would all be in trouble. Aghah's response remained muddled. By spying, he said he meant "helping to kill Iranians during the shah's time." If financial support were sent to Israel for "human needs," it would not be spying.

When Foxman reiterated his fear for the future of Iran's Jews, Aghah told him that, though no Iranian was allowed to take any hard currency out of the country, the Jews were free to leave, essentially saying they could leave without any money.

Bialkin ended the meeting by saying: "You, personally, Mr. Aghah, appear friendly. But I am still deeply troubled about what happened in connection with the execution of Elghanian. When we have a proper explanation, we hope to be able to be friendly, not before."

At the same time, members of the U.S. Congress voiced concern.

"Mr. Speaker, I was appalled to read in this morning's *Washington Post* of the execution of Habib Elghanian by the henchmen of the self-appointed ruler of Iran," Rep. Edward Stack of Florida said on the House floor May 10. He said Habib's "only crime was his devotion to his religion and his generosity to Jewish causes." For the tens of thousands of Jews in Iran, he added, the revolutionaries' action could be "their Kristallnacht, the fateful night when anti-Semitic mobs swept through Nazi Germany, and the world stood by in silence."

Stack concluded: "I call upon the president to warn the government of Iran that a repetition of this execution will lead the government of the United States to invoke economic sanctions . . ."[17]

A week later, on May 17, 1978, U.S. Sen. Jacob Javits and several others sponsored a bipartisan resolution that passed to express their opposition to the executions.

Supporting it in a floor speech, Sen. Robert Byrd of West Virginia lamented: "Unfortunately, at this time we speak almost alone. One would have thought that by now there would be a chorus of loud and persistent protests from around the world against the mock trials and executions by firing squad of at least 209 citizens in Iran. But I have heard no such protest. Why is there this reluctance to protest? Some have reported that it might be

---

17. Congressional Record - House Rec. 10734, "Day of Infamy in Iran," May 10, 1979.

because we are so dependent on foreign oil, that we dare not jeopardize the supply of oil."

Saying the revolutionary courts' judgments were based on hearsay and that no appeal was allowed, Byrd added: "One man was found guilty of 'economic imperialism.' His crime was that he was successful and that he gave money to Israel. This is not justice. Spokesmen in Iran say they are not bound by the trappings of Western justice. But Western standards are not at issue here. Human standards are the basic decency of due process that should be the right of every individual, everywhere."[18]

On May 24, Rep. Harold Hollenbeck of New Jersey introduced a House resolution denouncing Habib's summary trial and execution.[19]

By the last week of May 1979, Iranians gathered outside the new PLO headquarters and the U.S. Embassy in Tehran, chanting "Death to America," "Death to Israel" and "Death to Sadat," the Egyptian president who was negotiating a peace treaty with Israel.

On May 25, demonstrators placed effigies of Carter and Begin next to the U.S. Embassy wall to mimic condemned men before a firing squad. A large banner that read "Death to the American Senate!" hung over the effigies with another poster that had American and Israeli flags and a caricature of Habib.[20]

The Senate resolution infuriated Khomeini. Calling it "clear interference in Iran's internal affairs" and Javits himself a "notorious Zionist," he added, "The form and composition of the U.S. Senate is that they always support

18. Congressional Record - Senate, Rec. 11674-6 "Human Rights with Respect to Iran," May 17, 1979.

19. "Resolution blasting Iranian civil rights introduced in House," *Bergen Bulletin*, May 24, 1979.

20. "Clergyman shot in Iran protest," *News World Daily*, May 26, 1979.

Israel and Zionists, and the people of the Third World have always been suppressed by them."[21]

"Iran's revolutionary government, outraged by Senate criticism of its Islamic firing squads, told the United States yesterday to postpone sending a new ambassador to Tehran and warned that such 'interference' could lead Iran to 'limit' relations with Washington," wrote Edward Cody of *The Washington Post.*

"The Foreign Ministry's move, announced by the official Pars news agency, followed a stinging personal attack by Iran's Islamic patriarch, Ayatollah Ruhollah Khomeini, on President Carter, Sen. Jacob K. Javits (R-N.Y.) and the U.S. government in general," the article went on to say.[22]

"Why must we have any relationship with them? Our relationship with them is that of a tyrant with an innocent, that of a ravaged victim with a plunderer. We don't need America," Khomeini said. "It is they who need us. They want our oil."[23]

The execution and the resolution in tandem became a defining moment in the breakdown in relations between Iran and the U.S.

Caught off guard while they were working to save U.S. interests in Iran, Carter administration officials also viewed the resolution as interference. The head of the U.S. Embassy in Tehran from 1978 to 1980, Charles Naas, said in a 1988 interview published by the Foundation for Iranian Studies, "I was asked whether I thought the time was ripe to see Khomeini. This was in May, early May." He did, and arrangements for the meeting were made. "And then the Javits resolution passed in the Senate. It was one of those sort

21. "Ayatollah Takes Out After Javits; Denounces Senate as Zionist Tool," JTA, May 25, 1979.

22. Edward Cody, "Angry Iran Tells U.S. Not to Send New Ambassador," *The Washington Post*, May 21, 1979.

23. John Kifner, "Iran in a Protest Tells U.S. To Delay Sending New Envoy," *The New York Times*, May 21, 1979.

of things, it was a freebie for Senator Javits — and it was hell for me." He described thousands of Iranians "screaming outside our embassy. We were under a real threat of being attacked again. The resolution prevented me seeing Khomeini." It was, he said, "extraordinarily harmful."

I wrote to both Naas and the State Department's Henry Precht asking them if they could clarify the headaches posed by the resolution and President's Carter's stance on human rights.

Precht wrote back, copying in Naas, and began by relating his surprise at the Senate's action. He noted the rejection of Naas' and the appointed Ambassador Walter Cutler's meetings with Khomeini. And he added: "The U.S. was regarded by many as an enemy of the revolution and was hardly in a position to influence Iranian decisions on human rights (or any other matter). I don't think it takes anything away from President Carter's policy of advancing human rights that we were unable to move in that direction in the spring of 1979. As I have said, the Javits resolution was singularly unhelpful in that regard."

I wrote them back, explaining that I didn't envy the chaotic situation they were faced with. But as a granddaughter, journalist and U.S. citizen, I wondered if the government had been willing to turn a blind eye to what was going on to try to save its interests in Iran.

Precht responded: "First, although the revolution was indeed in great part about Iran achieving independence from U.S. influence, there is also always a pragmatic side to Iranians, including Khomeini. The U.S. was there, a great power that must be carefully handled. Better to have some guarded contact with them. That is my analysis based on what we knew of Khomeini's thinking. It may be wrong, as we had no access to him or most of the clerics around him.

"Second, we did not 'turn a blind eye' to human rights violations. We did not sacrifice human rights to the goal of improved relations with Iran. Rather, we kept it in the perspective of what might be accomplished in those undisciplined days when even Khomeini had difficulty controlling his followers."

Noting that for practical reasons the U.S. maintains relations with many nations that violate human rights, he said, "In hindsight, it might have been the better part of wisdom, had we shut down our embassy and waited for Iran to settle down. But in those Cold War days, Iran was terribly important to us and we felt obliged to work as best we could towards the goal of a better, more 'normal' relationship."

Naas also replied. Mentioning again the angry protests outside the embassy and noting repeated embassy efforts to get information on the safety of many individual Jewish Iranians, he also said that at one point, "I was informed personally by the Prime Minister that (and here my recollection varies a little from that of Mr. Precht) the assignment of Mr. Cutler as ambassador and my replacement was withdrawn as well as my first meeting with Khomeini. He was clearly saddened and said that the ayatollah at the outset was in favor of breaking all relations with the U.S. but was prevailed upon to relent. Thus, the resolution was the undermining of everything we — along with the secular government — had been trying to accomplish up until then."

The break in U.S.-Iranian relations has lasted for decades. To this day, Iranian policymakers cite the reaction to my grandfather's execution as a top reason — mangling the facts about both the execution and Senate resolution.

Hossein Mousavian, who served on Iran's nuclear diplomacy team in negotiations with the European Union and the International Atomic Energy Agency, cited the Javits resolution as the source of ongoing distrust in a 2014 book, *Iran and the United States: An Insider's View on the Failed Past and the Road to Peace.* He wrote: "Javits accused the Iranian government of killing Jews after they executed Habib Elghanian, a Jewish businessman. That condemnation stirred a great deal of resentment amongst the Iranian leaders. One revolutionary official told me that Elghanian was the only Jew who was executed at that time, and the reason was not because he was a Jew, otherwise thousands of Jews who lived in Iran should have been executed. Rather it was because he had close ties to the former regime."

Citing the Carter administration's human rights policy, too, Mousavian continued: "Ayatollah Khomeini and Iran's revolutionaries viewed this stance as a continuation of U.S. interference in Iran's domestic affairs. This perception would impact the Iranian leadership in two ways. First, they thought that Americans refused to acknowledge Iranian national identity, which entailed rejection of foreign domination and had been a major cause of the revolution. And second, the perception raised fears that the U.S. would not change its policy of interference in Iran's internal affairs. Interestingly, both of these perceptions persist today."[24]

There was other, continuing fallout from those fraught days. In August 1980, Rabbi Shofet left for Europe, urging Jews to leave Iran quickly. Of the estimated 80,000 to 100,000 Jews in 1979, more than half left Iran "uncertain and fearful about the future."[25] As the economic position of those remaining deteriorated, Jews in Iran were also singled out as a minority, and families were prevented from traveling out of Iran together.[26]

According to Iran's 2016 census, 9,826 Jews remain there.

Habib's execution also marked a turning point for Iran's economy. As Abbas Milani has written in *Eminent Persians*, between 1941 when the shah

---

24. Seyed Hossein Mousavian with Shahir ShahidSaless, *Iran and the United States: An Insider's View on the Failed Past and the Road to Peace*, (New York and London: Bloomsbury, 2014), p. 62.

25. Eliz Sanasarian, *Religious Minorities in Iran*, (Cambridge, U.K.: Cambridge University Press, 2006), p. 113.

26. Ibid.

took power and 1979, "the economy had taken giant strides, improving the lives of nearly every strata of society."[27]

"As the lives of the many Iranian industrialists, engineers, architects, and economic planners show, during the years between World War II and the Islamic Revolution, the efforts of this group helped transform Iran from a semi-feudal society to a contender to become 'a newly industrialized society.' Other countries in a similar position at the time, South Korea, Turkey and Taiwan, certainly made the transition. But the excesses of the Islamic Revolution aborted Iran's chances," Milani concluded.

Those excesses included my grandfather's execution.

The revolution and Khomeini's "economics is for donkeys" point of view provoked a brain drain, and today much of Iran's wealth is concentrated in the hands of hardline clerical leaders and the Islamic Revolutionary Guards Corps, the branch of Iran's military in charge of protecting the country's Islamic government. The very people who came to power to maintain social justice have amassed fortunes by engineering a corrupt system where largely they, their family members and their cronies can prosper.[28] Instead of investing in what's always been that nation's most valuable capital, the Iranian people, government officials obsess over its nuclear program. They blame Western sanctions for their economic woes rather than owning up to how they squandered Iran's chances of building a modern, diversified, export-based economy.[29]

---

27. Abbas Milani, "From Rags to Riches to Revolution, The Iranian Economy, 1941-1979," *Eminent Persians: The Men and Women Who Made Modern Iran 1941-1979*, Vol. 2 (Syracuse: Syracuse University Press and Persian World Press, 2008), p. 581.
28. Shahrzad Elghanayan, "Clerical Rule, Luxury Lifestyle," *The New York Times*, June 10, 2014.
29. Shahrzad Elghanayan, "How Iran Killed its Future," *The Los Angeles Times*, June 27, 2012.

Ironically, unlike my grandfather who built so much from nothing and refused to leave the homeland he loved, countless Iranian-born immigrants contribute their talents to new homelands around the world.

Gallery

Eliane and Fred's fake passport photos.

With my maternal grandparents Babaji and Mamanji in Tehran.

An Iranian Jewish woman places flowers on a grave in the Beheshtieh Jewish cemetery in downtown Tehran on Aug. 5, 2011. My grandfather is buried at Beheshtieh.

Iranian Jewish men recite a part of the Torah during Hanukkah celebrations at the Yousefabad Synagogue, in Tehran on Dec. 27, 2011. My maternal grandparents lived in Yousefabad and attended that synagogue until coming to California in 2005.

Afterword

When I set out to reconstruct my grandfather Habib's life, I felt that Iran belonged to me as much as I belonged to Iran. The more I delved into my family's and our former homeland's history, that feeling steadily ebbed. It's gone now.

In the midst of my research, I happened to watch the 2015 movie *Woman in Gold*, starring Helen Mirren as Maria Altmann, an Austrian-American Jewish refugee battling the Austrian government to recover the 1907 Gustav Klimt painting of her aunt, Adele Bloch-Bauer, which was stolen by the Nazis early in World War II. Until 2006, when Altmann won her case, the Austrian government displayed Klimt's painting at the Belvedere Palace in Vienna, publicizing it as a national treasure without acknowledging its provenance. Altmann wanted to get back what belonged to her family — but also to right a wrong.

Watching Tatiani Maslany's performance as the young Maria Altmann fleeing her home in Vienna during the war touched a nerve. I cried as I watched the scene, thinking about my uncle and aunt, Fred and Eliane, on the run in Tehran before they were able to escape. I thought of the countless

Jews who fled Iran, smuggled through Pakistan's bordering mountains on harrowing journeys in windowless vans, then on foot, some with just a suitcase, never to return home. I thought of my youngest aunt, my mother's sister Moji, 16 at the time of my grandfather's execution, who couldn't go back to school because she was related to Habib Elghanian. She fled Tehran, too, alone as a teenager.

It also made me think about the times I've seen my mother cry listening to Persian music or taking out old photographs, her heart aching for *home*.

As Khomeini's popularity grew before his return from exile in February 1979, some Jews left Iran with their assets. Many others fled immediately after my grandfather was executed, and others followed in the early 1980s, starting their lives over, mostly in Los Angeles and New York. David Menashri, a Tel Aviv University professor of Iranian Jewish history, told me that life for exiled Iranian Jews is much better now in many ways, because they are living in countries that allow them to flourish as Jews. He is right: Many have done extremely well.

But I have empathy for those who didn't have it in them to restart and rebuild their lives in a new country where they would have to learn a new way of life in their 50s, 60s and 70s. My own grandfather Habib, well into his 60s in 1979, didn't have it in him — and neither did my other grandfather, Babaji.

For decades, the post-revolution Iranian government wouldn't allow Jewish families to travel outside Iran together, which meant my mother's parents could never visit us together. My grandmother Mamanji came alone to the United States for a few short stays in the mid-1980s. For almost 30 years, we talked on the phone. She'd always sing to me the same songs she sang when I was a child, recount our old Tehran stories. *Yadesh bekheyr,* she'd sigh. "May those memories always stay sweet."

After my grandfather Habib's execution, the Revolutionary Guards' house-to-house searches lasted for months. Young armed men barged into homes looking for "evidence" connecting people to the old regime. They showed up at my mother's parents' house, examining the photos on their living room piano, wanting to know who everyone was. Later in the summer, worried about boxes of business documents my father had stored in his in-laws' basement when we left Iran in August 1977, my aunt Jeannette, painstakingly shredded documents with her hands and scissors before driving up the hills of the Yousefabad neighborhood in the dark, with plastic bags she threw into the then-undeveloped valley.

For a long time, Babaji was too scared and then too sick with lung problems to get himself smuggled out of the country. But after thieves kept breaking into their house, and even tying both my grandparents up and taking valuables, he was finally ready to try to escape with my grandmother. He resolved to sell the house, their beautiful two-story, four-bedroom home that had fallen into disrepair over the years, to a real estate developer who wanted to tear it down for a new building. My grandfather, who belonged to an era when a man's word was as good as his signature, made the mistake of sealing the deal with a handshake, and the guy turned out to be a shyster. With no signed papers, my grandfather agreed to live in an office space and get a monthly stipend from the man until the building was constructed. The developer would then give him two apartments and the rest of the money for the land. Shortly afterward, my grandfather suffered a heart attack, and the developer stopped paying him. He had bamboozled some government officials, too, and they put a lien on the uncompleted construction site.

My aunt Jeannette, who was living in Los Angeles, was finally able to persuade my grandfather to leave. She got green cards for both of my grandparents, and in 2005 brought them to the West Coast. When she arrived in Tehran, she saw that the office space where the developer had put them up had a bathroom with a sink and a toilet but no bathtub. They washed with a hose hung on one of the bathroom walls attached to the sink, slept on two small folding beds and made food in an office kitchenette. What little remained of their old life surrounded them in boxes and plastic bags.

When my grandparents landed at JFK airport in New York, in the hubbub and all the excitement of our long-awaited reunion, my grandfather kissed everyone, including my mother — though he didn't recognize her initially, and wondered where she was. He hadn't seen her since the morning we left Tehran more than a quarter-century earlier.

When they settled here, I'd visit them often in Los Angeles. I'd ask my grandmother what life had been like since the revolution. She talked about waiting in long lines for food and scary nights during the 1980-88 Iran-Iraq war when they had to take shelter from bombings. She told me how they made ends meet; she would knit children's clothing and sew patchwork quilts with my grandfather from scraps she had stored over the years, and go from store to store to try selling their wares.

She also described the difficulties she had dealing with bureaucrats when she needed to go to a government office with her passport. On the document, her name was followed by *Kalimi*, a Farsi word for Jewish. That her religion was stamped on her passport filled me with revulsion. But she was resilient, like all our ancestors, in dealing with bigotry. Her stock answer when they'd throw her religion in her face: "As far as I know, there is one God, and he belongs to all of us. If you have a problem with me being Jewish, you need to take that up with him. I don't know what else to tell you."

At the same time, I understood how much she missed her friends, her home, *her life.*

All of that was taken away, and not just from my grandmother. The Iranian government stole everything my grandfather Habib spent his lifetime building; my father and his siblings can't travel to Tehran to visit their parents' graves; my mother isn't allowed to walk the streets she knew and loved.

And yet over time, even losses like this somehow grow benumbing and recede, allowing us to build our future.

Iran is no longer mine, as I have said. As I have delved into our former homeland's record of injustices, to us and so many others, I've stopped yearning for this faraway land where I'd never have the opportunity to flourish because of my religion or my gender. That kind of yearning is nothing more than toxic romanticism. Home, I've realized, is the place where freedom, equality, the rule of law and a secular government are promises enshrined in a Constitution and in laws — no matter how imperfect the achievement of those ideals may be.

Today, the relationship between Iran's rulers and citizens is like that of a parent to children; people are infantilized. Simple choices that adults should be able to decide for themselves, from choosing what to wear if you're a woman to whom to openly love if you're gay, are verboten. No longer mine, Iran belongs to the people who are there. For their sake, I wish with all my heart that Iran's leaders' hearts would grow. When citizens demand civil or political rights, Iran's rulers trot out tired conspiracy theories: The protests are fomented from outside, by evil Americans, evil Westerners, evil Israelis — as though Iranians have no free will. Every time I read that someone's accused of being a Zionist spy in Iran, all the alarms go off. The accused is doomed because the claims against them are nebulous and pathologically anti-Israel. For Iran, where revolution after revolution has failed, the only path to a promising future has to come from compromise, sharing power, giving people freedom and a massive reckoning with a long history of injustices.

Maybe Iran's nearly 10,000 remaining Jews will one day flourish again, but for now their future looks like that of the nearly extinct Jewish communities of many other Middle Eastern countries. In a few generations, there will barely be any Iranian Jews left as we all assimilate in our new homelands.

As I finally close the Iranian chapter of my life by fulfilling my promise to not let the injustice of my grandfather's execution be forgotten, I know that I belong to America and that America belongs to me. Iran lives in the albums I made with my mother. I might still take them out, but the images will no longer evoke sorrow, only passing memories of ancient times.

Who's Who

Nikkha, aka Nikkou Jan, aka Mahsoltan: Habib's wife

Ostad "Oussa" Babai: Habib's father
Khanoun Jan: Habib's mother
Haim-Saghi: Habib's maternal grandfather

Saltanat: Habib's sister
John: Habib's oldest brother
Davoud: Habib's second oldest brother
Nourollah: Habib's younger brother
Sion: Habib's younger brother
Nejatollah, aka Nejat: Habib's younger brother
Attollah, aka Eddy: Habib's youngest brother

Hajji Mirza Agha, aka Mirza: Habib's maternal uncle, father-in-law
Hajji Aziz: Habib's maternal uncle, Mirza's brother

Fereydoun, aka Fred: Habib's oldest son
Karmel: Habib's second son, author's father
Mahnaz: Habib's daughter
Sina: Habib's youngest son

Shamsi: Habib's secretary

Acknowledgments

For their support, time and talent, I'd like to thank:

My editor Chris Sullivan. *Titan* could not have been in better hands.

My publisher Peter Costanzo, for taking on this project and giving it a home at The Associated Press.

My writers' group, Theasa Tuohy, Kay Williams and Pat Carlson, for offering insights into early drafts and encouraging me to keep going. I cherish every Thursday we worked late into the night at Kay's place.

Theasa, for bringing me into the group and for all the energy and thought she put into helping me tell my grandfather's story.

Rosemary Ahern, for fine-tuning my book proposal; Santiago Lyon for feedback on my manuscript.

Patrick Sison, first and foremost for his friendship, and for my portrait.

Alicia Tatone for the book cover; Kara Haupt for her art direction as we fine-tuned it.

Aryeh Levin, for time and generosity in sharing his family history and entrusting me with his research.

Lotfollah Hay and Hechmat Kermanshahchi, for talking to me at length about my grandfather.

282

Acknowledgments

For help with my research and interviews, in person, on the phone, by mail, email and on Skype: the photographer Abbas, Ervand Abrahamian, Amir Afkhami, Shaul Bakhash, Susan BenNoon, Kamran Beroukhim, Ruhollah Cohanim, Mehrdad Cohen, Meir Ezri, Arsalan and Faramarz Gueola, Serge Klarsfeld, A. H. Ladan, Dan Mariaschin, David Menashri, Abbas Milani, Charles Naas, Nasser Oliaei, Manouchehr Omidvar, Liam O'Murchu, Mansour Pouretehad, Henry Precht, Eli Roshkhodesh, Homa Sarshar, Liz Schultz, Houshang Seyhoun, Yadollah Shakib and Orbel Yaghoobinasab.

The French Jewish community, for honoring the age-old tradition of being their brothers' and sisters' keepers by watching out for Iran's Jewish community.

Corinna Barsan and Chantal Kordula, for going above and beyond with advice and counsel in the publishing process.

Dusan Vranic, for his friendship and the roof over my head in Jerusalem.

Anja Niedringhaus, whose life's work was filled with heart and courage and who helped me understand my grandfather's dedication to his work, to those he wouldn't leave behind, and his inability to watch events unfold from the outside.

My cheerleaders, Bethany, Brooke, Courtney, Donna, Doris, Geraldine, James, Kathy, Khaleh T., Lara, Laura, Lindara, Markus, Melissa, Rachel, Sophie, Stephanie, Surahy, Valerie, Vania, and Yas.

Amir and Nasser Victory, Fereshteh and Behrouz Shokati, for assistance with my research and Farsi newspaper translations.

Uncles Sion and Eddy, Khaleh Pari and Iraj Elghanian, for sharing family stories.

My very deepest gratitude to Pari Elghanian, for entrusting me with her father's journal.

Uncle Fred and Aunt Eliane, for reopening a painful chapter in their lives. I will always cherish my visit to Ohio.

Aunt Mahnaz, for her determination, hard work keeping our family together and sharing her father's letters. I admire her strength and grit. My appreciation to Simon for sharing his memories of the revolution.

Aunt Sheryl, for sharing photographs and memories.

Cousins Danny, Dariush, Diana, Shahab, Shahrooz, Aaron, Barry, Michelle, Nicole and their spouses, for their constant encouragement and help going to Israel.

The Alaghband, Amirianfar, Gueola, Jalili, Javaheri, Morovati, Nekoukar families, for all their love, warmth and support.

Aunt Jeannette, Uncle Johnny and Aunt Mojgan and her family — Uncle Ramin, and cousins Dara and Layla — whom I love dearly for being with me through every celebration and heartache of my life.

My brother Shahram, sister-in-law Carol, and the O's, for boundless love that fuels the sputtering engine, for every summer trip, dinner and good times.

My mother, Helen, for unconditional love and for encouraging me to always study. We walked so many streets in Manhattan together. I treasure every step, listening to memories of Iran. And I'm forever grateful for instilling in me a passion for photographs.

My father, Karmel, for bringing us to New York and teaching me to "Stand Firm as an Oak." I will always cherish our day trip to Nyack. This book was a grand journey for us. Despite living across the country, he always was a text message away.

Acknowledgments

My husband Douglas J. Rowe, who played the most important role in making *Titan* possible, from telling me to go for it, to becoming my de facto agent, to countless miles around the park, trips to the shore, to Philly, and dozens of Broadway plays. The light, love and laughter he brings to our life helped keep me going and growing. He was my sounding board, listened to my night thoughts, shared invaluable insights and paid special attention to narrative momentum.

He not only has "a good face" but a big heart that sparkles in the merriest of snow globes.

About the Author

Award-winning American journalist Shahrzad Elghanayan works at NBC News as a senior photo editor. Previously, she was at Bloomberg News and The Associated Press, where she was a supervisor on the national photo desk. Before her journalism career, she assisted with research at the human rights organization Freedom House.

Her op-eds have appeared in *The New York Times*, *The Washington Post*, *Los Angeles Times* and CNN.com.

Born in Tehran and raised in Manhattan, she graduated from the Lycée Français and has a B.A. in political science from Columbia University. She lives in New York with her husband Douglas J. Rowe, a longtime journalist.

Photo Credits

Pages 54 (top), 55, 125, 127, 128, 130 (top), 135, 136, 228, 229, 230, 232, 233, 234, 235, 236, 237, 238, 239, 273, 274.
Courtesy of AP Photo Archives

Pages 54 (bottom), 58.
Courtesy of Center for Iranian Jewish Oral History

Pages 57, 59, 60, 61, 124, 126, 129, 131, 133, 134 (top), 226, 227, 231, 240, 241, 272.
Courtesy of Elghanayan Family Collection

Page 56.
Courtesy of Victory Family Collection

Page 130 (bottom).
Courtesy of Shahnaz Ghodsian

Page 132 (bottom).
Courtesy of Meir Ezri

Pages 132 (top), 134 (bottom).
Courtesy of Nasser Oliaei

Pages 134 (top), 231.
Courtesy of Sheryl Elghanayan

Page 286.
Patrick Sison

CPSIA information can be obtained
at www.ICGtesting.com
Printed in the USA
LVHW080712211221
706816LV00014B/499/J